Children before God

Children before God

Biblical Themes in the Works of
John Calvin and Jonathan Edwards

JOHN MᶜNEILL

Foreword by David F. Ford

PICKWICK *Publications* · Eugene, Oregon

CHILDREN BEFORE GOD
Biblical Themes in the Works of John Calvin and Jonathan Edwards

Pickwick Publications
An Imprint of Wipf and Stock Publishers
199 W. 8th Ave., Suite 3
Eugene, OR 97401

www.wipfandstock.com

PAPERBACK ISBN: 978-1-4982-8106-5
HARDCOVER ISBN: 978-1-4982-8108-9
EBOOK ISBN: 978-1-4982-8107-2

Cataloguing-in-Publication data:

Names: McNeill, John.
Title: Children before God : biblical themes in the works of John Calvin and Jonathan Edwards / John McNeill.
Description: Eugene, OR: Pickwick Publications, 2017 | Includes bibliographical references and index.
Identifiers: ISBN 978-1-4982-8106-5 (paperback) | ISBN 978-1-4982-8108-9 (hardcover) | ISBN 978-1-4982-8107-2 (ebook)
Subjects: LCSH: Children—Religious aspects—Christianity | Calvin, Jean, 1509–1564 | Edwards, Jonathan, 1703–1758. | Bible—Theology
Classification: BT705 M330. 2017 (print) | BT705 (ebook)

Manufactured in the U.S.A.   NOVEMBER 6, 2017

"My babe so beautiful! it thrills my heart
With tender gladness, thus to look at thee"
(S. T. Coleridge, "Frost at Midnight," *PW 171* 48–49)

Contents

Foreword

BY PROFESSOR DAVID F. FORD

There are several deep roots feeding John McNeill's book—the Bible, his years working with children, a great deal of pastoral experience, intensive academic study and reflection, and engagement with God. McNeill's gift is to let them all nourish him as he seeks a twenty-first century Christian wisdom about children.

At the heart of his approach is a biblical wisdom, with original, subtle interpretations of four well-chosen passages about Moses, Samuel, Jeremiah, and Timothy. Their meaning is opened up tantalisingly, and never wrapped up. By the end of the book we have been given a rich set of concepts and insights through which to think and imagine 'children before God'—but no neat package. Rather like the coming of a new child into our life, we have been given something that cries out for our active, thoughtful response, one that stretches our capacities of imagination, intellect, and feeling in an open-ended way, and requires readiness for surprises.

Above all, this is a deeply theological work. It draws on two of the finest Christian theologians, John Calvin and Jonathan Edwards, but also freely critiques and supplements them. McNeill enters into their radical seriousness about God as the source and goal of all creation, God's reality as a living, loving presence that affects everything, and God's knowledge, wisdom, glory and beauty. He shows how Calvin and Edwards fragmentarily and imperfectly, but also richly and suggestively, begin to think about children in the light of this God, and McNeill himself risks going beyond them. He reaches back to the Bible, forward to later theologians, and beyond theology to other discourses about children.

There is also evident all through the book the accompaniment of the late Daniel (Dan) W. Hardy. He was one of my most important theological conversation partners too, and it is good to see John McNeill taking up his thinking. Dan loved to open up the levels and complexities of topics, trying to do justice to their depth and breadth. McNeill has proved a worthy student of his.

Dan was also my father-in-law, and as my wife and I look forward to the birth in the coming weeks of our daughter's first child, Dan's first great-grandson, I appreciate the way this book has helped to prepare us for his birth by sharing a theological wisdom about children that is indebted to Dan and so many others.

David F. Ford
Selwyn College, Cambridge University
July 2017

Preface

This study looks into theological issues that have arisen within Calvinian epistemology in relation to children. In the Introduction, I trace a historical trajectory to current Calvinian fundamentalist teaching in relation to children which I deem theologically reductionist in terms of both its language and its methodology, thus presenting a theological problematic. In chapter 1 I explore the language and imagery used of children in four biblical infancy narratives, and understand these to be theologically normative. In chapter 2 I go back to the roots of the Calvinian tradition and explore John Calvin's dialectical epistemology, which, I argue, provides a working framework in which children can be posited in relation to God. In chapter 3 I look at how Calvin's theological anthropology is actually mapped out, with particular reference to children, and conclude that his theological methodology, using the categories of sin and grace, forces him to use "harsh" language in reference to children. In chapter 4 I explore briefly some of the Calvinian language used by Thomas Boston and Jonathan Edwards in relation to children, before going on to expound Edwards's theological aesthetics, and argue that therein may lie a critical tool in which children can be construed in language that is more in keeping with the biblical language and imagery of children described in chapter 1. Finally, in chapter 5 I seek to delineate a biblical hermeneutic of wisdom by which the biblical infancy narratives can be read, and begin the process of tracing providential activity, understood in terms of a divine causality of life, in child development studies. I conclude that a theology of children should include an affirmative theological and biblical language of children that does not negate God's salvific purposes for children, rather is conducive to it. I offer this piece of research as a reparative exercise within Calvinian epistemology that gives Calvin his due but arguably goes beyond him.

Acknowledgments

I am deeply grateful to the late Rev. Prof. Daniel (Dan) W. Hardy for the time I spent sharing with him many aspects of my thoughts with regard to children which he described as "intuitive." He was the perfect conversational partner and my respect for him knows no bounds. I was one of his last research students along with Rev. Dr. Jason A. Fout whose friendship I continue to value. It felt very fitting that Professor David F. Ford would write the Foreword as he initially took me into his Systematic Class at Cambridge University and included me in his Home and Scriptural Reasoning groups in which both he and Dan took a leading role. I am grateful to Rev. Dr. Stephen Plant for encouraging me to reflect on my work with children in the Shetland Islands which acted as the initial spur for my research; he also pushed me toward submission which in the end gained me a Cambridge PhD. I acknowledge with grateful thanks Rev. Prof. George M. Newlands who initiated the process to publication after querying me in his inimitable way, 'Whatever happened to your work with Dan Hardy?' during a Society of the Study of Theology conference in Nottingham, to which I replied, 'It is all on my computer!' (Dan and Stephen had earlier nominated me to SST membership at the Exeter conference.) I have valued the input over time of Rev. Dr. George Bailey, Rev. Dr. Paul Ellingworth, Rev. Dr. James M. Gordon, Prof. Tom Greggs, Rev. Aboseh Ngwana, Dr. Jackie Potts, Prof. Kenneth A. Kitchen, Prof. Andrew F. Walls, Prof. Haddon Willmar, and Prof. Randall C. Zachman, several of whom kindly read a draft and offered comment. My external examiners at Cambridge Rev. Dr. John Bradbury and Prof. Paul T. Nimmo provided valued critique in my PhD viva and encouraged me to continue to develop my thought in this area of research. I would also like to acknowledge the support of staff and students at Wesley House, Cambridge, and the support of many in the Leeds North East and North of Scotland Mission Circuits where I have served as a Methodist minister. In particular I would like to mention the support of members of Crown Terrace Methodist Church, Aberdeen scattered near and far. For financial assistance I am grateful to Formation in Ministry, Methodist Church House; the Westhill Endowment Trustees; and the Bethune-Baker Fund Trustees. I am indebted to Drs. James K. Aitken and Razvan Porumb for meeting some of my accommodation needs in Cambridge. I am also grateful for the use of library facilities at Tyndale House and Westminster College, Cambridge; Cambridge University Library; Leeds University Brotherton Library; and Aberdeen University Library. Finally, I would like to express my deepest gratitude to my family and friends, particularly my parents James and Aileen McNeill who have been there for me every step of the way.

Abbreviations

Ad Hebraeos—Thomas Aquinas. *Ad Hebraeos*. In *Super Epistoloas S. Pauli Lectura*, edited by P. Raphaelis Cai, 2:335–506. Rome: Marietti, 1953; ET, *Commentary on the Epistle to the Hebrews*. Edited and translated by Chrystostom Baer. South Bend, IN: St. Augustine's, 2006.

ANF—*The Ante-Nicene Fathers: Translations of the Writings of the Fathers down to A.D. 325.* 10 vols. Edited by Alexander Roberts and James Donaldson. Revised by A. Cleveland Coxe. Peabody, MA: Hendrickson, 1994.

Ant.—Josephus. *Jewish Antiquities*, Books I–III. Translated by Henry St. John Thackeray, in LCL 242.

AR—Samuel T. Coleridge. *Aids to Reflection*. Edited by John Beer. In Vol. IX of *CC*.

ARG—*Archiv für Reformationsgeschichte.*

AT—*Acta Theologica.*

BHS—*Biblia Hebraica Stuttgartensia.* Edited by Karl Elliger and Wilhelm Rudolph. 5th rev. edn. Stuttgart: Deutsche Bibelgesellschaft, 1997.

Bib. Ant.—Pseudo-Philo. *Liber Antiquitatum Biblicarum.* Translated by Daniel J. Harrington. In *The Old Testament Pseudepigrapha*, edited by James H. Charlesworth, 297–377. New York: Doubleday, 1985.

BL—Samuel T. Coleridge. *Biographia Literaria*. Edited by James Engell and W. Jackson Bate. In Vol. VII/1–2 of *CC*.

b.Sotah—*The Talmud of Babylonia: XVII. Tractate Sotah.* Translated by Jacob Neusner. Chico, CA: Scholars, 1984.

BTB—*Biblical Theology Bulletin.*

BTh II—*Briefwechsel Karl Barth–Edward Thurneysen, 1921–1930.* Zürich: TVZ, 1974.

CAD—*The Assyrian Dictionary of the Oriental Institute of the University of Chicago, A–Z.* Edited by Ignace J. Gelb et al. 26 vols. Chicago: Oriental Institute, 1956–.

CBQ—*Catholic Biblical Quarterly.*

CC—*The Collected Works of Samuel Taylor Coleridge.* 16 vols. in 34 parts. Edited by Kathleen Coburn. Bollingen Series 75. London: Routledge, 1969–2002.

CD—Karl Barth. *Church Dogmatics.* 5 vols. in 14 parts. Edited by Geoffrey W. Bromiley and Thomas F. Torrance. Translated by G. T. Thomson et al. Edinburgh: T. & T. Clark, 1936–77.

CEF—Child Evangelism Fellowship.

CL—*The Collected Letters of Samuel Taylor Coleridge.* Edited by Earl L. Griggs. 6 vols. Oxford: Clarendon, 1951–71.

CM—Jean Calvin. *Institution de la Religion Chrétienne.* Edited by Jean Cadier and Pierre Marcel. 3 vols. Geneva: Labor et Fides, 1955–58.

CN—*The Notebooks of Samuel Taylor Coleridge.* 5 vols. in 10 parts. General editor Kathleen Coburn. London: Routledge, 1957–2002.

CNTC—John Calvin. *Calvin's New Testament Commentaries.* 12 vols. Edited by David W. Torrance and Thomas F. Torrance. Various translators. Grand Rapids: Eerdmans, 1959–72.

CO—John Calvin. *Ioannis Calvini opera quae supersunt omnia.* 59 vols. Edited by Johann W. Baum et al. Braunschweig: Schwetschke, 1863–1900; published as vols. 29–87 of *Corpus Reformatorum.*

Comm. Pss—John Calvin. *A Commentary on the Psalms.* 4 vols. Revised and edited by Thomas H. L. Parker. Translated by Arthur Golding. London: Clarke, 1965.

Conferences—John Cassian. *The Conferences.* Translated by Boniface Ramsey. New York: Paulist, 1997.

COR—John Calvin. *Ioannis Calvini opera omnia denuo recognita et adnotatione critica instructa notisque illustrate: Series I, Institutio Christianae Religionis; Series II, Opera exegetica Veteris et Novi Testamenti.* 10 vols. to date. *Series III, Scripta ecclesiastica.* 2 vols. to date; *Series IV, Scripta didactica et polemica.* 5 vols. to date. *Series V, Sermones.* 1 vol. to date. *Series VI, Epistolae.* 1 vol. to date. *Series VII, Varia.* 1 vol. to date. Various editors. Geneva: Droz, 1992–.

COTC—John Calvin. *Calvin's Old Testament Commentaries.* 2 vols. Edited by David F. Wright. Various translators. Carlisle, UK: Paternoster, 1993.

CTJ—*Calvin Theological Journal.*

CTL—John Calvin. *Selected Works of John Calvin: Tracts and Letters.* 7 vols. Edited by Henry Beveridge and Jules Bonnet. Various translators. Edinburgh: Calvin Translation Society, 1844–58. Reprint, Grand Rapids: Baker, 1983.

CTS—John Calvin. *The Commentaries of John Calvin.* 22 vols. Various translators. Edinburgh: Calvin Translation Society, 1843–55. Reprint, Grand Rapids: Baker, 1989.

CTT—*Calvin: Theological Treatises.* Edited by John K. S. Reid. Library of Christian Classics. Philadelphia: Westminster, 1954.

CW—Kahlil Gibran, *Collected Works.* London: Everyman's Library, 2007.

d'Aubigné—J. H. Merle d'Aubigné. *History of the Reformation in Europe in the Time of Calvin.* 8 vols. Vols. 6–8 translated by William L. R. Cates. London: Green, Longman, Roberts & Green, 1863–78.

DBW—Dietrich Bonhoeffer Werke. 17 vols. Edited by Eberhard Bethge et al. Munich: Kaiser, 1986–99.

DBWE—Dietrich Bonhoeffer Works. 17 vols. Various editors and translators. Minneapolis: Fortress, 1996–2014.

De Officiis—Cicero. *De Officiis.* LCL 30. Translated by Walter Miller.

De la Recherche—Nicolas Malebranche. *De la Recherche de la vérité.* In Œuvres Tome 1. Edited by Geneviève Rodis-Lewis. Paris: Bibliothèque de la Pléiade, 1979; ET, *The Search After Truth.* Edited and translated by Thomas M. Lennon and Paul J. Olscamp. Cambridge: Cambridge University Press, 1997.

Doumergue—Émile Doumergue. *Jean Calvin, les hommes et les choses de son temps.* 7 vols. Lausanne: Bridel, 1899–1927.

DS—Dominican Studies.

DT—"Dialektische Theologie" in Scheidung und Bewährung 1933–1936, Edited by Hrsg. Walther Fürst. Theologische Bucherei 34. Munich: Kaiser, 1966.

ECS—Eighteenth-Century Studies.

Enneads—Porphyry on the Life of Plotinus and the Order of His Books. *Ennead* I.1–9. LCL 440. Translated by Arthur H. Armstrong.

ET—English Translation.

EQ—Evangelical Quarterly.

EvTh—Evangelische Theologie.

Exodus Rabbah—Midrash Rabbah: Exodus. Translated by Simon M. Lehrman. London: Soncino, 1961.

Four Sermons—Quatre sermons traictans des matieres fort utiles pour nostre temps, avec briefve exposition du Pseaume LXXXVII. Geneva: Estienne, 1552; ET, *Faith Unfeigned: Four Sermons concerning Matters Most Useful for the Present Time with a Brief Exposition of Psalm 87.* Translated by Robert White. Edinburgh: Banner of Truth Trust, 2010.

FP—Faith & Philosophy.

FragG&G—Karl Barth. *Fragments Grave and Gay.* Translated by Eric Mosbacher. London: Collins, 1971.

GNB—Good News Bible.

HJ—Heythrop Journal.

HTR—Harvard Theological Review.

IB—The Interpreter's Bible. 12 vols. Edited by George A. Buttrick et al. New York: Abingdon, 1952–57.

ICC—International Critical Commentary.

IDB—The Interpreter's Dictionary of the Bible. 4 vols. Edited by George A. Buttrick et al. Nashville: Abingdon, 1962.

IJPS—International Journal of Practical Studies.

Institutes—John Calvin. *Institutes of the Christian Religion* [1559]. 2 vols. Edited by John T. McNeill. Translated by Ford L. Battles. Library of Christian Classics 20–21. Philadelphia: Westminster, 1960. Unless otherwise indicated, quotations from the *Institutes* are from this edition.

Institutes (1536)—John Calvin. *Institutes of the Christian Religion: 1536 Edition.* Translated and annotated by Ford L. Battles. London: Collins Liturgical, 1986.

Institutes (1539)—John Calvin. *Institutes of the Christian Religion of John Calvin, 1539: Text and Concordance.* 4 vols. Edited by Richard F. Wevers. Grand Rapids: Meeter Center for Calvin Studies at Calvin College & Seminary, 1988.

Institutes (1541)—Jean Calvin. *Institution de la Religion Chrétienne (1541).* 2 vols. Edited by Olivier Millet. Geneva: Droz, 2008; ET, *Institutes of the Christian Religion: 1541 French Edition.* Translated by Elsie A. McKee. Grand Rapids: Eerdmans, 2009.

Institutes (1560)—John Calvin. *Institution de la Religion Chrétienne (1560).* 5 vols. Edited by Jean-Daniel Benoit. Paris: Vrin, 1957–63.

IRM—*International Review of Mission.*

IS—*Idealistic Studies.*

JAAC—*Journal of Aesthetics and Art Criticism.*

JAOS—*Journal of the American Oriental Society.*

JBL—*Journal of Biblical Literature.*

JBR—*Journal of Bible and Religion.*

JCL—*Journal of Child Language.*

JETS—*Journal of the Evangelical Theological Society.*

JHI—*Journal of the History of Ideas.*

JHP—*Journal of the History of Philosophy.*

JPS—Jewish Publication Society.

JRT—*Journal of Reformed Theology.*

JR—*Journal of Religion.*

JRE—*Journal of Religious Ethics.*

JRT—*Journal of Religious Thought.*

JSR—*Journal of Scriptural Reasoning.*

JSSR—*Journal for the Scientific Study of Religion.*

JTS—*Journal of Theological Studies.*

KgS—Immanuel Kant. *Kant's Gesammelte Schriften.* 29 vols. in 34 parts. Edited by von der Deutschen (formerly Könliglichen Preuissischen) Akademie der Wissenschaften. Berlin: Reimer, later de Gruyter, 1902–.

KBL—Eberhard Busch. *Karl Barths Lebenslauf: Nach seinen Briefen und autobiographischen Texten.* 2nd rev. ed. Munich: Kaiser, 1976; ET, *Karl Barth: His Life from Letters and Autobiographical Texts.* Translated by John Bowden. London: SCM, 1976.

KD—Karl Barth. *Die kirkliche Dogmatik.* 5 vols. in 14 parts. Zollikon: Evangelischen Buchhandlun, 1932–70.

KJN—*Kierkegaard's Journals and Notebooks.* 11 vols. Edited by Niels J. Cappelørn et al. Princeton: Princeton University Press, 2007–.

KJV—King James Version.

KW—*Kierkegaard's Writings.* 26 vols. Edited and translated by Howard V. Hong and Edna H. Hong. Princeton: Princeton University Press, 1978–2000.

LCL—*Loeb Classical Library.* Cambridge, MA: Harvard University Press, 1912–in progress.

LJW—*The Letters of John Wesley, A.M.* 8 vols. Edited by John Telford. London: Epworth, 1931.

LSJ—Henry G. Liddell, Robert Scott, and Henry S. Jones. *A Greek-English Lexicon.* 9th ed. Oxford: Clarendon, 1996.

LW—*Luther's Works: American Edition.* Vols. 1–30: Edited by Jaroslav Pelikan. St. Louis: Concordia, 1955–76. Vols. 31–55: Edited by Helmut T. Lehmann. Philadelphia: Fortress, 1957–86. Vols. 56–82: Edited by Christopher B. Brown. St. Louis: Concordia, 2009–.

LXX—Septuagint.

MAJT—*Mid-America Journal of Theology.*

Moses—Philo. *Moses I and II.* In LCL 289:274–95. Translated by Francis H. Colson.

MPL—Jacques–Paul Migne. *Patrologia Latina.*

MS—*Medieval Studies.*

MT—Masoretic Text as found in BHS.

MT—*Modern Theology.*

MTP—Charles H. Spurgeon. *The Metropolitan Tabernacle Pulpit.* 63 vols. London: Passmore & Alabaster, 1861–1917.

M. Trin.—Bonaventure. *Quaestiones disputatae de mysterio Trinitatis.* In *Doctoris seraphici S. Bonaventurae opera omnia,* edited by the Fathers of the Collegium S. Bonaventurae (Ad Claras Quas), 5:45–115. Quaracchi: Collegium S. Bonaventurae, 1891; ET, *Disputed Questions on the Mystery of the Trinity.* Translated by Zachary Hayes. New York: Franciscan Institute, 2000.

NA—Erwin Nestle, Kurt Aland et al., eds. *Novum Testamentum Graece.* 28th rev. ed. Stuttgart: Deutsche Bibelgesellschaft, 2012. All Greek references in the text are taken from this edition unless otherwise noted.

NC—*Nineteenth Century.*

NEQ—*New England Quarterly.*

NIV—New International Version.

NPNF²—*A Select Library of the Christian Church: Nicene and Post-Nicene Fathers: Second Series.* 14 vols. Edited by Philip Schaff and Henry Wace. Peabody, MA: Hendrickson, 1994.

NRSV—New Revised Standard Version.

NT—Emil Brunner and Karl Barth. *Natural Theology: Comprising "Nature and Grace" by Professor Dr. Emil Brunner and the Reply "No!" by Dr. Karl Barth.* Translated by Peter Fraenkel. London: Centenary, 1946.

NTG—Johann A. Bengel. *Novum Testamentum Græcum manual.* Tübingen: Heerbrandt, 1790.

OC—Jean-Jacques Rousseau. *Œuvres complètes.* 5 vols. Paris: Pléiade, 1959–95.

OS—John Calvin. *Ioannis Calvini Opera Selecta.* 5 vols. Edited by Peter Barth and Wilhelm Niesel. Munich: Kaiser, 1926–52.

Pap.—*Søren Kierkegaards Papirer.* 16 vols. Various editors. Copenhagen: Gyldendal, 1968–78.

Pesh—Marinus D. Koster. *The Old Testament in Syriac according to the Peshiṭta Version.* Part 1, fasc. 1. Exodus. Leiden: Brill, 1977.

PR—*Philosophical Review.*

PRRD—Richard A. Muller. *Post-Reformation Reformed Dogmatics: The Rise and Development of Reformed Orthodoxy, ca. 1520 to ca. 1725.* 4 vols. 2nd ed. Grand Rapids: Baker, 2003.

PrTR—*Princeton Theological Review.*

PW—Samuel T. Coleridge. *Poetical Works.* Edited by J. C. C. Mays. In Vol. XVI/1–6 of *CC.*

RB—Karl Barth. *Die Theologie der Reformierten Bekenntnisschriften, 1923.* Edited by Eberhard Busch. Zürich: TVZ, 1998; ET, *The Theology of the Reformed Confessions, 1923.* Translated by Darrell L. Guder and Judith J. Guder. Louisville: Westminster John Knox, 2002.

RC—*Reformed Confessions of the 16th and 17th Centuries in English Translation.* 4 vols. Edited by James T. Dennison, Jr. Grand Rapids: Reformation Heritage, 2008–14.

Republic—Plato. *The Republic,* books I–IV. LCL 237. Translated by Paul Shorey.

RS—*Religious Studies.*

RT—Karl Barth. *Revolutionary Theology in the Making: Barth–Thurneysen Correspondence, 1914–1925.* Translated by James D. Smart. Richmond: John Knox, 1964.

SAT—Die Schriften des Alten Testaments.

SB—Hermann L. Strack and Paul Billerbeck. *Kommentar zum Neuen Testament aus Talmud und Midrasch.* 6 vols. München: Beck, 1926–61.

SC—John Calvin. *Supplementa Calviniana, Sermons inédits.* 10 vols. to date. Edited by Erwin Mühlhaupt et al. Neukirchen-Vluyn: Neukirchener, 1936–.

SCG—Thomas Aquinas. *Liber de Veritate Catholicae Fidei contra errores Infidelium qui dicitur Summa contra Gentiles,* books 1–4. Rome: Marietti, 1967; ET, *Summa contra Gentiles.* 5 vols. Translated by Anton C. Pegis. Notre Dame, IN: University of Notre Dame Press, 1975.

SCJ—*Sixteenth Century Journal.*

Sententiarum Libri quatuor—Petrus Lombardus. *Sententiae in IV Libris distinctae.* 2 vols. Edited by Ignatius Brady. Spicilegium Bonaventurianum 5. Rome: Collegium S. Bonaventurae ad Claras Aquas, 1971, 1981; ET, Peter Lombard. *The Sentences, Books 1–4.* Translated by Giulio Silano. Toronto: Pontifical Institute of Medieval Studies, 2008–2010.

Sermons on Hezekiah's Song—John Calvin. *Sermons of John Calvin, upon the songe that Ezechias made after he had bene sicke, and afflicted by the hand of God, conteyned in the 38. Chapiter of Esay* (1560). In *The Collected Works of Anne Vaughan Lock,* edited by Susan M. Felch, 4–71. Tempe, AZ: Arizona Center for Medieval and Renaissance Studies, 1999.

SJT—*Scottish Journal of Theology.*

ST—St. Thomas Aquinas. *Summa Theologiæ: Latin Text and English Translation, Introductions, Notes, Appendices, and Glossaries.* 60 vols. Edited by Thomas Gilby et al. London: Eyre & Spottiswoode, 1963–74.

Strom.—Clement of Alexandria. *Stromateis,* books I–III. Translated by John Ferguson. Washington, DC: Catholic University of America Press, 1991.

SWF—Samuel T. Coleridge. *Shorter Works and Fragments.* Edited by H. J. Jackson and J. R. De J. Jackson. In Vol. XI/1–2 of *CC.*

SZT—Karl Rahner. *Schriften zur Theologie.* 16 vols. Einsiedeln: Benziger, 1954–1984.

TC—Karl Barth. *Die Theologie Calvins.* Edited by Hans Schioll. 1922. Zürich: TVZ, 1993. ET in *The Theology of John Calvin.* Translated by George W. Bromiley. Grand Rapids: Eerdmans, 1995.

Themistocles—Plutarch's Lives: *Themistocles.* In LCL 47:1–92. Translated by Bernadotte Perrin.

TI—Karl Rahner. *Theological Investigations.* 23 vols. Various translators. London: DLT, 1961–84.

TS—*Theological Studies.*

TSL—*Tennessee Studies in Literature.*

TT—Samuel T. Coleridge. *Table Talk.* Edited by Carl Woodring. In Vol. XIV/1–2 of *CC.*

USQR—*Union Seminary Quarterly Review.*

Vg—Vulgate translation of the Bible.

WA—Martin Luther. *D. Martin Luthers Werke: Kritische Gesamtausgabe.* 90 vols. Weimar: Böhlau, 1883–2009.

Wadding—Joannis Duns Scoti. *Doctor Subtilis, Ordinis Minorum, opera omnia.* 22 vols. Edited by Luke Wadding. 1639. Reprint, Paris: apud Ludovicum Vivès, 1891–95.

WBBW—*The Works of Benjamin Breckinridge Warfield.* 10 vols. New York: Oxford University Press, 1931.

WBC—Word Biblical Commentary.

W.G.Th.—Karl Barth. *Das Wort Gottes und die Theologie.* Munich: Kaiser, 1924. ET, *The Word of God and Theology.* Translated by Amy Marga. London: T. & T. Clark, 2011.

WJE—The Works of Jonathan Edwards. 26 vols. Various editors. New Haven: Yale University Press, 1957–2008.

WJEO—The Works of Jonathan Edwards Online. Vols. 27–73. http://edwards.yale.edu/.

WMQ—William & Mary Quarterly.

WSA—The Works of Saint Augustine: A Translation for the 21st Century. 42 vols. to date. Edited by Edmund Hill and John E. Rotelle. New York: New City, 1990–.

ZAW—Zeitschrift für die alttestamentliche Wissenschaft.

ZDT—Zeitschrift für dialektische Theologie.

Zohar Exodus—The Zohar. Translated by Harry Sperling and Maurice Simon. London: Soncino, 1934.

Introduction

The Problem of the Child
in the Calvinian Tradition

"You are the bows from which your children
as living arrows are sent forth."[1]

Thinking theologically about children has been a particular area of interest for me ever since I was a full-time children's worker in the Shetland Islands, working with around four hundred children for over three years in which I purposively, and providentially some would argue, indwelt the phenomenon.[2] Many people from a wide-range of backgrounds in Shetland look back at my work with children with great affection and deemed it a huge success, measured in terms of what the children I worked with have gone on to do in their lives, and also in terms of the integration of the churches and the communities in which

---

1. Gibran, "On Children," in *CW* 107.

2. This is how Dan Hardy described my line of work (pers. comm.). Dan had in mind Michael Polanyi's concept of "personal knowledge," using the Johannine language of "indwelling" (cf. John 17:20–23). For example: "Indwelling, as derived from the structure of tacit knowing, is a far more precisely defined act than is empathy, and it underlies all observations, including all those described previously as indwelling." Polanyi, *Tacit Dimension*, 17. Further: "[I]nto every act of knowing there enters a passionate contribution of the person knowing what is being known, and (. . .) this coefficient is no mere imperfection but a vital component of his knowledge." Polanyi, *Personal Knowledge*, viii. Like Polanyi, Hans-Georg Gadamer raised fundamental questions concerning "the scientific concept of objectivity" when he claimed: "What is known (. . .) certainly also embraces the being of the scientist, for he too is a living creature and a man." Gadamer, *Truth and Method*, 268, 449. For Gadamer the hermeneutical task is located, not in linear cause-and-effect, but in the iterative interplay between *interpretandum* and *interpretans*.

I worked, namely in Burra, Gott/Girlsta, Nesting, Scalloway, Vidlin, and Whiteness/Weisdale.

My life-long "faith seeking understanding" project, as my doctoral supervisor Dan Hardy called it, seeks to allow my experience of working with children in Shetland to disclose its intrinsic intelligibility vis-à-vis the frame of reference involved. In this I have sought to move beyond impressionistic guess-work, even if highly informed, as well as abstract analysis as found in much child developmental literature today, to the investigation of human existence as lived experience, "a turning from the phraseological to the real."[3] Consequently, the theological task I have set myself has been to try and make sense of whatever "*tacit knowledge*"[4] I may have gained from working with children, appropriating biblical, theological, and empirical resources in order to make such knowledge more explicit, recognizing that "intuitions without concepts, or concepts without intuitions"[5] is hardly a viable way forward.

Under the guidance of Dan Hardy, I decided that my main theological interlocutor for the doctoral phase of my project would be John Calvin. In many ways, he would not have been my natural first preference but working in the contexts I have been in, mainly in the Scottish Highlands and Islands where Calvin has had a pervasive hand theologically speaking, it made sound, logical sense. It would be fair to say that I have seen firsthand the ripple effects of Calvinian thinking on children in the Scottish rural context, albeit largely in what I would describe as reductionist terms which I will shortly delineate. Not only has Calvin much to say about children

---

3. *DBWE* 8:358 [*DBW* 8:397]. There is a social and context-relative aspect to what could be called my "critical realist" account of children along the lines that Hilary Putnam explains: "The realist explanation, in a nutshell, is not that language mirrors the world but that *speakers* mirror the world—i.e. their environment—in the sense of *constructing a symbolic representation of that environment*." Putnam, *Meaning and the Moral Sciences*, 123; italics his. Tom Wright defines "critical realism" as "the process of 'knowing' that acknowledges *the reality of the thing known, as something other than the knower* (hence 'realism'), while also fully acknowledging that the only access we have to this reality lies along the spiralling path of *appropriate dialogue or conversation between the knower and the thing known* (hence 'critical')." Wright, *New Testament and the People of God*, 35; italics his. This is not to privilege one account (of children "as they are" in this instance) over another; rather, it is more about what Richard Boyd advocates, that this, in general terms, "affords epistemic access to kinds which are 'natural' in the sense of corresponding to important causal features of the world." Boyd, "Metaphor and Theory Change," in Ortony, ed., *Metaphor and Thought*, 392.

4. Polanyi claims "*tacit knowledge* to comprise two kinds of awareness, *subsidiary awareness* and *focal awareness* (. . .) A *wholly* explicit knowledge is unthinkable." Polanyi, *Knowing and Being*, 144; italics his.

5. Kant, *Critique of Pure Reason*, B314 [*KgS* 3:213.34–35].

in his writings, he is also the fountain of a tradition stretching back to the Reformation which historically has found a natural habitat in Scottish theological soil.

Evidently Calvin took an interest in how a child was formed, advocating: "As the majority of children are not always a source of joy to their parents, a second favour of God is added, which is his forming the minds of children [*dum liberos format*], and adorning them with an excellent disposition, and all kinds of virtues."[6] Calvin's noetic understanding of child development takes into account that a child's mind can be shaped in a particular way, which ideally for him was in the ways of godliness. How he could practically support such a forming of children's minds was of critical importance to him,[7] to the extent he created the Consistory of Geneva in 1541 in order to oversee the morality of the city including that of family life,[8] and he promoted school reforms such as the establishment of the Academy of Geneva in 1559.[9] In relation to the church, he developed infant baptism formulae[10] and various forms of catechesis deemed suitable for children.[11] Calvin's interest in catechesis for children and in their general education arguably indicates an emphasis on his part on children's cognitive development as well as in forming a correct understanding of the Christian faith as he understood it.

However, the modern context in which I engaged with children was one in which I found resources which tended to belie their theological

6. *Comm. Ps* 127:3, *CTS* 6:110 [*CO* 32:324].

7. Cf. Pitkin, "The Heritage of the Lord," 160–93; Pitkin, "Children and the Church in Calvin's Geneva," 144–64.

8. Cf. Watt, "Calvinism, Childhood, and Education," 439–56; Watt, "Childhood and Youth in the Geneva Consistory Minutes," 43–64.

9. Cf. Naphy, "The Reformation and the Evolution of Geneva's Schools," 185–202.

10. Cf. Spierling, *Infant Baptism in Reformation Geneva*.

11. Article 3, "Church Order" (1537) prescribed catechetical instruction of children. *CTT*, 54 [*OS* I:375]. For Calvin "the Church of God will never preserve itself without a Catechism," *CTL* 5:191 [*CO* 13:71–72]. Further: "[W]hat agreement in doctrine our Churches had amongst themselves cannot be observed with clearer evidence than from the Catechisms." *CTT*, 90 [*OS* II:73.22]. Catechetical instruction was not limited to church authorities; parents and schoolmasters also had a role in instructing children in the Christian faith. As Calvin states: "When God has given a man children, it is not only that he should have charge to give them bread to eat, but good instruction is the chiefest." *Sermons on Timothy & Titus*, no. 39 (1 Tim 5:7–12), 475.b.23–27 [*CO* 53:473]. Cf. References to the sixteenth-century English translations of Calvin's sermons on Deuteronomy, Job, Timothy, and Titus are comprised of page number, column (a/b), and line numbers. For all citations to these translations, I have modernized the spelling and altered the punctuation without intending to lose the sense of the original translations. See Calvin Primary Sources in the Bibliography for full details.

ancestry in Calvin. In many ways I felt like I was working in a theological vacuum which led me to develop my own resources, albeit soaked in prayer and reading Scripture. At the same time, I was conscious of the theological tone of what children's resources were available to me which sat uneasily with my understanding of what the Bible said of children, of which more of in chapter 1 of my book. Allow me to explain this tension further.

I was aware that certain twentieth-century self-proclaimed Calvinist fundamentalist[12] exponents posited children in relation to God by using what could be described as narrowly construed categories of sin and grace, with the direct intent, in their terms, to "get the child to *accept* salvation (. . .) *It is not enough to tell the child that he should accept Christ, we must get him to do it then and there.*"[13] Sam Doherty, a former National and European Regional Director of the "Child Evangelism Fellowship" (CEF) in Ireland, in his definition of "the doctrine of total depravity—and original sin," states: "*All* children are therefore spiritually dead, and they will all die physically— as a result of sin. Because *all* children are spiritually dead, they are outside God's kingdom, and they are all LOST as far as their position is concerned."[14] The organization he worked for has published a variety of children's evangelistic material including *The Wordless Book Visualized*[15] and *The Wordless Book Song*,[16] which begins:

> My heart was black with sin,
>
> Until the Savior came in;
>
> His precious blood, I know,
>
> Has washed me white as snow.

The Wordless Book was originally developed by Payson Hammond in the mid-1860s with the support of the itinerant evangelist Dwight L. Moody and the Baptist preacher Charles H. Spurgeon to help illiterate people, including children, gain some understanding of the gospel message. It had three colored pages: black to represent the sinful nature of humanity by nature, red to represent the blood of Christ, and white to represent the perfect

---

12. Cf. Noll, *Scandal of the Evangelical Mind*, chap. 5.

13. Overholtzer, *A Handbook on Child Evangelism*, 17; italics his.

14. Doherty, *Children: A Biblical Perspective*, 185; Doherty, *How to Evangelize Children*, 9; emphasis and capitals his. Cf. John Wesley's counter: "One of Mr. Fletcher's *Checks* [*to Antinomianism*] considers at large the Calvinistic supposition, 'that a natural man is *as dead as a stone*;' and shows the utter falseness and absurdity of it; seeing no man living is without some preventing grace; and every degree of grace is a degree of life." *LJW* 6:239; italics his.

15. Overholtzer, *Wordless Book Visualized*.

16. Johnston, *Wordless Book Song*.

righteousness of God.[17] Spurgeon refers to it in a message given to hundreds of orphans on January 11, 1866:

> I daresay you have most of you heard of a little book which an old divine used constantly to study, and when his friends wondered what there was in the book, he told them that he hoped they would all know and understand it, but that there was not a single word in it. When they looked at it, they found that it consisted of only three leaves; the first was black, the second was red, and the third was pure white. The old minister used to gaze upon the black leaf to remind him of his sinful state by nature, upon the red leaf to call to his remembrance the precious blood of Christ, and upon the white leaf to picture to him the perfect righteousness which God has given to believers through the atoning sacrifice of Jesus Christ his Son.[18]

Moody used it in at least one occasion to address a children's meeting in Liverpool during February 1875 where an estimated 12,000 were present, as his son records: "Mr. Moody gave an address founded on a book with four leaves—black, red, white, and gold—with a sort of running interchange of simple yet searching questions and answers. Responses were very promptly given."[19]

In this light, *The Wordless Book*[20] could be understood to be a form of catechetical exercise. For Spurgeon, the color "black" would have meant for him a means of accommodating Calvin's doctrine of total depravity which

17. Hammond was instrumental in helping Josiah Spiers establish the Children's Special Service Mission (CSSM) in 1867. Cf. Pollock, *Good Seed*, 15–18. Spurgeon refers to Hammond's services at his church on November 8, 1868. Sermon #840, *MTP* 14:625. Hammond modified the book in 1875 by adding a fourth color gold to represent the glories of heaven.

18. Sermon #3278, *MTP* 57:565.

19. Moody, *Life of Dwight L. Moody*, 198–99. Although Spurgeon publicly endorsed Moody's ministry, he was somewhat critical of its tendencies. Murray, *Forgotten Spurgeon*, 177–79. Sir George Adam Smith, also an admirer of Moody and who saw him close up during his Edinburgh campaign in 1874, makes this critical remark of some of Moody's co-laborers: "A young man who had not heard Moody, but who was awakened and anxious, listened for several evenings to these speakers. He saw them whittle away one after another of the essentials of faith, and call him to a reception of salvation in which there was neither conscience nor love nor any awe." Smith, *Life of Henry Drummond*, 58. David Breed sums up: "['Moodyism'] meant much that was intensely earnest, vital and evangelical; but it meant much also that was crude, mistaken and divisive (. . .) But in course of time the defects of the system began to involve its decay. Mr. Moody himself seemed to realize this." Breed, "The New Era in Evangelism," 230–31.

20. In 1939, CEF began to print *The Wordless Book* with a fifth color green representing Christian growth. Overholtzer, *From Then Till Now*, 152.

taught the totalizing effects of original sin on human nature.[21] That doctrine did not mean, however, as we shall see in chapter 3 of my book, that human nature had become depraved with reference to its total intent, rather to the extent of its reach, to "all parts of the soul,"[22] "from the top of our heads to the tip of our toes,"[23] so that no faculty in human nature (none of which had been destroyed) had escaped its corrupting influences.[24]

In contrast, Doherty in his writings gives a wooden, literalist, absolutist, substantialist[25] and essentialist[26] reading of the customary Calvinist rhetoric of total depravity, collapsing it into one whereby original sin has corrupted human nature both to the maximal extent and intent of its reach so that the heart is understood to be utterly depraved, "black" in an unqualified sense. Unlike Calvin as we shall see, Doherty in his many writings offers no discussion of the *imago Dei*, no understanding of faculty psychology in terms of the understanding and the will, no *sensus divinitatis* or *semen religionis* implanted within every human being by God.[27] In effect Doherty describes children in a theological vacuum.

However, Doherty would not be the first to treat Calvin's systematics in such a degenerate manner, as George MacDonald of Huntly hints at in his earliest novel:

> The cause of this degeneracy they share in common with the followers of all other great men as well as of Calvin. They take up what their leader, urged by the necessity of the time, spoke

21. The book in his view was only a reminder—and what it reminded him of Spurgeon could spell out in words. Spurgeon's preaching was full of imaginative suggestions and human sensitivity, and was not a linear formulaic teaching like Doherty's.

22. *Institutes* II.1.9 [*OS* III:236].

23. *Sermons on Genesis*, no. 33 (Gen 6:5–8), 557 [*SC* XI/1:369.12–13].

24. William Wilberforce spells out the doctrine thus: "[M]an is an apostate creature, fallen from his high original, degraded in his nature, and depraved in his faculties; indisposed to good, and disposed to evil; prone to vice, it is natural and easy to him; disinclined to virtue, it is difficult and laborious; that he is tainted with sin, not slightly and superficially, but radically and to the very core." Wilberforce, *A Practical View of Christianity*, 14–15.

25. In contrast, Calvin, who, in reference to natural vitiation, asserts that "it is an adventitious quality which comes upon man rather than a substantial property which has been implanted from the beginning." *Institutes* II.1.11 [*OS* III:240.17–20].

26. Susan Gelman: "Essentialism is a reasoning heuristic that allows us to make fairly good predictions much of the time, but it should not be confused with the structure of reality." Gelman, *Essential Child*, 324. Interestingly, Henry Wellman comments: "Children have an entity notion of mind [a form of essentialism], adults more a process one." Wellman, *Child's Theory of Mind*, 118.

27. The same could be said of the CEF "Statement of Faith" (Part E) in relation to its theological anthropology of children. Cf. Doherty, *How to Evangelize*, 144.

loudest, never heeding what he loved most; and then work the former out to a logical perdition of everything belonging to the latter.[28]

Pertinent in this regard are the remarks of Karl Barth on the historical demise, as he saw it, of "regular dogmatics" as achieved, for instance, by Calvin, resulting in "an individualistic simplification and abridgement of all questions which has given a journalistic impress to modern Evangelical dogmatics (. . .) Would that we had even reached the point where we again regarded regular dogmatics as at least an admonitory ideal worth striving after!"[29]

Without Calvin's training in rhetorical eloquence and his expertise in philology, Doherty has not maintained his method of balancing theologically sophisticated logic with Scriptural argumentation, and thus ended up with less-guarded, linear-sequential, one-to-one correspondence statements between words or concepts and the realities they attempt to express. A hermeneutical methodology of dividing biblical phenomena neatly into antithetical categories ("black" and "white"), in conjunction with a form of pedestrian biblicism by which, based on a certain understanding of the Reformation principle *sola Scriptura*,[30] the biblical text is forced to support a preconceived belief-system can be discerned in these patterns of thought.[31]

---

28. MacDonald, *David Elginbrod*, 1:93. In a later novel MacDonald writes: "The ruin of a man's teaching comes of his followers, such as having never touched the foundation he has laid, build upon it wood, hay, and stubble, fit only to be burnt. Therefore, if only to avoid his worst foes, his admirers, a man should avoid system. The more correct a system the worse will it be misunderstood; its professed admirers will take both its errors and their misconceptions of its truths, and hold them forth as its essence." *Weighed and Wanting*, 2:172. MacDonald (1824–1905) was brought up in an atmosphere of strict Calvinism in Huntly, Aberdeenshire, which he reacted to in his adult life. Coleridge also reacted to a particular form of Calvinism current in his day. In the following remark he seems to indicate a downward trajectory from Calvin on his understanding of human determinism to that of Edwards: "Now as the difference of a captive and enslaved Will, and *no* Will at all, such is the difference between the *Lutheranism* of Calvin and the Calvinism of Jonathan Edwards." *AR* 160; italics his.

29. *CD* 1/1:276–77 [*KD* 1/1:293].

30. William Chillingworth's dictum: "The BIBLE, I say, The BIBLE only is the Religion of Protestants!" *Religion of Protestants*, 56; capitals his. Charles Simeon comments: "God has not revealed His truth in a system; the Bible has no system as such. Lay aside system and fly to the Bible; receive its words with simple submission, and without an eye to any system. Be Bible Christians and not system Christians." Brown, *Recollections of the Conversation Parties of the Rev. Charles Simeon*, 269.

31. Harry Kennedy claims: "Solitary proof-texts have wrought more havoc in theology than all the heresies." Kennedy, *St. Paul's Conceptions of the Last Things*, 310. Ian Paul argues that Calvin was "opposed to all fundamentalist habits of the mind because they attempt to collapse the Scriptures onto a literalist plane of expedient apprehension." Paul, *Knowledge of God*, 40. For George Lindbeck: "Fundamentalist literalism,

Invariably such thinking leads to dehumanized, impersonalistic dogmatic assertions which short-circuit the search for deeper ontological foundations and create a false dichotomy between thought and existence.[32] As Jim Loder argues: "It leads to using prestructured conceptions in an attempt to manipulate an infinitely rich and variegated natural order and to control intrinsically open-ended events."[33] Dan Hardy goes further:

> Resting in such notions, whether scientific or theological, as if they were "facts," involves treating the particular meaning ascribed to them as *equivalent* to that to which they refer, as if the referents themselves were as accessible as the meanings ascribed to them. In effect, this *confines* the referents to the limitations of the referring expressions.[34]

On this basis, purely logical cognitive propositions, even with biblical proof-texts, do not bear the weight of truth-meaning, for they, in the words of Lindbeck, "create rigidities that harbor the seeds of their own destruction."[35] Moreover, they do not sufficiently construe or describe life in all its richly differentiated and beautiful complexity; instead they employ shallow description which "inevitably twists, deforms and falsifies reality."[36] What needs to be taken into account by such proponents as Doherty is that the processes of truth-making defy rationalistic linear forms of logic by going beyond them.[37] Or to put it another way, the dynamics of faith con-

like experiential-expressivism, is a product of modernity." Lindbeck, *Nature of Doctrine*, 51.

32. In many ways, the same theological criticism of Doherty could be directed at theologies of children which do not use biblical categories of sin and grace at all. Jerome Berryman's *Godly Play* program, for example, does not have a Fall narrative. Instead, narrowly construed categories of "innate spirituality" and "relational consciousness" are used, but again within a theological vacuum, for example: "[Innate spirituality] is an entirely natural universal human predisposition (. . .) and a biologically in-built constituent of what it is to be human." Hay and Nye, *Spirit of the Child*, 144, 155.

33. Loder and Neidhardt, *Knight's Move*, 7.

34. Hardy, *God's Ways with the World*, 233; italics mine. Arguably the same thought can also be applied to the following "Logical Positivist" statement: "In science there are no 'depths'; there is surface everywhere (. . .) Everything is accessible to man; and man is the measure of all things." Neurath and Cohen, *Otto Neurath*, 306. Cf. Anglo-American analytic philosophy of religion's preoccupation with the cognitive or informational meaningfulness of religious utterances from which conclusions are drawn with "a considerable degree of confidence" and which require no further examination, an avenue that arguably leads to simplicity and abstraction from reality. Alston, "Two Cheers for Mystery," 99.

35. Lindbeck, *Nature of Doctrine*, 127.

36. Loder and Neidhardt, *Knight's Move*, 9.

37. For Kierkegaard, following Hugo de St. Victor: "With respect to the things that

tradict complete systematization, or at least relativize it, but a reasonable account of faith, without being absolutized, remains legitimate. Tom Torrance would go along with this line of thought for he, like his *Doktorvater* Barth, "moves decisively beyond the limitations of overly logical systematizations of Calvin, (. . .) but his own work still emphasizes close and well-defined logical connections."[38]

More constructively, Loder argues that proper systematic theologizing requires divergent or creative thinking which depends on insight, perceives wholes, and is gestalt-intuitive.[39] I would also argue for a broader, more holistic understanding of knowledge (avoiding "hypostatizations or 'substance-like' thinking"[40] or "hollowness of abstractions")[41] which is contingent on the generative and dynamic power of wisdom. This demands "a wisdom interpretation of scripture"[42] which reads the biblical text with "total imaginative seriousness"[43] and reconciles or integrates[44] the activity of the heart (cordial knowledge) with the activity of the head (intellective knowledge), such as Samuel T. Coleridge advocates:

> For the writings of these mystics acted in no slight degree to prevent my mind from being imprisoned within the outline of any single dogmatic system. They contributed to keep alive the *heart* in the *head*; gave me an indistinct, yet stirring and working presentment, that all the products of the mere *reflective* faculty partook of DEATH, and were as the rattling twigs and sprays in winter, into which a sap was yet to be propelled, from some root to which I had not penetrated, if they were to afford my soul either food or shelter. If they were too often a moving cloud of smoke to me by day, yet they were always a pillar of

---

surpass reason, faith is in fact not really supported by any reason, because reason does not comprehend what faith believes; but nevertheless here there is also a something through which reason becomes determined or is determined as honoring the faith that it nonetheless is incapable of grasping fully." *KJN* 7, Notebook 15:25, 20 [*Pap.* X2 A 354]. Loder would add: "to move into complementarity is the only way to keep faith with reason and at the same time complete the knowing act as inclusive of faith." *Knight's Move*, 87.

38. Hardy, "T. F. Torrance," in Ford, *Modern Theologians*, 173; cf. Torrance, *Calvin's Doctrine of Man*, Preface.

39. Loder and Neidhardt, *Knight's Move*, 268–70.

40. Hardy, *God's Ways with the World*, 247.

41. *LS* 28.

42. Ford, *Christian Wisdom*, 52.

43. Moberly, "To Hear the Master's Voice," 461n44.

44. "[T]he persuasion of the Holy Spirit [working on the human spirit] schools simultaneously the two distinct modes of human knowing." Paul, *Knowledge of God*, 6.

fire throughout the night, during my wanderings through the wilderness of doubt, and enabled me to skirt, without crossing, the sandy deserts of utter unbelief.[45]

Having shared something of the background to my area of research in these opening remarks, indicating that it began from my praxis of working with children which then brought certain areas of tension to the surface as I gave thought to my experience, I was encouraged by Dan Hardy to begin my reflection by looking in a theological manner at various biblical narratives both in the Old and the New Testaments which arguably reflect, rather than sideline, children's own actions, meanings and culture, and which allow interpretation as dynamically contingent events in the real world of space and time which could be deemed a form of biblical realism. It was then that I realized that in Calvin's opening remarks in his *Institutes* that therein may lie a framework (what I call a form of "dialectical epistemology") in which children could be construed in relation to God in an expansive rather than an inhibitive manner. I also considered that this framework potentially offered an alternative way to the more usual practice of forcing knowledge of children from "the *new* world of the Bible"[46] into a separate realm from that of the empirical as gained through the exact sciences. Dan Hardy encouraged me to follow my line of thinking here.

However, as I began to gather data from Calvin's œuvre which refer to children (see chapter 3), I began to see more and more that there was a real problem here, for although his framework could be deemed expansive, his language of children could be deemed reductionist, particularly when contrasted to the biblical language I had already explored. But instead of understanding Calvin to be merely theologically reductionist in his use of language (as I would argue is the case for Doherty), I suggest that Calvin used a form of rhetorical hyperbole in order to heighten his soteriological claims.

After working with Calvin, I began to trace a Calvinian historical trajectory in relation to children in the eighteenth-century writings of the Revs. Thomas Boston of Ettrick and Jonathan Edwards of Northampton (see chapter 4). It was then that I began to note within the Edwardsean corpus that therein may lie a critical tool, namely his aesthetics, by which children

---

45. *BL* I 152; capitals and italics his. Cf. Coleridge: "Believe me, Southey! a metaphysical Solution, that does not instantly *tell* for something in the Heart, is grievously to be suspected as apocry[p]hal." *CL* II 961; italics his. Blaise Pascal: "We know the truth, not only through reason, but also through the heart. It is through the latter that we know first principles, and reason, which has part in it, tries in vain to challenge them." Pascal, *Pensées* S142/L110.

46. *W.G.Th.*, 26; ET, 23; italics his.

could be construed in language more in keeping with the biblical material, in particular that of Moses. By linking Edwards's aesthetics (primary and secondary beauty) to Calvin's dialectical epistemology (knowledge of God and humanity), Edwards's aesthetics could be seen to correct both his and Calvin's dogmatic use of language of children in relation to God.

My final move (chapter 5) is an attempt to expand Calvin's dialectical framework in order to develop a theology of children and childhood which integrates biblical categories of sin and grace, but not in a narrowly construed sense, and which upholds biblical language and imagery of children. I then explore a biblical *"hermeneutic* of wisdom"[47] in relation to children, thus beginning the process of developing an *a posteriori* epistemological account of how a child develops, understanding "a child is a life-history in the making, formed by God's providence."[48] A key question I raise here is what could be considered to be conducive for the fullest maturation of children which involves more than their cognitive structures of intelligence.[49]

Some of the germane theological questions which lie at the heart of my project are these: What is a child's "normal development"? What does God think of children? What possible intentions does God have for developing children in a fully realized sense? My ultimate aim is to delineate a soteriological environment (language and imagery are both important in this regard) which enables children to discover their "fundamental beauty as human beings"[50] as part of God's salvific purposes for their lives.

47. Hardy, *God's Ways with the World*, 246; italics his.

48. Dan Hardy (pers. comm.). Barth defines "providence" as "the superior dealings of the Creator with His creation, the wisdom, omnipotence and goodness with which He maintains and governs in time this distinct reality according to the counsel of His own will." *CD* 3/3:3 [*KD* 3/3:1]. Cf. Eric Erikson's definition of human life: "[T]he accidental coincidence of but one life cycle with but one segment of history." Erikson, *Childhood and Society*, 232. According to Barth's theological criteria, this definition lacks due providential attentiveness and care.

49. For James Hadfield: *"Maturation is the development of innate patterns of behaviour in ordered sequence."* Hadfield, *Childhood and Adolescence*, 48; italics his. For Margaret Donaldson the maturational process is the means by which children "become competent, self-determining, responsible beings." Donaldson, *Children's Minds*, 126. For Frances Wickes: "[O]ur goal is to help in the creation of a free individual." Wickes, *Inner World of Childhood*, 35. My theological issue with these definitions is that they draw attention to the child's natural "innateness" or "self-determination" as if these alone allow the child to achieve full maturity, without taking into account providential activity. For my purposes, Jerome Kagan offers a better definition of maturation, "a special organization, slow growth, and connectedness." Kagan, *Nature of the Child*, 75.

50. Vanier, *Becoming Human*, 34. Many of these questions first struck me after I helped taking aid relief to orphaned children in Romania on various occasions. I remember being struck by those I saw tied up in their cots, many of whom were mentally as well as physically malformed. It was evident to me even then that human life which

All of this discussion has important implications for children's nurture and education within the home, the church, the academy, and broader society today.

---

finds itself rootless can lead to a dehumanised state of development. Simone Weil puts this very well: "To be rooted is perhaps the most important and least recognized need of the human soul. It is one of the hardest to define. A human being has roots by virtue of his real, active and natural participation in the life of a community which preserves in living shape certain particular treasures of the past and certain particular expectations of the future (. . .) Every human being needs to have multiple roots. It is necessary for him to draw wellnigh the whole of his moral, intellectual and spiritual life by way of the environment of which he forms a natural part." Weil, *Need for Roots*, 43.

Chapter I

Biblical Language and Imagery of Children

The wisdom & graciousness of God in the infancy of the human species—
its beauty, long continuance &c &c.[1]

Without going into the historicity of the individual infancy narratives I shall explore, I take all the children so described as "real" children, rather than seeing them, for example, as "embodiments of God's hopes for us."[2] Further, I look at these narratives recognizing that each child had a very particular history in terms of God's redemptive purposes in and for the world. This leaves then the issue of how to move from the particular to the general[3] in order to construct, if it is a distinct possibility, a theology of any child born in space and time. According to Hardy:

---

1. Coleridge on 'Infancy & Infants,' *CN* I 330.

2. Moltmann, *In the End—the Beginning*, 17.

3. Loder claims that it is the "journey into the depth of particularity that yields final universality." Loder and Neidhardt, *Knight's Move*, 275. Francis Watson justifies a claim to a universalistic, extrasystematic biblical hermeneutic, as opposed to a particularized, intrasystematic biblical hermeneutic thus: "Theology must reject a hermeneutic that condemns the biblical texts to narcissist self-referentiality. What is needed, however, is not a return to non-narrative theology but a better theology of the Christian narrative, and this will inevitably remain indebted to earlier work in this field even as it attempts to remedy its deficiencies. Hence the appropriate procedure is to attempt to show that *a claim to universality is inherent in Christian narrative*, and that this particular narrative therefore refuses the particularity which is here imposed upon it." Watson, *Text, Church and World*, 137; italics mine; cf. Barth's christological reworking of Calvin's doctrine of election, in *CD* 2/2.

13

> Hebrew understanding (. . .) always finds the universal in the
> particular (. . .) [I]t begins from the particular in its spatio-
> temporal location (. . .) this "location" or particularity is then
> expanded in praise to be "everywhere," without displacing other
> particularities. The universal is therefore a world of particulars,
> each contingent upon its place yet joined by an expanding truth
> found in the praise of God.[4]

One biblical text which may exemplify such an "expanded" move is
where Jesus takes *a* child and places it in the midst of his disciples.[5] This
text seems to imply he could have taken any child and still have made the
same point. On this basis, MacDonald contends: "The lesson will be found
to lie not in the *humanity*, but in the *childhood* of the child."[6] In other words,
there is something particular about any child born into a spatio-temporal
location, which is why Jesus took a child and not an adult and placed it in
the midst. MacDonald argues that this particularity is "the divine idea of
childhood"[7] which can never be annihilated from the heart of any child as it
is an intrinsic part of the *imago Dei*.

I take it to be theologically normative to explore knowledge of children in the biblical material in order to set forward a standard with which
to compare what Calvin and Edwards (my main theological interlocutors)
have said of children in relation to God. As this is ultimately an epistemic
exercise, the next step will be to map out a theological framework in which
such knowledge can be placed, but I did not want the biblical material to
be framework-dependent even if the framework is deemed deep and expansive; that is, the information gained by this means from each biblical
narrative would be evident only in a contrived task situation. Rather, I
have sought to allow each narrative to speak in accordance with its own
respective nature. A comparison can be drawn here to Calvin's conundrum,
whether knowledge of God or humanity comes first, as one form of knowledge has an impact on the other. But in the order of right biblical thinking (I
am proposing a form of biblical theology), the biblical narrative must come
first, a further reason for the placing of this chapter at the start of this study.

The four biblical infancy narratives I have chosen to look at in this
chapter seem to me to use specific language of children in relation to God,
which arguably bears epistemological possibilities hardly drawn out by

4. Hardy, *God's Ways with the World*, 248.

5. Matt 18:2.

6. "The Child in the Midst," *Unspoken Sermons First Series*, 6; italics his.

7. Ibid., 5. MacDonald goes on to argue: "Childhood belongs to the divine nature."
Ibid., 19.

biblical exegetes. They are also texts that Calvin addressed in either his commentaries or sermons, thus providing a fruitful way of engaging with Calvin's exegesis, allowing one to see to what extent he allowed the "plain sense" of the text to speak for itself (always his ideal)[8] or whether he allowed his systematics, deliberately or otherwise, to impose on the text a structure alien to its own intrinsic integrity.[9]

MOSES

There are various words used in the canonical texts that refer to Moses as a new-born child: in the MT טוֹב [ṭôb], and in the LXX and Greek New Testament ἀστεῖος. This is how they are found in context:

> Now a man from the house of Levi went and married a Levite woman. The woman conceived and bore a son; and when she saw that he [Moses] was a fine [טוֹב] baby, she hid him three months.[10]

> By faith Moses was hidden by his parents for three months after his birth, because they saw that the child was beautiful [ἀστεῖον]; and they were not afraid of the king's edict.[11]

> At this time Moses was born, and he was beautiful [ἀστεῖος] before God.[12]

There are various theological issues that arise from these texts, namely the language which is used to describe Moses as a new-born child, particularly as he is posited in relation to God, and what this may say about the Calvinian use of language in relation to children which I will explore later, and secondly, the form of discernment[13] or seeing which is understood in

---

8. Calvin only allowed for allegorical interpretation when certain exegetical conditions were met; cf. *Comm. Minor Prophets*, 1, Budé's "Preface," CTS 13:xxvi–xxvii [CO 42:107–8].

9. Cf. Lindbeck's assertion: "[I]t is the text which absorbs the world rather than the world the text." *Nature of Doctrine*, 118.

10. Exod 2:1–2. All biblical quotations are taken from the NRSV translation unless otherwise indicated.

11. Heb 11:23.

12. Acts 7:20.

13. The issue of discernment (seeing with the eyes of God) is taken up by Walter Moberly in his monograph *Prophecy and Discernment*.

relation to children, and how this may help in how children can be seen today. To begin this discussion, this is how Calvin comments on Exod 2:2:

> There is no doubt but that God had adorned him with this beauty, in order the more to influence his parents to preserve him (. . .) since they had good hopes of the deliverance promised to them, their courage was increased by the additional motive of his beauty, and that they were so attracted to pity, that all obstacles were overcome (. . .) In fine, the love which his beauty awakened was so far from being a part of faith, that it deservedly detracts from its praise; but God, who, in his wonderful wisdom, makes all things to work for the good of his chosen ones, sustained and strengthened their tottering faith by this support.[14]

Here Calvin interprets the "beauty" with which God adorned the child Moses purely on a physical level (how he appeared), suggesting that this was to be taken as a sign and symbol of hope to the child's parents of what they should do with their child, namely "preserve him" at all costs from any danger that could potentially befall him. It was this that gave them the energy and resilience to go to such great lengths to hide him in a papyrus-reed container, carefully waterproofed with hot tar and pitch, among the bulrushes along the river Nile.

According to Calvin's interpretation, the focus is more on the parents' actions rather than on the child itself, the description of the child serving only as a means to an end, which certainly is in keeping with the earlier presentation of how the midwives behaved and of the role of the women in these early chapters of Exodus in thwarting Pharaoh's oppression. There is thus a simple cause-and-effect logic to Calvin's way of thinking about this text.[15]

However, this seems to me to beg the question as to why the text is so specific in the way it describes the child, for, after all, is it not the case that "every baby is beautiful to its mother anyway" [Car quel enfant, fût-il laid, n'est pas beau aux yeux de sa mère?], as Išo'dad of Merv (Bishop of Ḥĕdhatha) rhetorically remarks.[16] In other words, do not all babies, regardless of how they appear, naturally elicit compassion and care from their mothers no matter the cost that this may involve? Why then does the text say that Moses was "good" or "beautiful"? Would his mother have discarded him if he had not been so? Surely not. It is here that the Rabbinic commentator Nahmanides takes this thought one step further in the following suggestive midrash:

---

14. *Comm. Exod* 2:2, CTS 2:42–43 [CO 24:23].

15. Cf. Cassuto, *Commentary on the Book of Exodus*, 18.

16. Van den Eynde, ed., *Commentaire d'Išo'dad de Merv sur l'Ancien Testament*, 3:3; cf. Salvesen, *Symmachus in the Pentateuch*, 67n14.

It is well known that women love their children, beautiful or not, and they would all hide them to the best of their ability; there was no need to say that he was beautiful to explain why she hid him. The reason why this detail was included is that she saw in him an *unprecedented beauty* and thought that a miracle might be done for him, and he would be saved. So she set her mind to devise a plan.[17]

Nahmanides hints here that there is something more pertinent than just a perceived physical beauty or just the actions which followed the perception going on in this text; rather, the text draws attention to the child in itself and not merely to its physical appearance (although it did have a causal role to play). This, Calvin does not seem to have grasped or at least to have made any attempt to uncover. But Calvin is not alone in this kind of interpretation. Indeed, he follows in a long line of Jewish commentators who held a similar understanding.

Philo of Alexandria, for example, first mentions Moses's physical appearance in relation to what his parents saw in him at his birth, recording: "Now, the child from his birth had an appearance of more than ordinary goodliness," and on that basis his parents acted, "as long as they could actually set at nought the proclamations of the despot."[18] Philo seems to indicate here that it was what Moses's parents saw in their new-born baby which motivated them to go against the king's edict that all Hebrew male babies must be slaughtered, and that instead they sought to preserve his life. The second mention of the child's beauty is recorded by Philo after Pharaoh's daughter surveyed his overall appearance "from head to foot"; consequently "she approved of his beauty and fine condition."[19] Philo makes one further reference to Moses's appearance as a child where, after he was weaned by his natural mother, he is described as "noble and goodly to look upon."[20]

Flavius Josephus, using the same LXX text as Philo, also interprets the beauty of the child purely in physical terms but avoids using the distinctive LXX word ἀστεῖον. In his discussion of this matter, he frequently draws attention to the people who "saw" this beauty but not necessarily his parents. To begin with, it is Pharaoh's daughter who sees the beauty:

[S]he, at sight of the little child, was enchanted at its size and beauty; for such was the tender care which God showed for

17. Carasik, ed., *Commentators' Bible: The JPS Miqra'ot Gedolot: Exodus*, 9; italics mine.

18. *Moses* I.3 (9).

19. *Moses* I.4 (14).

20. *Moses* I.5 (18).

Moses, that the very persons who by reason of his birth had de-
creed the destruction of all children of Hebrew parentage were
made to condescend to nourish and tend him.[21]

Not only is it Pharaoh's daughter who sees the beauty, but Josephus
then turns attention to those who passed by him in normal everyday life:

> When he was three years old, God gave wondrous increase to his
> stature; and none was so indifferent to beauty as not, on seeing
> Moses, to be amazed at his comeliness. And it often happened
> that persons meeting him as he was borne along the highway
> turned, attracted by the child's appearance, and neglected their
> serious affairs to gaze at leisure upon him: indeed childish charm
> so perfect and pure as his held the beholders spell-bound.[22]

In effect, the beauty of the child is discerned by quite a range of people,
not just his mother[23] or indeed just his parents.[24] Finally, Josephus refers to
how Pharaoh's daughter presented the child to her father, telling him that
she had "[brought] up a boy of divine beauty and generous spirit."[25]

As we have seen, Nahmanides hints that there is something more
significant going on in the text. The question thus arises, what is it about
the child that draws such an appraisal? There have been a number of Rabbinic exegetical attempts to understand what Moses's mother saw when she
first looked upon her child on account of which she sought to save him
from Pharaoh's death decree, revealing that interpreters have not restricted
themselves to what could be called a 'simple' explanation of the text. Sarna
suggests that the MT word [טוֹב], usually translated "goodly" [ṭôb], could
also in this context connote "robust or healthy."[26] Although William Propp
suggests that it more likely means "viable, healthy," he does consider that it
could alternatively connote "beauty,"[27] comparing it to 1 Kgs 20:3 where it
is translated "goodliest."

The LXX translation of the Hebrew word טוֹב in Exod 2:2 is ἀστεῖον.
It is not easy to see why the writer chose this LXX word. The second-cen-
tury Greek translations of Aquila of Sinope and Symmachus the Ebionite

21. *Ant.* II.9.5 (224–25).

22. *Ant.* II.9.6 (230–31).

23. Exod 2:2.

24. Heb 11:23.

25. *Ant.* II.9.7 (232); cf. Acts 7:20.

26. Sarna, *JPS Torah Commentary: Exodus*, 9.

27. Propp, *Anchor Bible: Exodus 1–18*, 149.

rendered טוֹב literally as ἀγαθός and καλός respectively,[28] either of which, rather than the MT, may have influenced Jerome's Vulgate translation of *elegantem*. John Wevers sees the LXX's use as "idiomatic" and somewhat dismissively concludes: "The tradition offers little of interest."[29] This is hardly respectful to the way many Jewish Rabbinic commentators have treated the text, as we shall see. Rather, the difficulty in the text seems to have indicated to them that there was something significant going on, and consequently they were attentive to its potential meaning.

Redaction analysis suggests that the whole clause in Exod 2:2—"she saw that he was good and she hid him"—echoes a key phrase which is repeated seven times in the divine verdict in the first Genesis creation narrative: "God saw that [it] was good."[30] Like God, Moses's mother also looked and examined her work of creation, and consequently deemed it "proper and correct."[31] Sarna suggests that the hinted parallel between the two texts indicates that the birth of Moses should be read on a par with "the dawn of a new creative era."[32] Likewise, the midrash claim (R. Shemoth), "When Moses was born, the whole house was filled with light,"[33] bears a striking resemblance to Gen 1:4 which says: "And God saw the light, that it was good [טוֹב]."

R. Judah claims that, based on the use of the Hebrew word *ṭôb*, *ṭobiah* was Moses's original name as received from his parents.[34] Other interpretations include the child Moses being described as beautiful as an angel of God in the sight of his parents,[35] and Pseudo-Jonathan speaking of him as "a steadfast child/a boy full of vigour" [*br qyywm*].[36] In the early church

28. Field, *Origenis Hexaplorum quae supersunt*, 1:82.

29. Wevers, *LXX: Notes on the Greek Text of Exodus*, 12.

30. Gen 1:4, 10, 12, 18, 21, 25, 31.

31. *Rashbam's Commentary on Exodus*, 20.

32. Sarna, *JPS Torah Commentary, Exodus*, 9.

33. *Exodus Rabbah* i.20; *b.Sotah* 12a; *Zohar Exodus* 11b; cf. *Bib. Ant.* IX.13, 15. This light is identified with the divine presence in the midrash on Exod 2:6: "Said R. Yose b. R. Hanina, 'She [Pharaoh's daughter] saw the Presence of God [*Shekhinah*] with him.'" *Exodus Rabbah* i.24; *b.Sotah* 12b.

34. "R. Meir says, 'His name was "good" [*Tob*].' R. Judah says, 'His name was "The Lord is good" [*Tobiah*].' R. Nehemiah says, 'He was worthy of prophecy.'" *b.Sotah* 12a.

35. *Jalkut Rubeni* f.75.4; *Pirḳe de-Rabbi Eliezer* XLVIII.

36. Otherwise translated: "[H]e was viable." *Targum Pseudo-Jonathan, Exodus*, II, 164n7; cf. Vermes, *Scripture and Tradition in Judaism*, 185n1; Le Déaut, *Targum du Pentateuque*, 2:20–21.

tradition, Clement of Alexandria refers to him as "a child of noble birth,"[37] and Eusebius of Emesa refers to "the grace that rested upon him."[38]

By linking the Exodus text back to the first Genesis creation narrative, perhaps there is an indication that there was something about this child which was of primary significance, pointing beyond the merely physical interpretation as articulated by many commentators as we have seen. The theological conundrum, however, is whether Moses's mother saw her child in ethical terms (if so, the Hebrew word should be translated "good"), or in aesthetic terms (if so, the Hebrew word should be translated "beautiful"). Rabbi Ezra comments that the word literally means "good," that in reference to a mature man, "good" could refer to his intellectual or spiritual qualities, but in reference to a child, it could only refer to its physical attributes,[39] which again begs the question as to why the text is so specific about the child. All that Rabbi Ezra can offer by way of response to this question is that it must mean that Moses "was better than all who are born," i.e., that "[h]e was better looking than any other child,"[40] which, in the light of what I have said of caring mothers, is hardly a suitable retort.

On the other hand, Walter Brueggemann draws attention to Gen 1:31 where, at the conclusion of the sixth day of creation, Yahweh exclaimed, "It was very good," and interprets this to be "likely an aesthetic judgment,"[41] in effect, a response to a brilliant act of creation, rather than an ethical appraisal. In this, Brueggemann draws from Samuel Terrien who argues that the aesthetic dimensions of the God of wisdom and the work of this God of wisdom readdresses and checks excessive ethical readings of the biblical narrative such as the Creation and Wisdom accounts.[42]

If this is so, could it then be said that the sense of beauty or loveliness on the part of the created order evoked from God's side a doxological response to what he had created, indicating a sense of satisfaction on his part, a glad acknowledgement of success? In support of this interpretation, Brueggemann suggests that both here and in other places in Scripture, a glad affirmation of creation is moved more by awe and delight than by ethical insistence or demand. Thus for example, Prov 8:30–31, in speaking of creation, culminates in a statement of "delight" and "dancing," which can be

37. *Strom.*, I.23 [*ANF* 2:658].

38. *Catena Sinaitica* E 21; cf. Petit, ed., *Catena Graecae*, 2:276.

39. Ibn Ezra, *Commentary on the Pentateuch*, 34.

40. Ibid., n49.

41. Brueggemann, *Theology of the Old Testament*, 251; cf. Claus Westermann renders this: "It is very good (beautiful)." *Genesis 1–11*, 167.

42. Terrien, *Elusive Presence*, chap. 7.

construed more as an aesthetic response than an ethical one.[43] Based on this reading, perhaps Exod 2:2 is simply another instance of someone, in this case Moses's mother, delighting in what she "saw" in her child, an important point which I will pick up shortly.

Heb 11:23 follows the LXX rather than the MT (which tells the story throughout with Moses's mother as the subject) in assigning responsibility for the decision of defying the royal edict to both Moses's parents (Amram and Jochebed),[44] as do Philo,[45] Josephus,[46] Pseudo-Philo,[47] and the Peshiṭta Syriac text.[48] The fact that their decision to take such risks was based on what they "saw" [εἶδον] in their child, that he was "uncommonly striking" [ἀστεῖον], does not seem to solely rest on human pride (after all he was "their" child), but rather that the "beauty" they discerned in him indicated to them that there was something about the child which by the "modality of faith"[49] enabled them to enter into the providential purposes of God for their child.[50]

Thomas Aquinas indicates that the text implies a causal connection between divine sovereignty (as indicated by the child's beauty) and human behavior (the parents' response to the beauty), when he says: "And so from his beauty they judged that there was some power of God in him, for they were rude rustics, sweating in the work of clay and brick."[51] The outcome was favourable to all concerned.[52] Certainly the text gives no hint that his parents were given any other special revelation regarding their child, such as later occurred with regards to the birth of Samson.[53] So what form of discernment could their seeing their child as "beautiful" be described as?

---

43. For Brueggemann, the ethical "issues in the [Pauline, juridical] categories of sin and grace." *Theology of the Old Testament*, 344.

44. Exod 6:30.

45. *Moses* I.1 (7)—"his father and mother"; *Moses* I.1 (9)—"his parents."

46. *Ant.* II.9.4 (217–19).

47. *Bib. Ant.* IX.5.

48. Pesh, 118.

49. WBC 47b:369.

50. Aquinas comments: "From this we are given to know that although faith is about invisible things, yet we can struggle to faith through certain visible signs." *Commentary on the Epistle to the Hebrews*, 251 [*Ad Hebraeos* 612].

51. Ibid.

52. Bruce, *Acts of the Apostles*, 217–18; Williamson, *Philo and the Epistle to the Hebrews*, 469–70; D'Angelo, *Moses in the Letter to the Hebrews*, 38–42.

53. It was the view of Josephus that there had been such an extraordinary communication to Amram in a dream. *Ant.* II.9.3 (210); cf. Judg 13:2–5.

This is where Acts 7:20 seems to me to be theologically pertinent to this overall discussion.[54] The Acts text comes in the middle of Stephen's address before the Jewish Sanhedrin in which he claimed that Moses as a baby "was beautiful before God" [ἦν ἀστεῖος τῷ θεῷ]. The word ἀστεῖος comes again from the LXX version of Exod 2:2. LSJ interprets the LXX word in physical terms, putting it under the heading "of outward appearance" then suggesting it means "pretty, graceful."[55] Contrariwise, Kingsley Barrett argues that "the latter seems particularly unsuitable for a new-born infant," and therefore that "Luke possibly means that Moses was an entirely satisfactory child, without physical or mental handicap."[56] Other English translations of this text frequently suggest that this relates to something out of the ordinary about Moses's physical appearance, that he was "no ordinary child," or, alternatively, that he was "fair in the sight of God" (NIV).

However, these comments do not immediately explain the significance of what the Acts text might actually be saying about the Exodus event. The text, I suggest, is not telling us something about the physicality of the child, nor indeed (prophetically) what is going to become of the child; rather, the text is saying something about the child itself by positing the child in relation to God, that the theological construal of the child is "beautiful before God." On this basis, not even Mary D'Angelo's translation that the child was "divinely beautiful" is theologically adequate or sufficient.[57]

Looking more closely at the actual wording in this expression, we have the dative opinion or respect [τῷ θεῷ] with reference to God, translated "in God's eyes," which may reflect an idiomatic way of expressing an emphatic, almost superlative, quality in Hebrew,[58] leading Frederick Bruce to state: "Such expressions (. . .) were often used with elative force (. . .) As the LXX examples indicate, this is a Semitic idiom."[59] As if to indicate this, it has been translated "exceeding fair" (KJV) and "a very beautiful child" (GNB).

Ben Witherington goes further: "The expression conveys more than just the idea of how God views someone. It speaks of a character trait which is deemed good and approved by God."[60] However, Witherington's ethical

---

54. Calvin preached on this text but made no reference to how the child Moses is described. He basically takes the narrative to be an encouragement for faith; cf. *Sermons on Acts of the Apostles*, no. 32 (Acts 7:20–22), 437–51 [*SC* VIII:281–89].

55. LSJ 1:260; cf. Plutarch, *Themistocles* V.4 (16) where Bernadotte Perrin translates it "clever".

56. Barrett, *Critical and Exegetical Commentary on the Acts of the Apostles*, 1:353.

57. D'Angelo, *Moses*, 39.

58. Cf. Jonah 3:3.

59. Bruce, *Acts of the Apostles*, 197.

60. Witherington III, *Acts of the Apostles*, 269n298.

appraisal does not seem to take into account that this is a baby that is being spoken of, not an adult whose "character trait[s]" would be more apparent. This is where Brueggemann's argument may prove useful, that this should be read (at least partly) as an aesthetic judgment, that God "saw" this child as he "saw" creation, and consequently named it "beautiful."[61]

Hence, what is theologically significant about these texts is not what could be understood merely on a physical level, which is temporal and fleeting (although it could include this), nor what it could have indicated to the onlookers (although again this could have had a part to play), but rather naming/affirming/construing the child as "beautiful" by positing it in relation to God. The use of such aesthetic language in the biblical text has thus epistemological weight, providing knowledge of the child not otherwise gained by any other method, including the empirical.

What is further illuminating about these texts is that this theological understanding of the child was identical with that of the child's mother (MT) and with that of its parents (LXX). In effect what we have here is a form of godly seeing or discernment, seeing something or someone as God sees them, having the mind of God on the matter, sharing precisely the same kind of knowledge.[62] That this form of "personal knowledge" seems to have come to the parents intuitively is something I want to pick up shortly.

Moses himself seems to have become more aware of this "personal knowledge," that he "possessed a visible sign of God's elective favour,"[63] in the process of his maturation and development into adulthood. The question therefore arises as to how Moses gained such knowledge and tacit awareness? Was there a point in his development when he became aware of who and what he was in the sight of God? Could this have been in the time of his earliest consciousness, though perhaps in an implicit mode, when he was embraced in the bosom of his mother when she saw him to be "beautiful"? Hans Urs von Balthasar would seem to argue thus, for according to his

---

61. Jacques Maritain uses an ontological argument to come to the same conclusion: "[I]n the eyes of God all that exists is beautiful, to the very extent to which it participates in being. For the beauty that God beholds is transcendental beauty, which permeates every existent, to one degree or another." Maritain, *Creative Intuition in Art and Poetry*, 163. Edwards's aesthetic theory offers a similar argument. See below, chap. 4. However, Edmund Newey argues that when Friedrich Schleiermacher's use of the verb *glauben* in his Christmas Eve novella is stressed, "that is when the beautiful and the divine in the child are perceived not ontologically but sophiologically, when the child is seen as an image of the divine potential in humanity rather than as divine in herself." Newey, *Children of God*, 111.

62. Edwards defined truth as "the consistency and agreement of our ideas with the ideas of God." *WJE* 6:341–42.

63. WBC 47b:370.

theological understanding, when a mother turns in love toward their child, the two become one, that is the child becomes one with the mother in her love but still remains separate from her, which in turn enables the child to discover their identity or, at the very least, helps to form it.[64] For Moses, perhaps in the depths of his soul, there slumbered an awareness of who he was in the sight of God by the way his mother looked at him which, as we have seen, was a form of godly discernment.

Needless to say, in spite of all the calamities of his life, and the inevitable strain of giving up a comfortable existence in Pharaoh's palace to live in tents in the land of Midian, God had his hand upon Moses right from the start of his life. Moses was under the protective eye of "the providence of God," as Philo and Josephus both note concerning Moses's origins;[65] his education in the royal palace was with the intended aim of "the improvement of the mind," but he showed throughout his studies an instinctive genius and great abilities which for Philo equipped him to "carve out much that is new in the way of knowledge."[66]

When it came to putting this "personal knowledge" of who he was in the sight of God, which he did not gain by his Egyptian education, into practice, Moses took matters into his own hands and killed an Egyptian,[67] all along supposing that his kinsfolk would understand who he was, namely a deliverer sent by God, but nothing more specific than this. Certainly the text does not explicitly state that God told him this information directly, which only happened later in the "divine-human encounter" at the burning bush,[68] which

64. Von Balthasar, *Unless You Become Like This Child*, 16–18. A similar thought is expressed by George MacDonald: "[T]he sky over him is his mother's face; the earth that nourishes him is his mother's bosom (. . .) Her face is God, her bosom Nature, her arms are Providence—all love—one love—to him an undivided bliss." *Dish of Orts*, 44. Further, "The child was compelled to love; he could not help it. The beginning of his love to his mother was just the beginning of that which was in the infinite, all-embracing love towards everything that feels. The smallest spark of love was from God, and if it were in the poorest and most selfish heart, it was the presence of the divine origin in that heart." MacDonald, "Dr. George MacDonald in Aberdeen," 3. Early "mutuality" or "intersubjectivity" between mother and child is understood to be integral to a child's development including learning of language; cf. Bruner, "The Ontogenesis of Speech Acts," 1–19; Trevarthen, "Communication and Cooperation in Early Infancy: A Description of Primary Intersubjectivity," 321–47; Trevarthen, "The Foundation of Intersubjectivity: Development of Interpersonal and Cooperative Understanding in Infants," 316–42; Schaffer, *Child's Entry into a Social World*, chap. 4.

65. *Moses* I.4 (12, 17); *Ant.* II.9.7 (236). Philo adds: "God makes all that He wills easy, however difficult be the accomplishment." *Moses* I.5 (19).

66. *Moses* I.5 (22).

67. Exod 2:11–14.

68. Exod 3:1—4:17; Brunner, *Divine-Human Encounter*.

again begs the question of when that happened. This "personal knowledge" (which seemingly had gone public) is also inferred by the remark from one of his own kindred the day following the murder when he referred to Moses as "a prince" and "a judge."[69] The overall sense of the text of Exod 1–3 seems to indicate that Moses intuitively knew who he was (a deliverer) and that this was something which he was nurtured in from his birth.

In terms then of the dialectical relationship between God and Moses, God had an intimate knowledge of Moses right from his birth which his parents somehow had come into possession of. By seeing him as God saw him, they set him on a path toward true self-knowledge as determined by his relationship to God. From Moses's perspective, the development of his knowledge of God and of himself seems to have been gradual, coming to some sort of peak when he took matters into his own hands in the killing of the Egyptian, then slowly subsiding until God called him from the burning bush. Moses was preserved in this knowledge, it seems, by holding on to how he had been seen at the start of his life. The relationship between God and Moses was thus not a static one but dynamic, ever opening up new possibilities and disclosures in terms of knowledge of God and of himself, a dialectical relationship which was both personalistic and objectivistic—an "I-and-Thou" relationship.[70]

A practical implication of this discourse is that, on the basis of Išo'dad of Merv's remark "every baby is beautiful to its mother anyway," perhaps the reason why mothers often bond with their new-born children is that, like Moses's mother, they too have a form of "personal knowledge," that they see their child the way God sees them, which can be properly construed and named as "beautiful." There is therefore more truth in Margaret Hebblethwaite's remark than she may have originally realized:

> Every mother knows reverence at the creation of her new-born baby, who is so obviously a person from the first moment she sees him. More reverence still would a mother feel if she could already see with the eyes of God all that her little child would grow to—the talent and beauty and strength and love that are already written into his make-up.[71]

69. Exod 2:14. The accuser may have said more than he realized.
70. After Martin Buber's I and Thou.
71. Hebblethwaite, Motherhood and God, 94.

SAMUEL

Arguably in 1 Sam 3:3 we have another pericope which focuses sharply on the theological issues I am seeking to raise in my overall discussion, namely, how a child can be properly construed in relation to God, and what the appropriate language is to describe such a construal. This is what the text says: "[T]he lamp of God had not yet gone out, and Samuel was lying down in the temple of the LORD, where the ark of God was."

In a homily never before translated into English on the child Samuel sleeping before the Ark of the Covenant, Calvin draws attention to what he believed to be theologically significant about this narrative:

> Behold, what is to be learned from these words, when God is said to have appeared to Samuel in the temple and the sanctuary as he was sleeping? For if God had appeared to him while he was awake, if he had responded with prayers and with an empty speech, it would have seemed that Samuel had prepared himself justly, and as a result had been heard by God. But with him sleeping, he could not be said to have been heard. What then? Surely God heard even the prayers of his own people? Truly. But not for that reason did he anticipate [the prayers]. For our prayers cannot come from anywhere else but from our faith, but faith is from God, and accordingly while God hears the prayers of his own people, he even anticipates them. Wherefore we must fix this higher in our minds, and ascend to this one source of divine grace, we who were known by God at the time when we did not know him. This is what Paul teaches the Galatians, when he says: "You, before you knew God, who were you?" But he teaches that knowledge of the Galatians is to be from faith. And it was on this account, lest they attribute that [their faith] to their own wisdom and industry, he says that it was mentioned that they were known by God and anticipated at the time of their blindness and ignorance. So, brothers, let us contemplate the grace of God as though represented on a canvas, and let us recognize that he himself watches over us even as we are sleeping, and though we do not know him, nor think about him, let us remind ourselves that God anticipated us.[72]

72. My translation. The Latin text reads: "*En quid ex verbis illis discendum, quum dicitur Deus apparuisse Samueli in templo et sanctuario dormienti. Nam si vigilanti, si precibus et orationi vacanti respondisset, merito Samuel sese praeparasse, et a Deo exauditus fuisse videretur: sed dormiens exauditus dici non potuit. Quid ergo, nonne suorum etiam preces Deus exaudiit? Nae: verum non ideo non praevenit. Neque enim preces nostrae possunt aliunde quam a fide manare, fides vero a Deo est, ac proinde suorum preces Deus dum exaudit, etiam eos praevenit. Quare mentibus nostris altius istud infigendum,*

Calvin here focuses on the fact that Samuel was a "sleeping child," rather than a "wakened child" in the temple, which he takes to be a fitting illustration of the position "people" should take in relation to God, in effect low and humble on the ground, as it is God who anticipates or goes before people's prayers or faith, and not vice versa. For Calvin, if this had been a "wakened child," the text could then have been read to suggest that people could bring something to merit favor from God, which for Calvin was anathema, for there was nothing that could be deemed worthy of making such an approach. In other words, what was at stake was the glory of God which, as we shall see, is a guiding principle in Calvin's theologizing and form of piety.[73]

But this is where it seems to me the shape of Calvin's dialectical epistemology,[74] somewhat ironically, took him away from the "plain sense" of the text and, in effect, led him to allegorize it. Using a "sleeping child" to put people in their place, as it were, does not necessarily serve the text's purposes, nor does it say anything about the child in the narrative. Indeed Calvin says nothing of why it may be significant that this was a "child" that was lying before the Ark of God, nor does he comment on the strangeness of the text, namely why a child was sleeping in such a holy place to begin with, a practice that would have been deemed inappropriate according to Jewish orthodoxy.

In order to begin this discussion, I would like to draw attention to a pertinent comment by Robert Gordon on this text:

> While Samuel's sleeping arrangements *within* the temple turned out to be an embarrassment to some ancient guardians of orthodoxy, something may be implied in the statement that the young man Joshua "did not depart from the tent (*sc.* of meeting)" (Ex. 33:11). Blushes are spared, nevertheless, if Samuel slept in an adjacent room or area, as Driver (. . .) suggests and as the Targum takes pain to explain ('and Samuel was sleeping in the court of the Levites and the voice was heard from the temple of the Lord'). Even the Massoretic punctuation of the verse, by putting

---

et ad hanc unam divinae gratiae scaturiginem adscendendum, nos a Deo cognitos quo tempore illum nesciebamus. Id Paulus ad Galatas docet, quum ait: Vos antequam Deum cognosceretis, qui eratis? Cognitionem autem illam Galatarum esse docet ex fide. Atque idcirco ne suae sapientiae et industriae illam tribuerent, nominatim illos a Deo cognitos et praeventos tempore caecitatis et ignorantiae ipsorum dicit. Itaque, fratres, hic tanquam in tabula depictam gratiam Dei inspiciamus, et nobis dormientibus ipsum pro nobis vigilasse agnoscamus, et quum non eum noscemus, nec de ipso cogitaremus, nos tamen quaesivisse memori mente reponamus." Homilies on 1 Samuel, no. 13 (1 Sam 3:1–10) [CO 29:380].

73. See below, chap. 2.

74. Ibid.

the half-way pause (*'athnah*) after *lying down*, reflects unease at
the plain sense of the text.[75]

Gordon intimates that "the plain sense of the text" suggests that it was
the very Holy of Holies which the child Samuel used as his sleeping-quar-
ters, even if this sounds strange and embarrassing to orthodox regulatory
practice. How such a circumstance could arise can only be suggested on the
basis of what happened preceding this account, namely of how the relationship between the child and the Lord had been formed.

Knowing that the Lord alone is the giver of life, Samuel's mother Hannah cried to the Lord Almighty for a child.[76] But Hannah also recognized that
a relationship with the Lord involved giving, not just taking. She thus made
a vow to present the child to the Lord for all the days of his life.[77] In other
words, she understood the two-way relationship between the human and the
divine was fundamental to a properly construed way of human life with its
rich possibilities. Even the naming of the child, Samuel, suggests intonations
of Hannah's bold request and the Lord's gracious response, with the name
possibly derived from the Hebrew phrase meaning "asked of the Lord."[78]

Samuel as a child was dedicated to the Lord even before he was conceived in his mother Hannah's womb, and after he was weaned he was
handed over to the service of the sanctuary at Shiloh to work under Eli the
high priest. In the first three chapters of 1 Samuel there are a number of texts
that refer specifically to the growth and development of the child Samuel in
his work at Shiloh, in contrast to the degeneracy and under-development of
Eli's two sons. What is interesting here is that this growth is posited within
Samuel's relationship with the Lord sequentially: "[T]he boy Samuel grew
up in the presence of the LORD;"[79] "the boy Samuel continues to grow in
stature and in favor with the LORD and with the people;"[80] "As Samuel grew
up, the LORD was with him."[81] The first two references come before the
night he was called in the sanctuary when he was sleeping, and the last reference comes after. In other words, it seems that the writer/editor of these
texts wants to draw attention to the fact that growth in true knowledge and

75. Gordon, *1 & 2 Samuel*, 89; italics his; cf. Driver, *Notes on the Hebrew Text*, 42.

76. 1 Sam 1:10–11.

77. 1 Sam 1:11, 22, 28.

78. 1 Sam 1:20.

79. 1 Sam 2:21.

80. 1 Sam 2:26.

81. 1 Sam 3:19.

understanding only comes in relationship to/with the Lord, even though the child did not have "personal knowledge" of the Lord before he was called.[82]

The narrator contrasts this picture of Samuel as a child living, ministering, and growing before the Lord with that of Eli's sons who violated this relationship, forsaking their responsibilities, and thus put themselves in the position of "death" (as opposed to "life" in the case of Samuel). All their actions in the temple demonstrated their arrogance and pride, marking them out as degenerate priests whose fate was to be determined by the Lord,[83] in contrast to Samuel's attitude of being a willing, faithful minister in the temple. Each got what he deserved, for the Lord promised to honor those who honored him, and those who despised him the Lord would despise in return.[84] The question could be asked, why did Eli's sons turn out the way they did in contrast to Samuel? Was this something to do with the way they were brought up? If so, this shows the cruciality of Hannah's attentive actions in weaning her child in the presence of the Lord. But the most important thing she could be said to have imparted to him was not essentially "knowledge" per se, but living a life as lived before the Lord. Perhaps her willingness to pay the price of handing her child over to the Lord was rewarded in the way Samuel turned out. The sense of death to self in her was a source of life to her child.[85] There may too have been pain to Samuel in the letting go of his maternal and family ties, with all their caring and nurturing qualities, qualities which he may not have received, at least to the same extent, in his living with Eli. Nonetheless, Hannah had given him foremost to the Lord, and the Lord took responsibility for him in return.

With respect to Calvin, perhaps this is why the child was allowed to sleep before the ark of the Lord, where the presence of the Lord, marked by the Shekinah glory, could be sensed and realized, for the child was disciplined in the ways of the sanctuary. At least Samuel was in the right place in which to hear God speak, such that John Schroeder comments:

> It is worthy of comment that the boy has been so trained in the service of the sanctuary that he can respond when the hour arrives. Many a man, distressed to feel that God is alien to him, has actually never so disciplined himself in the observances of religion as to be ready for a revelation.[86]

82. 1 Sam 3:7.

83. The Lord would use the Philistines to kill them.

84. 1 Sam 2:1–10.

85. Cf. John 12:24.

86. *IB* 2:892. See my argument later in this chapter where Timothy grew up in an environment to know the Holy Scriptures.

In other words, the child's ears had been finely attuned through disciplined formation to hear the Lord speak. It is as if the Lord took on the role of Samuel's mother, so that it was his voice he now heard rather than his mother's, thus enabling him to grow continually. The historical and natural trajectory of Samuel's transformation from *na'ar* [נַעַר, "child/boy"] to *nābî'* [נָבִיא, "prophet"][87] thus reveals the Lord's propensity for confounding human systems, bypassing the favoured for the least, which from a human side was activated by Samuel's dedication and his ministering to the Lord. This, to take Calvin's point on board, did not merit him the Lord undertaking for him, but it certainly put him in the position where the Lord could anticipate on his behalf. With maturity came responsibility, and with that came recognition: "[A]ll Israel from Dan to Beersheba knew that Samuel was a trustworthy prophet of the LORD."[88]

The relationship between the child and the Lord can thus be construed as contained within the context of the Lord's blessing, but from the child's point of view, this was more narrowly focused on the tasks at hand such as keeping the lamp of God alight within the sanctuary. Indeed, the lamp of God can be seen as an allegory of the presence of the Lord lighting up the child's way, providing him with the resources to grow and develop both in relationship to the Lord and to the people whom he served. As a child he grew in his responsibilities; so too it seems did the Lord on Samuel's behalf. In time, people were to sense this about Samuel, that "the LORD was with him."[89]

A continuous causality of life can be discerned in Samuel's life, the responsibility and care for this passing from the Lord to Hannah then back to the Lord again, so that Samuel was resourced and equipped to be the person he became. There is no sense of this chain of events being interrupted or broken, a testimony both to Hannah and the Lord's faithfulness to Samuel. Samuel's natural dependency as a child on others for his well-being could have been dislocated or harmed in the move from his mother's home to the temple, but the Lord ensured that he was never alone.

The sequence of events in Samuel's childhood, in a continuous, developing, progressive, and dynamic sense, can be mapped out as follows: He was asked of the Lord by his mother Hannah; his birth was a pure gift from the Lord;[90] he was given back to the Lord;[91] he worshipped the Lord;[92] he

---

87. 1 Sam 3:20.
88. 1 Sam 3:20.
89. 1 Sam 3:19.
90. 1 Sam 1:20, 27.
91. 1 Sam 1:28.
92. 1 Sam 1:28.

ministered to/before the Lord;[93] he grew up in the presence of the Lord;[94] and he continued to grow both in stature and in favor with the Lord and with the people.[95]

In the midst of this sequence comes this text which I now want to be attentive to: "Samuel was lying down in the temple [הֵיכַל, *hêkal*] of the Lord, where the ark of God was."[96] Two issues arise from this text, one about what might be called the geographical location of Samuel's movement in the Tent of Meeting at Shiloh, the other about what this might say about the person who was doing such an action, namely a child.[97] This is how Henry Smith interprets the text:

> It is evident that Eli and Samuel slept in adjoining rooms, if not in the same room. Samuel, at least, lay in the apartment in which the Ark stood (. . .) The sanctuary is here called a *temple* as in 19. The sleeping of an attendant near the Ark, as a servant sleeps near the monarch so as to serve him, seems to show preëxilic custom, but how it shows this account to be pre-Deuteronomic I do not see (. . .) *The Ark of God* is here mentioned for the first time.[98]

We are not told how it came about that the child Samuel slept by the Ark. However, there is no sense of any unease or discomfort from the child's perspective, indeed not even of the honor this would normally have induced. Rather, there is something natural about Samuel's actions, as if it was his right and duty so to do. According to Jewish practice, only the High Priest could enter the Holy of Holies once a year with the blood of a sacrificial lamb which was then sprinkled on the mercy-seat above the Ark between the two cherubim, the place where the Shekinah glory appeared.[99] To do otherwise warranted the death penalty.

But for the child Samuel, instead of this being a place of death, it was a place of life, of happenings, of surprises.[100] So the question arises, what

93. 1 Sam 2:11, 18; 3:1.

94. 1 Sam 2:21.

95. 1 Sam 2:26.

96. 1 Sam 3:3.

97. For critical literature on the significance of this text, see, for example, Batten, "The Sanctuary at Shiloh, and Samuel's Sleeping Therein," 29–33; Bourke, "Samuel and the Ark: A Study in Contrasts," 3–103; Driver, *Notes on the Hebrew Text*, 42; Kirkpatrick, *First Book of Samuel*, 26.

98. Smith, *A Critical and Exegetical Commentary on the Books of Samuel*, 26; italics his.

99. Cf. Exod 40:34–35.

100. Cf. 2 Cor 2:16.

allowed Samuel to lie in such a place without being smitten dead? Further, it seems that Eli was quite comfortable with this arrangement, and certainly made no attempt to stop Samuel from lying down in such a place. Was it the fact that Samuel was a child and not an adult that allowed him such access? Certainly there was nothing in the laws and regulations about children entering the Holy of Holies in the Pentateuch.

In this place, the Lord audibly called the child three times;[101] he then stood by him as in a vision and called him.[102] For Samuel this was no dream, for he arose each time and ran to Eli to ask who had called him. The child finally identified whose voice it was calling him with the help of Eli (who showed at last some form of discernment), but Samuel showed all along his eagerness (an open, willing disposition) to respond each time before he finally said the words: "Speak, for your servant is listening." Here he missed out the word for "Lord" which Eli advised him to use, perhaps indicating his lack of personal knowledge of the Lord up to this time, knowledge now received by a revelatory word from the Lord.

With regards to the form of discernment, it seems that Eli did not have enough spiritual discernment to understand what was going on when Hannah first prayed for a child at the temple; indeed he thought her to be drunk. It seems that Eli did not understand piety, and his accusation of her was insensitive and false. Ironically, although Eli falsely judged Hannah in this instance, when it came to his two sons who were degenerate and exploitative having no respect for the Tent's cultic rules, Eli showed his spiritual ineptitude by hardly doing anything to stop them. And when Samuel came to him after God had called out Samuel's name the first two times, Eli sent him back to bed not realizing that it was the voice of God that Samuel had heard. In contrast to Eli, Samuel was in the right place to hear God's voice, and although it took him a little time to recognize that it was God that was calling him, nonetheless he could still hear God's voice (unlike Eli). Arguably, Samuel's growth and spiritual maturation is narrated in counterpoint to Eli's irresponsibility and ultimate fall.

It seems that the reason why God did not speak to Eli the high priest, but rather to his servant boy Samuel, was because Eli was terribly compromised by sin. On the other hand, there was nothing in Samuel to hinder him from hearing from God. What Samuel became and achieved had its roots in his early life. His achievements as an adult were the inevitable result of the great potential which existed in the situation surrounding the family to which he belonged, the circumstances accompanying his birth, and his

101. 1 Sam 3:4, 6, 8.
102. 1 Sam 3:10.

early training.[103] Ultimately his achievements can be traced to his childhood environment, which in effect gives the Lord the credit for the grown man's success as it was the Lord who took responsibility for his growth and development. It could thus be said, following Jürgen Moltmann: "[Human wisdom] begins with respect for the primordial memory of life embedded in the natural processes, and with what Albert Schweitzer called reverence for life, as the foremost commandment which follows from the right to life."[104]

Although this Samuel text does not use explicit language of the child, nonetheless the language of the narrative is theologically significant at least in this wise: nothing in the text undermines the child in its "right to life"; rather, it is conducive towards it. It is Samuel's mother, and ultimately the Lord, who in the Samuel narrative respect the child in its "right to life," and provide an environment in which the child could grow up "in the discipline and instruction of the Lord,"[105] in effect to proper human maturation as the Lord willed for him.

JEREMIAH

The next biblical pericope can be found in Jer 1:4–8 which reads as follows:

> Now the word of the LORD came to me saying, "Before I formed you in the womb I knew you, and before you were born I consecrated you; I appointed you a prophet to the nations." Then I said, "Ah, Lord GOD! Truly I do not know how to speak, for I am only a boy [נַעַר, na'ar]." But the LORD said to me, "Do not say, 'I am only a boy'; for you shall go to all to whom I send you, and you shall speak whatever I command you. Do not be afraid of them, for I am with you to deliver you," says the LORD.

This is part of what Calvin has to say on this text in the second lecture of his series on Jeremiah's prophecy:

> We mentioned yesterday the reason why JEREMIAH refused the office of teaching, even because he thought himself unequal to the work; and for this reason he called himself a child, not in age, but in knowledge. Hence the word "child" is to be taken metaphorically; for thereby the Prophet confessed that he was not sufficiently qualified as to knowledge and practice. Some, as

---

103. Cf. Greßmann, *Die älteste Geschichtsschreibung und Prophetie Israels*, in SAT II/1:4.

104. Moltmann, *Science and Wisdom*, 29.

105. Eph 6:4.

I have said, have unwisely applied this to his age. Though then he was of a mature age, yet he called himself a child, because of his unskilfulness, and because he possessed not the gifts necessary for an office so important.[106]

Just like the Samuel text I looked at previously, Calvin does not countenance what this text could have meant if it spoke of a literal child rather than, according to his interpretation, a metaphorical one. It could even be suggested, on Calvin's behalf, that if Jeremiah had been a literal child in the text, the glory of God would have been heightened (Calvin's primary concern),[107] as a helpless, vulnerable child cannot claim anything other than dependency for its growth and welfare, which for Calvin would have been God's sovereign purposes for Jeremiah's life. However, reading this text through a child-centered hermeneutic could provide richer insight into how this child could be construed in relation to God.

The account of Jeremiah's calling to the vocation of prophet of the Lord is extremely concise and dense in this text, which conveys the dynamics of the dialogue and struggle of Jeremiah to ascertain his identity and call from God. First of all he was told that, before he was born, even before he was conceived, he was set aside for the role of a prophet.[108] Although the verse may imply some form of theological determinism or foreknowledge (Calvin's contention on the reading of this text), this need not necessarily be seen to be its sole or primary purpose. From one perspective, the initial words to Jeremiah seem to present him with a *fait accompli*, that he was set aside to be a prophet even before his birth, and that he could do nothing about it. Yet, in the dynamics of the dialogue, while the opening words present Jeremiah with an overwhelming sense of God's purpose, they still required a response from him to follow and obey. The undertones throughout the text could thus be construed as those of human freedom and the capabilities of the recipient to consent or dissent to the divine call. Yet Jeremiah's response, involving his cognitive, affective, and volitional faculties sufficiently developed, once it was freely and positively given, must have been (in a continuous sense) strengthened by the opening words of the dialogue, that the call was not of his own making, nor the consequence of divine whim or fancy, but the expression of a firm purpose and resolve from God's perspective. Although, in freedom, Jeremiah could have resisted the call, it is equally clear that he could only discover the mean-

---

106. *Comm. Jer* 1:7, *CTS* 9:39 [*COR* 6/1:27.215–222].

107. See below, chap. 2.

108. According to Louis Brodie, the language here is similar to the "Hymn to Wisdom" in Prov 8:22–30. Brodie, "Creative Writing: Missing Link in Biblical Research," 34–39.

ing of what and who he was in the sight of God by his affirmative response to the call. In other words, the call construed the significance of his life in relation to God even before he was born. In effect it gave him his identity.

Taking this one step further, even before God began to form Jeremiah as a foetus in his mother's womb, he "knew" him and took an intense interest in him. Such "personal knowledge" led the Psalmist to say:

> O Lord, you have searched me and known me (. . .) Such knowledge is too wonderful for me; it is so high that I cannot attain it (. . .) For it was you who formed my inward parts; you knit me together in my mother's womb. I praise you, for I am fearfully and wonderfully made. Wonderful are your works; that I know very well. My frame was not hidden from you, when I was being made in secret, intricately woven in the depths of the earth. Your eyes beheld my unformed substance. In your book were written all the days that were formed for me, when none of them as yet existed.[109]

It seems that for Jeremiah it was crucial that, in order for him to be an instrument that could be used for divine purposes, he needed to know, even as a young boy, that he was known by God, that it was God who took the initiative (a gratuitous gift) even when he knew nothing about it. In all this Jeremiah's response to the call had to be accommodated to his development, but it did not ultimately depend on this. The call was *a priori* to his development. His growth and development thus took place within the context of the knowledge that God had of him; his call in turn led him to a deeper knowledge of God. To decontextualize this *duplex cognitio* of one-inside-the-other (knowledge of self inside knowledge of God) would have emptied the meaningfulness of both forms of knowledge. God's knowledge of him, constituted by the communicated word of God, could be construed as affirmative with positive implications in terms of his self-knowledge in relation to God.

This biblical notion of identity being declared *a priori*[110] before a child can comprehend or apprehend its meaning can also be found in many other narratives: of Samson where an angel told Samson's mother that "the boy shall be a nazirite to God from birth";[111] of the Psalmist who speaks of God as the one who "knit me together in my mother's womb";[112] of John the Baptist where again an angel told his father Zechariah that he would be "filled with the Holy Spirit, while yet in his mother's womb";[113] and of Paul who

109. Ps 139:1, 3, 13–16.
110. Cf. Eph 1:4.
111. Judg 13:5.
112. Ps 139:13.
113. Luke 1:15.

speaks of being "set apart, even from [his] mother's womb."[114] As previously argued, the infancy narratives of Moses and Samuel also both infer an identity directed by God from birth which provided them with true knowledge of themselves in relation to God.[115]

The words, "I knew you" [יְדַעְתִּיךָ], according to Hebrew understanding, express much more than intellective or cognitive recognition. Rather, they express an intimacy, indeed union, between the one who knows and the object that is being attended to.[116] In order that the object may know, and knowing may appropriate another being to himself, the object of his knowledge must be given to him. But from God's perspective, he alone can know what has not yet come into being for his knowledge is creative, in that, in the act of knowing he creates what he knows. He did not choose Jeremiah in his existence as a child; rather he knew him even before his mother could have conceived him. Herein is a form of "tacit knowledge" which is affirmative to the object of the knower.

When God says that he "formed" [אֶצָּרְךָ] Jeremiah in his mother's womb, the idea is that of the craft of an artist such as a potter working with clay.[117] The same verb is used to describe how God "fashioned" the animals from the earth and how he "formed" the first man with the clay of the ground.[118] But Jeremiah is not simply just a piece of clay or earth; he is intrinsically given in his formation an immaterial sense of dignity which would subsequently affect his material life on earth. Such is the significance of the dialectical relationship between God the knower and Jeremiah the child, the object of the knowing.[119]

Of all the Hebrew prophets, Jeremiah seems to have been the most conscious of the compelling character of his call. When it first came to him, he tried to evade it on the grounds of his youth and inexperience, but the word of God was in his mouth, and his fears were postulated as groundless.[120] Later, when he tried to escape from his vocation and determined never again to utter the prophetic word, he found a fire burning in his bones, an inner constraint that he was powerless to subdue or negate altogether.[121] When

---

114. Gal 1:15.

115. Cf. Isaiah 49:1b—"The Lord called me before I was born, while I was in my mother's womb he named me."

116. Gen 4:1; Amos 3:2.

117. Cf. Jer 18.

118. Gen 2:7.

119. Cf. Vischer, "The Vocation of the Prophet to the Nations," 310–11.

120. Jer 1:4–19.

121. Jer 20:9; cf. Paul's statement to Timothy (2 Tim 1:6): "[K]indle afresh/stir up the gift of God which is [*a priori*] in you." I will look at this in the next biblical pericope.

he described the word of God as a fire and a hammer,[122] which was all-consuming and all-shattering, and against which he was helpless, he was but describing what he had known to be intrinsic to his identity and purpose.

It is this sense of a divine purpose that is more profoundly characteristic of what could be called a higher prophecy than mere frenzy. Relevant to this is Jeremiah's regular complaint that his contemporaries were stealing one another's oracles,[123] and uttering their own thoughts rather than the word of the Lord.[124] Instead of knowing the direct constraint of the Spirit of God upon their lives which Jeremiah had even from his childhood, they were looking around for their oracles. They could thus be described as mere members of a profession, and not people who knew their identity and purpose in life.

The Hebrew word for "prophet" [נָבִיא, nābî'], according to William Albright, derives its meaning from either the Akkadian verb nābû, meaning "to call to duty," or the noun derived from the verb nibîtu, meaning "the one called by the great gods," which led Albright to suggest that "[t]he correct etymological meaning of the word is rather 'one who is called (by God), one who has a vocation (from God).'"[125] A similar passive etymology was proposed by Alfred Guillaume who argued that the nābî' "is the passive recipient of something which is manifested in his condition as well as in his speech (. . .) one subject to the inspiration of a god or demon."[126] However, on the basis of more recently published second millennium BC Syrian texts from Mari and Emar, Daniel Fleming argues that the West Semitic (Syrian) usage of nābû "is best understood as one who invokes the gods, and the noun should be an active participle from the verb nābû, 'to name.'"[127] He concludes that this term (and that of munabiātu) "offer the first direct evidence for religious personnel etymologically related to the Hebrew nābî'."[128] The Assyrian Dictionary also provides an active etymology to the meaning of nābû, namely "to invoke (a deity)."[129]

Jeremiah could therefore be theologically construed as someone called by God even before he was born (passive sense) and who thereupon calls upon God (active etymological sense) in order to speak the divine word

122. Jer 23:29.

123. Jer 23:30.

124. Jer 23:16.

125. Albright, *From the Stone Age to Christianity,* 303; Albright, "The Archaeological Background of the Hebrew Prophets of the Eighth Century," 133; Albright, *Archaeology and the Religion of Israel,* 24.

126. Guillaume, *Prophecy and Divination among the Hebrews,* 112–13.

127. Fleming, "The Etymological Origins of the Hebrew nābî'," 218.

128. Fleming, "Nābû and Munabbiātu," 183.

129. *CAD* 11.1:35.

to Judah and the nations of the world. He took responsibility for his own actions and thus was not an "ecstatic prophet" as many of the false prophets were, but at the same time he was totally dependent upon God for both his identity and enabling. This is the distillation of Jeremiah's years of reflection on his call, and though it is supplemented with various visions, it is significant that the consciousness of God as someone over against him even before his birth, as a genuine and invincible otherness, is placed first in the order of his recollection.

As already has been suggested, the importance of this should not be minimized. This was a genuine "divine-human encounter" with massive ramifications for Jeremiah's life. Emil Brunner's statement is pertinent here: "The Biblical conception of truth is: truth as encounter (. . .) Faith, which appropriates God's self-revelation in His Word, is an event, an act and that a two-sided act—an act of God and an act of man. *An encounter takes place between God and man.*"[130] But this event in Jeremiah's life should not be construed in a narrow interventionist sense, disrupting his growth and development; rather, this reflected a story of the continuing grace of God upon Jeremiah's life, coming to him from the outside, leading him to affirmation of who he was in the sight of God. For Jeremiah the central point of this encounter was the word of the Lord which came to him. As Brunner writes: "An exchange hence takes place here which is wholly without analogy in the sphere of thinking. The sole analogy is in the encounter between human beings, the meeting of person with person."[131]

As I begin this discussion with reference to the glory of God displayed in human weakness, the question arises if there is something about the weakness and vulnerability of the child even in its mother's womb with which God identifies himself? According to Paul, God chooses the weak and despised in order to confound the mighty and proud.[132] Could the child then be seen as the archetype of human weakness and vulnerability which God looks upon with sympathy and compassion and not with condemnation? In all this Jeremiah's growth and formation as a child in relation to God was of vital importance for his subsequent ministry. He was to become an intense human persona, humanly weak yet divinely invincible, his love for God's people tender and pure, his eyes streaming with tears at the sight of what would become of God's people yet sparkling with fiery prophetic indignation against their sins and abominations.

---

130. Brunner, *Divine-Human Encounter*, 6, 53; italics his.

131. Ibid., 59.

132. 1 Cor 1:27–28.

TIMOTHY

In the following discussion, I intend to look at what Calvin said or wrote about Timothy within the Pauline correspondence,[133] for therein Timothy is referred to as a developing child and arguably these letters are about growth and development of human life to a mature form. Arguably, these letters to Timothy provide a suitable basis, with Calvin as a conversation partner, on which to explore further the issue of how a child can be construed in relation to God, and which can also help to delineate the kind of soteriological context which proved to be conducive to Timothy's growth and development from infancy to adulthood. The key text reads as follows:

> But as for you [Timothy], continue in what you have learned and firmly believed, knowing from whom you learned it, and how from childhood [βρέφους] you have known the sacred writings that are able to instruct you ["make you wise"], for salvation through faith in Christ Jesus.[134]

This is how Calvin comments on this text:

> The fact that he [Timothy] had been accustomed from his boyhood to read the Scriptures was also a powerful urge to fidelity, for this long established habit can make a man much better prepared to meet any kind of deception. It was a wise care that in ancient times was taken to make sure that those who were intended for the ministry of the Word should from their boyhood be instructed in the solid doctrine of godliness, and should drink deep of the sacred writings, so that when they came to fulfil their office they should not be untried apprentices. Thus if anyone has a[c]quired from his youth a knowledge of the Scriptures he should count it a special blessing of God.[135]

Here Calvin argues that key to Timothy's growth to maturity and wisdom even from childhood was his living and breathing "the sacred writings," namely the Jewish Scriptures. What Calvin does not explore is how Timothy as a child, when his cognitive faculties were insufficiently developed, and the Scriptures could interact, but what Calvin does suggest is that

---

133. For my present purposes, I take it for granted that the letters to Timothy are written by the apostle Paul. This is what Calvin says of Timothy: "As for me, I know that I have profited, and do daily profit more by this Epistle, than by any book of the Scripture, and if every man will look into it diligently, I doubt not but he shall find the like." *Sermons on Timothy & Titus*, no. 1 (2 Tim 1:1–2), 659.b.34–40 [CO 54:5].

134. 2 Tim 3:14–15.

135. *Comm. 2 Tim* 3:15, CNTC 10:329 [CO 52:382].

the Scriptures did perform a key role in enabling Timothy to become the person he became, a man of faith and fidelity.

Right from the outset of his second letter to Timothy, Paul declared Timothy to be his "beloved child" [ἀγαπητῷ τέκνῳ],[136] an expression or term of endearment, approval, affirmation, intimacy, and affection, which may indicate a filial obligation on Paul's part in his relationship with Timothy, as well as point toward the vital role that Paul himself had played in the growth and development of the "honest/sincere faith"[137] which Paul discerned in him. It is not likely that Paul was directly involved in the beginnings of Timothy's life of faith,[138] for when Paul first met him on his second missionary journey in Asia Minor, Timothy was already a "disciple" of a believing mother and grandmother,[139] and was well spoken of by believers both in Lystra and Iconium.[140] But Paul did lay his hands on him,[141] which raises the question, what did this action imply in relation to Timothy's development?

Certainly it seems to have conferred a certain gift or favor upon Timothy, which Paul possibly relates to the Holy Spirit.[142] But that does not imply that Timothy had not received the gift of the Holy Spirit already, otherwise Luke would have likely indicated this in his narration of events in the book of Acts.[143] It is plausible that Paul's perhaps more private and personal action of laying his hands on Timothy should be seen as a direct parallel with the church's more public and collective action of ordination when the body of elders laid their hands on Timothy prophetically conferring on him a similar, if not the same, gift,[144] all of which suggests that this particular

136. 2 Tim 1:2; 1 Cor 4:17; cf. 2 Tim 2:1—"my child [μου τέκνον]"; 1 Tim 1:2—"my loyal/true child [γνησίῳ τέκνῳ]."

137. 2 Tim 1:5.

138. Cf. Knight, *Pastoral Epistles*, 63–64; Marshall, *A Critical and Exegetical Commentary on the Pastoral Epistles*, 356; Fee, *God's Empowering Presence*, 759n13. Oberlinner completely denies the supposition. *Die Pastoralbriefe*, 5n10. However, in 1 Cor 4:17, Paul refers to Timothy as "my true son in the faith" indicating that he did have some part in Timothy's spiritual development.

139. 2 Tim 1:5.

140. Acts 16:1–2.

141. 2 Tim 1:6.

142. 2 Tim 1:7.

143. Luke does mention Paul having Timothy circumcised for the sake of the Jews but that is all. In a later event, Luke mentions that Paul came across certain disciples in Ephesus who had not even heard of the Holy Spirit (Acts 19:1–7) but Timothy does not seem to fall into that category.

144. 1 Tim 4:14. For more on this argument see, for example, Marshall, *A Critical and Exegetical Commentary on the Pastoral Epistles*, 564; Fee, *God's Empowering Presence*, 772–73.

action of Paul's was related to Timothy's calling to the Christian ministry rather than simply to his more personal salvific needs, not that these should be postulated as unrelated.

Moreover, Paul did not assume that he had done all the work in bringing Timothy to faith, but that God had been at work in Timothy right from the outset of his life in answer to the prayers and faithfulness of both his mother Eunice and grandmother Lois. It is clear that Paul did not underestimate the part that Timothy's maternal line had played in Timothy's earliest development, for it was they who had been largely responsible for his learning of "the holy Scriptures" in the early years of his life,[145] his father being a non-believing Greek. It was this maternal line which seems to have been the particular human agency through which Timothy had come into possession of "the promise of life in Christ Jesus."[146]

Interestingly, there is no hint here of a drastic, interventionist understanding of grace in relation to the child Timothy, rather a sense of continuity in his growth and maturation which gently opened Timothy up to the salvific purposes of God. Perhaps then Paul's apostolic "laying on of hands" could be seen as an acknowledgement or affirmation that God had already given this gift to Timothy,[147] as well as an affirmation of what his maternal family had done for him.[148]

The expression "salvation that is in Christ Jesus"[149] can be construed as another way of describing what this "promise of life" was.[150] Calvin comments: "God admits into possession of salvation those to whom He gives a share in his Gospel, for the Gospel reveals to us God's righteousness which guarantees an entrance into life."[151] And further: "Since the preaching of the Gospel brings life, he [Paul] rightly concludes that God regards all men as being equally worthy to share in salvation."[152] Here Calvin suggests that the key function of the gospel is to bring people into "life," a particular form of knowledge that was salvific rather than merely intellective. This is an important point to bear in mind in terms of the soteric environment in which Timothy was brought up.

145. 2 Tim 3:14–15.

146. 2 Tim 1:2. By this eternal life is meant; cf. 1 Tim 1:16; 6:12; Titus 1:2; 3:7; Rom 8:2; Gal 2:20. This is put into effect in this present age for those who have believed in Christ but which also carries on, in a continuous sense, into the age to come (1 Tim 4:8).

147. Num 27:18–23.

148. Cf. Deut 34:9.

149. 2 Tim 2:10.

150. 2 Tim 1:1; cf. 1 Tim 4:8.

151. *Comm. 1 Tim* 2:3, *CNTC* 10:208 [*CO* 52:268].

152. Ibid.

In Paul's experience, salvation was both dynamic and life-transforming. One of the marks of his apostleship was that he sought to bring others to the One who said, "I came that they may have life, and have it abundantly" [περισσὸν, "in all its fullness"].[153] Salvation in the New Testament is presented, through the verb or noun, as a past fact,[154] a present experience,[155] or a future hope,[156] but never in a propositionally static sense. All these aspects are woven into a holistic understanding of God's gift of deliverance to a humanity bound to sin, and the destruction of those death-dealing forces which drag humanity down to total depravity (as understood in a Calvinian sense). And the amazing thing is, even as a child, Timothy had entered this "living way,"[157] and had become a partaker of eternal life.

What is interesting about Timothy is this did not happen to him all of a sudden as an adult believer when his cognitive and affective faculties had become sufficiently developed, but in the early stages of his development, and that in a continuous, dynamic sense,[158] for "before he came to the years of discretion,"[159] he had been "nourished on the words of the faith and of the sound teaching that [he] followed,"[160] similar in value and practice to the Jewish form of instruction in Torah which took place from early childhood.[161]

Referring to Timothy's maternal line, Calvin comments: "[Paul] sets before him [Timothy] his grandmother, Lois, and his mother, Eunice, by whom he was reared in his infancy in such a way that he could suck in godliness along with his mother's milk."[162] In similar wise, but with one notable difference, in a sermon on the same text, Calvin said: "Having been rightly instructed in the faith from your infancy, and having, so to speak, sucked in sound doctrine with your mother's milk, and having made till now continual progress in it, take pains."[163] Here Calvin interchanges the concepts

---

153. John 10:10b.

154. Titus 3.5; Eph 2:5, 8.

155. Phil 2:12.

156. Rom 13:11.

157. Heb 10:20.

158. 2 Tim 3:15.

159. Sermons on Timothy & Titus, no. 23 (2 Tim 3:14–15), 924.b.19–20 [CO 54:274].

160. 1 Tim 4:6.

161. It was the Jewish parents' duty to instruct their child in the Law from the age of five; cf. Philo, De Legatione Ad Gaium 16 (115); Josephus, Apion I.12 (60); Pirke 'Abot V.21 (SB III:664–66).

162. Comm. 2 Tim 1:4, CNTC 10:292 [CO 52:348].

163. Comm. 1 Tim 4:6, CNTC 10:242–43 [CO 52:298]; cf. "And therefore he had been faithfully brought up, and instructed in the doctrine of God, and in true religion, even from his mother's breasts as it were." Sermons on Timothy & Titus, no. 23 (2 Tim

of "godliness" with "sound doctrine," perhaps indicating his more cognitive understanding of how a child develops, a point which I will address shortly.

At any rate, the net result was that Timothy was enabled to grow in his understanding and knowledge both of God and of himself as a sinner in the sight of God, and of what Christ had done for him in order to bring him salvation.[164] Thus the Scriptures had made him not just knowledgeable (involving his cognitive faculties) but also "wise for salvation"[165] (involving all his faculties).[166]

What is particularly fascinating is how Paul construes what salvation means in Timothy's particular case. Many commentators on Paul's two letters to Timothy understand Paul to be solely addressing Timothy's cognitive faculties, based on the fact that he frequently exhorts Timothy to lay hold of and teach the "sound words" or "doctrine" of the Christian faith. Arguably, however, Paul's instructions to Timothy can be construed in a different fashion. I would understand him to be working on the premise of a divine causality of life, and not merely a cognitive apprehension of truth (at least not on its own—it takes the presence of the other in order for this to function properly),[167] which he discerned to be *ipso facto* operating in Timothy's life which Paul sought to encourage and nurture in his continual maturation into the fully particular human being that God intended. How this conveyance or communication of life became operative in Timothy's childhood could potentially make an interesting case scenario of the kind of relationship which God can have with any child, with its developmental and providential implications.

Another way of describing what was causally at work in Timothy's young life is "the power of God,"[168] based on a divine happening, namely

3:14–15), 924.a.3–8 [CO 54:273].

164. 1 Tim 1:15.

165. Cf. Ps 119:98 LXX (119:98 MT/ET)—"You have made me wiser than my enemies in your commandment, for it is mine forever."

166. This fits in with the following observation: "[E]ven though young children are limited to reasoning only about desires and emotions and perception, and at a nonrepresentational level, we see them as evidencing an important sort of sensible reasoning that considers and honors certain tenets of consistency and relevance within an individual's psychological states and actions." Bartsch and Wellman, *Children Talk about the Mind*, 159.

167. As if eternal life was solely an intellective pursuit of acquiring data. Indeed, Calvin rebuffs this reduction of faith to a mere assent to doctrine thus: "The Scholastics go completely astray, who in considering faith identify it with a bare and simple assent arising out of knowledge, and leave out confidence and assurance of heart." *Institutes* III.2.33 [OS 4:30]; cf. The Westminster divines (1643–47), who commended "not a brain-knowledge, a mere speculation (. . .) but an inward, a savoury, an heart knowledge." "Preface," *Westminster Confession of Faith*, 4.

168. 2 Tim 1:8.

the Incarnation, by which means God had through Christ "abolished death and brought life and immortality to light through the gospel."[169] And Paul encouraged his young charge to "be strong in [this] grace which is in Christ Jesus," for by doing so Timothy would gain the strength he needed in order to fulfill his ministry using all the gifts God had given him. Cognitive knowledge in the form of sound words had its part to play in Timothy's development, but that was not all he needed. His emotional and volitional capacities needed to be addressed as well in order that he would flourish in "all things"[170] as God intended.

Paul exhorted Timothy to believe firmly without wavering in the message he had heard,[171] otherwise he could end up a spiritual shipwreck like Hymenaeus and Philetus who had "swerved from the truth."[172] By being rooted and grounded in "the glorious Gospel of the blessed God,"[173] Timothy would find continual stability and strength to grow and develop as a Christian. As he had been nurtured and brought him up in the sacred writings of the Jewish Scriptures,[174] so in a somewhat similar fashion in terms of their spiritual maturation and enlightenment, Jesus had opened the Scriptures to the two disciples on the road to Emmaus, the result of which was they felt their hearts burning within them as Jesus talked with them on the way.[175] Here Scripture is seen as having a normative role in the forming and shaping of the human person, not simply in a notional or cognitive sense, but also affectively, touching the heart from which "flow the springs of life."[176]

It was by this means Timothy himself had received eternal life, a salvific dynamic in him given to him by God. Salvation thus as Paul conceived it was not static or substantive, but dynamic and relational, having "life-giving" [*vivificae illius*][177] consequences. With this salvific causality (oth-

169. 2 Tim 1:10.

170. 2 Tim 2:7.

171. 2 Tim 3:14.

172. 2 Tim 2:17.

173. 1 Tim 1:11.

174. Cf. Eph 6:4, where Paul encourages fathers to bring their children up "in the discipline and instruction of the Lord." Note: the Scriptures had the ability/power to lead him to salvation (continuity with the Pauline Gospel, Rom 1:16), in contrast to the impotence of the false teachers.

175. Luke 24:32.

176. Prov 4:23. Towner states: "Within Paul's anthropological teaching, and continuous with the biblical tradition and cultures that influenced him, the heart was regarded as the locus of the human personality and origin of the emotions and intentions." Towner, *Letters to Timothy and Titus*, 115; cf. Jewett, *Paul's Anthropological Terms*, 448; Marshall, *A Critical and Exegetical Commentary on the Pastoral Epistles*, 370.

177. *Comm. 2 Tim* 1:11, CNTC 10:298 [CO 52:354].

erwise known as "the help of the Holy Spirit")[178] operating in his heart and life, Timothy was given the ability to "avoid vain chatter," to "turn away from wickedness,"[179] to "cleanse [himself],"[180] and to "[s]hun youthful passions," as well as, more positively, to "pursue righteousness, faith, love, and peace, along with those who call on the Lord from a pure heart."[181] This was no mere natural or innate ability he had in and of himself, but was radically based on a gift given to him by God, which then put him under solemn obligation and necessity to work it out within the holy demands of God's righteous requirements. This was the kind of justifying and sanctifying grace which did not set aside the law of God but upheld it.[182] In this way, God's sovereign purposes and human responsibility are seen to be working together in tandem, with God's grace always going before (prevenient grace), upholding Timothy on his ongoing journey, just as Paul expressed it in his exhortation to the Philippians: "[W]ork out your own salvation with fear and trembling; for it is God who is at work in you, enabling you both to will and to work for his good pleasure."[183]

This divine causality of life operating in Timothy's heart more than likely began as a small seed planted in him even as a child by the Spirit of God which, aided by the scriptural environment in which he was brought up, enabled him to come to faith and grow thereby in the grace and knowledge of the Lord Jesus Christ. Paul's ministry to Timothy was thus one of confirmation and affirmation.

In his commentary and sermons on the letters to Timothy, Calvin arguably construed living faith in rather narrow terms, namely what the mind could understand (cognitive knowledge) rather than what I have termed a divine causality of life. But that is not to say that Calvin did not evaluate Timothy's early child formation as unproductive, for by it Timothy had gained certain qualities which were conducive to his coming to faith, as his mind gained the capacity to grasp truth. So Calvin comments on 2 Tim 1:5: "I take the meaning to be that Timothy, from his childhood, when he had not yet obtained a knowledge of the Gospel, was so imbued with reverence and faith in God, that it was a living seed [*vivum semen*] which later increased and grew."[184]

178. 2 Tim 1:14.
179. 2 Tim 2:19.
180. 2 Tim 2:21.
181. 2 Tim 2:22.
182. Cf. Rom 3:31.
183. Phil 2:12–13.
184. *Comm. 2 Tim* 1:5, *CNTC* 10:292 [*CO* 52:348]. 2 Tim 1:14.

Here Calvin does not go as far as to say that Timothy experienced salvation in its proper (in his terms) noetic sense as a child, yet the "fear of the Lord"[185] instilled into Timothy even as a child had a causal germinating effect which only needed a nurturing hand in order to achieve its end, namely "faith in Christ Jesus."[186] However, it could be argued that Timothy had an authentic faith already within him as a child (albeit something that cannot be construed solely in cognitive terms) which just needed further nurturing. Paul had his part to play in this development, but not necessarily to plant the seed of life in him as it already existed in him and only needed certain conditions for it blossom.[187]

The "honest/sincere faith" which Paul subsequently discerned in Timothy is depicted as an enduring, persevering characteristic, the aorist tense of the verb suggesting that this dynamic had its beginning in the life of God (an indication of divine causality), to which Paul must have felt a close affinity in terms of what he had also known in his own experience.[188] What these people round about Timothy could be said to have provided him with was a nurturing environment or context in which he could appropriate, in a continually more fully realized sense, the "gift" of God which was already within him. Knowing this to have happened to Timothy gave Paul the confidence to encourage his young charge "to rekindle, kindle, inflame"[189] this divine enabling within him.

Paul's use of the metaphor of a fire which needed to be kept aflame can also be translated "to fan fully into flame,"[190] "stir up," "revive," or "cultivate,"[191] which is at least linked to, if not identified with, the Spirit given by God to Timothy.[192] Walter Lock notes that it properly means "to stir up smouldering

185. Eph 6:4.

186. 2 Tim 3:15.

187. It is often those with Anabaptist tendencies who suppose that Timothy was not "saved" until he reached a certain consenting age of responsibility. But this is to read into the text something which is not necessarily there. It is also to understand salvation in *chronos* time rather than *kairos* time, and thus to limit it to human decision rather than to God's providential purposes, as Loder suggests: "One fundamental characteristic of God's time is that it uses the arrow of time to serve God's purposes. Thus, things happen providentially in 'the fullness of time' (*kairos*), as in the incarnation, or they happen suddenly (*exaiphanes*), reversing the apparent drift toward entropy, as in the resurrection." Loder and Neidhardt, *Knight's Move*, 140.

188. Marshall, *A Critical and Exegetical Commentary on the Pastoral Epistles*, 696; cf. Gal 1:15–16.

189. Ibid.

190. Ibid., 565, 596.

191. Roloff, *Der erste Brief an Timotheus*, 255.

192. 2 Tim 1:7.

embers into a living flame" with a possible cross-reference to the metaphor of the Spirit who is often imaged as fire.[193] It was this gift of God in Timothy which Paul desired him to keep burning brightly to its maximum potential and effect and not to let it smoulder away or die out completely. In terms of Timothy's service in the church, this potentially for Paul would make all the difference between his ministry being effective and life-imparting to others, or it being inept and death-dealing.[194]

What is fascinating here is how Paul argues his case with Timothy. What was happening in Timothy's life was not simply a static logical deductive self-induced occurrence, but rather a dynamic relational process, based on the premise of a divine causality or initiative[195] of charismatic life which had touched the inward parts of Timothy's personality.[196] One could say that for Timothy the energies with which life was teeming had become for him the energies of grace, and that the higher education he had received in the developmental sequence of his life had ultimately come from God, albeit through human agents who had nurtured him in the faith. To use an expression of Loder's, "the logic of the Spirit" had found residence in Timothy's inner being,[197] influencing his thoughts, motives, and emotions, bringing shape and structure to his outward and visible activities.[198] It was on this basis that Paul encouraged Timothy to recurrently "take pains with himself,"[199] in accordance with the power of God[200] working within him (i.e., "as God strengthens you to do so"),[201] for this was the only way by which Timothy could truly make spiritual progress and grow to maturity.[202] The direct effect

193. Lock, *A Critical and Exegetical Commentary on the Pastoral Epistles*, 85. Note: one can only revive something which is already there even if it is lying in a dormant condition. Fee, *God's Empowering Presence*, 785–89; Dunn, *Baptism in the Holy Spirit*, 167; cf. Acts 2:8; Matt 25:8; 1 Thes 5:19.

194. Cf. 2 Cor 3:6b.

195. 2 Tim 1:11.

196. Cf. Prov 4:23. The inward personality "represents the inward perspective of Christian existence in its totality." Marshall, *A Critical and Exegetical Commentary on the Pastoral Epistles*, 370. "[A] 'pure' heart (καθαρός, Tit. 1.15 note) is one which is not defiled by sin and self-seeking." Ibid., 370; cf. 1 Tim 1:5; 2 Tim 2:22.

197. 2 Tim 1:14.

198. Towner, *Letters to Timothy and Titus*, 458.

199. 1 Tim 4:16. Marshall, *A Critical and Exegetical Commentary on the Pastoral Epistles*, 571.

200. 2 Tim 1:7.

201. Cf. 2 Cor 8:3; Eph 3:20; Fee, *God's Empowering Presence*, 789–90; Marshall, *A Critical and Exegetical Commentary on the Pastoral Epistles*, 704.

202. Otherwise, Paul would have been arguing with Timothy in a flattened Pelagian manner.

of this dynamic relationality or synergy between divine causality and self-discipline[203] was a life in the Spirit at both the existential and practical level which bore fruit to the glory of God. So, for Howard Marshall, while the "stress here is on human effort, progress is ultimately the gift of God."[204]

In his first letter to Timothy, Paul used another strong active verb to encourage Timothy on his spiritual journey, namely "to take hold of [ἐπαγγελλόμενοι]," which he construed in terms of "the life that really is life."[205] In his letter to the Romans, Paul related these terms of "gift" and "eternal life" together when he expressed himself in the words "the gift of God is eternal life in Christ Jesus our Lord."[206] We could say then that the gift that was operating in Timothy was not something that was static or substantive, but dynamic and substantial. To use the metaphor used by Jesus, it was "a spring of water [in him] gushing up to eternal life."[207] Calvin defined this kind of life as "[consisting in] our participation in the image of God."[208] Timothy was in possession of this form of qualitative life, a life that nourished, sustained, and enabled him to grow to a fully mature person. This was subsequently to bear fruit in terms of Timothy's ministry, both as an evangelist working alongside Paul on his second missionary journey which took them into the European continent from western Asia,[209] and as a pastor working within the life of the church at Ephesus. All these human actions can be regarded as a genuine, authentic response to and outworking of the epiphany of God's grace operating in his life.[210]

The good news of God for Timothy then was both life-transforming and life-invigorating,[211] a message not simply consisting of words (cognitive knowledge), but in demonstration of the power of God,[212] otherwise known as Holy Spirit wisdom,[213] which had found permanent residence in Timothy's heart.[214] This divine causality of life within Timothy Paul described in

---

203. Cf. John Cassian, *Conferences* III.

204. Marshall, *A Critical and Exegetical Commentary on the Pastoral Epistles*, 570.

205. 1 Tim 6:19.

206. Rom 6:23.

207. John 4:15.

208. *Comm. 2 Tim* 1:10, CNTC 10:298 [CO 52:354].

209. Acts 16:1–3.

210. Cf. Eph 2:8–10.

211. 2 Tim 1:10.

212. 2 Tim 1:8; cf. 1 Thes 1:5.

213. 1 Cor 1:25.

214. 2 Tim 1:14.

three positive outward qualities of "power/strength/courage," "love,"[215] and "self-discipline/moderation/prudence/self-control."[216] Without this Spirit in him, Timothy may have gained cognitive knowledge of the Christian faith even in his early child development, but it cannot be argued that this form of knowledge would have given him the inner drive or momentum which the Spirit of life evidently gave him. In other words, Paul's words of encouragement to him did not necessarily impart life to him, but a combination of Paul's "sound/healthy words"[217] and the life already within him causally manifested itself in his outward actions construed in terms of "work of faith, labor of love and patience of hope,"[218] which were all proof of Timothy's election by God. The Greek verb used to describe this spiritual impetus is ἐνδυναμόω, meaning "to give strength, to empower,"[219] which is the same word used of Christ's action[220] and of God's,[221] and also of Paul's growth in confidence after his conversion.[222] In other words, those whom God calls he also strengthens and equips for the task.

Naturally speaking, Timothy was shy and reserved and so needed to be encouraged to exercise the gifts which Paul discerned in him. Hence the reason why Paul tells him that "God did not give [him] a spirit of cowardice, but rather a spirit of power and of love and of self-discipline."[223] Here Timothy was encouraged to realize in his personal and public life what was in him "an abundance [*pleroma*] already there but also endlessly generative."[224]

When Paul further encouraged Timothy to "hold fast the form of sound/healthy words," Paul put this in the context of "faith and love in Christ Jesus."[225]

215. Cf. 1 John 4:18.

216. 2 Tim 1:7. Fee argues that the lower-case translation of the RSV and NIV, "For God did not give us a spirit of timidity, but a spirit of power, of love and of self-discipline" is unjustifiable, suggesting that the context demands something more like the GNB translation: "For the Spirit that God has given us does not make us timid; instead, his Spirit fills us with power, love, and self-control." There is a fundamental difference between the two readings: "This lower-case translation tends to obscure the fact that for Paul πνευματικός is primarily an adjective for the Spirit, referring to that which belongs to, or pertains to, the Spirit," and not to the interior life of the human person. Fee, *Listening to the Spirit in the Text*, 34.

217. 2 Tim 1:13.

218. 1 Thes 1:3.

219. 1 Tim 1.12.

220. 2 Tim 2:1, 4:17; Eph 6:10; Phil 4:13.

221. Rom 4:10.

222. Acts 9:22.

223. 2 Tim 1:7.

224. Ford, *Self and Salvation*, 115.

225. 2 Tim 1:13.

Calvin understood Paul to mean here that Timothy was not only to hold fast to the substance of the doctrine he had learned as a child but also "the very form of expression," as if this should be identified with his coming into "life." However, I would argue that if this was Paul's intention this would have encouraged Timothy meticulously to formulate notional propositional truth-claims, as if they, in and of themselves, could impart life or "health"[226] to the hearer, otherwise he would end up feeling guilty for misrepresenting Paul's very forms of expression. Put in its historical context, Calvin was contending with those he believed were skewing truth to the detriment of the hearer. But the danger in Calvin's line of argument is that, if taken to its logical conclusion, this could potentially do God's living truth an injustice for, as Marshall suggests, "[it can divert] people into intellectual arguments away from the concern for the Christian living which is the matter of supreme importance."[227] But more pertinently in light of my overall discussion, children in their early child development do not have the cognitive skills or ability to learn truth in this way, and so, if this was the only means whereby they could be wise to salvation, they would be deprived of what God could offer them, namely "life." But evidently this was not the case for Timothy, so he must have received "life" by some other means or at least by a more complex process.

I would suggest that there is another way of interpreting Paul's instruction toward Timothy. Paul himself said that "words" do not necessarily have the ability or capacity to encapsulate or indeed impart life or power to the hearer.[228] If this is so, it cannot be argued that Timothy was instructed solely to analyze and proclaim "words" as if they had an end in and of themselves. Indeed, Anthony Thiselton argues that "for Paul, it is not enough to proclaim the gospel only ἐν πειθοῖς λόγοις (1 Cor. 2:4; cf. v.1). Far from being 'power-laden,' λόγος actually stands in contrast to δύναμις."[229] For Thiselton, Gerhard von Rad, and by implication many other biblical scholars whom he does not name, had collapsed the proper dialectic of biblical words with the power of the word, revealing a narrowly construed notion of the biblical nature of language.[230] Word and power are not the one and the same thing in Thiselton's estimation, nor does it seem were they for biblical writers such as Paul.

On this basis, I would contend that Paul was instructing Timothy to use "sound/healthy words" which were already imbedded in a dynamic relationality of life ("faith and love in Christ Jesus"), which in turn could

---

226. *Comm. 2 Tim* 1:13, *CNTC* 10:301 [*CO* 52:357].

227. Marshall, *A Critical and Exegetical Commentary on the Pastoral Epistles*, 362.

228. Cf. 1 Cor 4:20; 1 Thess 1:5.

229. Thiselton, *Thiselton on Hermeneutics*, 66.

230. Ibid., 67.

perform their God-ordained function of imparting life to others.[231] In other words, life-saving truth may use words but it is not restricted by Paul's "very form of expression," which would have put severe limitations on Timothy as a messenger of the promise of life. Potentially he could have ended up like the scribes and Pharisees whom Jesus called "blind guides [who] strain out a gnat and swallow a camel."[232] Arguably, only affective grace, which may include words but not is bound by them,[233] could lead to the growth of faith and love as evidenced in Timothy's life.[234]

Calvin's interpretation of 2 Tim 1:13 is very much based in this context on his translation of the Greek word ἐν. He admits that the usual translation for this word is "with," based on the fact that it was linked to the Hebrew idiom בְ, which, if so, would suggest that Paul meant "that Timothy is to add to sound doctrine the affections of godliness and love."[235] However, while admitting this argument to be helpful, Calvin himself felt somewhat uneasy with it, believing as he did that this could undermine the nature of true doctrine and give too much leeway to his opponents[236] who did not engage with Scripture in the same manner as he did, and were thus prone to heresy. Instead, Calvin preferred to differentiate between doctrinal formulations and pious feelings in order that proper theological weight could be given to the former, in contrast to his opponents who placed it on the latter. So Calvin comments: "Paul has added this as a mark of sound doctrine to tell us what it contains and how it may be summed up, and he includes all this, as is his custom, under faith and love."[237]

Whilst acknowledging that Calvin offered important correctives to the thinking of his time, I would still contend that Calvin opened the possibility of understanding truth in a particular way which, if isolated from its historic context, could justify a methodology of construing truth purely in rationalistic, notional terms (a form of propositionalism) which arguably by themselves cannot offer "life" to the hearer, rather "the letter [that] kills."[238] In my opinion,

231. Cf. 1 Cor 8:1, noting the contrast between "knowledge which puffs up" and "love which edifies."

232. Matt 23:24.

233. Cf. the place of the sacraments in the life of the church.

234. 1 Tim 1:12.

235. *Comm. 2 Tim* 1:13, *CNTC* 10:301 [*CO* 52:357].

236. As seen in its historical polemical context.

237. Ibid.

238. 2 Cor 3:6. Watson makes this interesting remark: "It [Holy Scripture] is the vehicle of the life-giving Spirit of truth, but it is also the letter that kills." Watson, *Text, Church and World*, 60. The question arises, what makes the difference? One answer could be: "Humanity is called to 'know' God, to 'participate' in his life, to be 'saved,' not

it is vital to hold the two things together, not separating sound doctrine from the context of faith and love. Just as Calvin placed his anthropology within his soteriology,[239] so doctrine could be seen to be encompassed by faith and love ("speaking the truth in love"),[240] and so in effect it is "the word of life"[241] that is proclaimed and not the word solely. In this instance at least Calvin's interpretation could therefore be seen to be pneumatologically weak.[242]

Paul further told Timothy to present himself to God as a worker in God's service, "rightly dividing/explaining[243] the word of truth."[244] Paul already knew that Timothy had the primary prerequisite of life dwelling in him, so on this basis he sought to encourage Timothy to use all the hermeneutical, exegetical, and homiletical skills available to him but only as means to an end, to bring the word of life so that others could receive the same quality of life he had received. Paul used this dividing metaphor in order to underscore the "straightness" or correctness that should characterize Timothy's teaching ministry, as opposed to the "profane chatter"[245] of those who had "swerved/missed aim"[246] with regards to the truth, and had come up with inadequate, arcane, and deceptive formulations of the truth. This is how Calvin comments on 2 Tim 2:15:

> [Paul] advises Timothy to "divide aright" lest, like men without skill, he succeeds only in cutting the surface and leaves the inmost pith and marrow untouched. But I take what is said here to have general application and to refer to a judicious dispensing of the Word which is adapted to the profit of those who hear it. Some mutilate it, some dismember it, others distort it, others break it in pieces, some, as I have said, keep to the outside and never come to the heart of the matter. With all these faults he contrasts

---

simply through an extrinsic action of God's, or through the rational cognition of propositional truths, but by 'becoming God' [theosis]." Shier-Jones, Children of God, 198.

239. See below, chap. 3.

240. Eph 4:15.

241. Cf. "the Book of life"—Ps 119:28; Phil 4:3.

242. The antidotal newness of life is described in terms of the Holy Spirit; cf. Titus 3:5-7.

243. Literally "to cut a path in a straight direction." Marshall, A Critical and Exegetical Commentary on the Pastoral Epistles, 748-49. Or "to cut straight." Towner, Letters to Timothy and Titus, 521.

244. 2 Tim 2:15.

245. 2 Tim 2:16.

246. 2 Tim 2:18.

a right dividing, that is, a manner of exposition adapted to edify. This is the rule by which we should judge every interpretation of Scripture.[247]

Arguably what Calvin describes here is a particular dynamic which penetrates through "the surface/outside," which could be construed as "the words," to "the inmost pith and marrow/the heart of the matter," where the real source of life lies, namely in the vital energies of the life of God. Calvin construed saving faith in a similar outer/inner dialectic when he said: "[F]aith is not a wandering opinion, as when we have some bare understanding of the word of God (. . .) It is a lively knowledge [*cognoissance vive*] rooted in the heart."[248]

Calvin went on to compare the deadening effects of false doctrine to the disease of gangrene which destroys the body.[249] His critique here offers a corrective to those who minister doctrine (with reference to "the words") which "kills/brings forth death" if not done in the Spirit.[250] Moreover, just because a person's doctrine is "sound" (in the sense of being precisely and correctly formulated) does not mean that they have got the substance, which is "life."[251] When Paul encouraged Timothy to "preach the word,"[252] therefore, this could be understood to mean the Word of life which includes "sound (or healthful) doctrine,"[253] as Calvin helpfully interprets this, with reference to the "effect" produced, namely "instructing us in godliness."[254]

In his first letter to Timothy, Paul also advised him to teach doctrine with the aim of "godly edifying which is in faith."[255] In other words, Paul explicitly says that doctrine should only be seen as a means to an end, and if it does not serve the purpose of producing godliness and life, then it has failed "[its] purpose of eternal life."[256] So Paul encourages Timothy to live a

247. *Comm. 2 Tim 2:15, CNTC* 10:313–14 [*CO* 52:367–68]; cf. Johann Bengel's aphorism: "Apply yourself wholly to the text, and then apply all its subject matter to yourself." [*Te totum applica ad textum: rem totam applica ad te.*] *NTG* Preface (1734), §XII.

248. *Sermons on Timothy & Titus*, no. 3 (1 Tim 1:5–7), 29.a.29–32, 36–37 [*CO* 53:32].

249. *Comm. 2 Tim 2:17, CNTC* 10:314 [*CO* 52:368].

250. 2 Cor 3:6.

251. Cf. John 6:62.

252. 2 Tim 4:2.

253. 2 Tim 4:3.

254. *Comm. 2 Tim 4:3, CNTC* 10:334 [*CO* 52:386]. To this I would add doctrine which nurtures godliness and a wholesome life.

255. 1 Tim 1:3–4.

256. 1 Tim 1:16. John Zizioulas points out that truth (in its truest sense) brings forth life: "To be saved from the fall, therefore, means essentially that truth should be fully applied to existence, thereby making life something true, i.e. undying. For this reason the

life of godliness for it "is valuable in every way, holding promise for both the present life and the life to come."[257] Sound doctrine and words without the life-giving Spirit could never serve this end, and someone like Timothy would certainly not have been "nourished on the words of the faith and of the sound teaching"[258] in the manner that Paul knew Timothy had been even from his childhood if the Spirit had not moved upon him and dwelt within him.

Calvin picks up further on the "effect produced" when he comments on 2 Tim 4:3:

> In addition, since the Gospel is unimposing and humble in its outward appearance, its teaching fails to satisfy either our curiosity or our pride. There are very few endowed with a taste for spiritual things so that they relish newness of life and all that belongs to it.[259]

Here Calvin does make it clear that the words (doctrine) require a "spiritual taste" (a work of the Holy Spirit) in order for them to produce the desired effect, namely "life."

When examining Paul's advice to Timothy to "[a]void the profane chatter and contradictions of what is falsely called knowledge; by professing it some have missed the mark as regards the faith,"[260] Philip Towner never suggests that the false "knowledge" of the teachers could be orthodox in word (cognitive knowledge) but wrong in spirit (affective knowledge).[261] Instead Towner takes a positive line with regards to a construal of cognitive knowledge which appeals to the mind when he states:

> Thus "sound teaching" is a way of describing the approved apostolic teaching, which is positively health-producing. The implied polemical contrast is that the opponents' "other" doctrines are infectious, diseased, and capable of destroying the spiritual health of those who come under their influence.[262]

Fourth Gospel identifies eternal life, i.e. life without death, with truth and knowledge. But it can be accomplished only if the individualization of nature becomes transformed into communion—that is, if communion becomes identical with being. Truth, once again, must be communion if it is to be life." Zizioulas, *Being as Communion*, 105.

257. 1 Tim 4:8.

258. 1 Tim 4:6. An image of feeding and rearing children.

259. *Comm.* 2 Tim 4:3, CNTC 10:334–35 [CO 52:387].

260. 1 Tim 6:20–21.

261. Towner, *Letters to Timothy and Titus*, 432–34.

262. Ibid., 130–31.

Commentators such as Towner do not seem to make a clear distinction between what I term cognitive knowledge and affective knowledge and so fall into the trap of interpreting Paul purely in cognitive terms. However, I would argue that the proper balance is to hold both the mind and the senses as activated by the Spirit together, otherwise the polarizations and stagnations of dogmatism (giving priority to the intellect) or scepticism (giving priority to the senses) will invariably and inevitably creep in, leading to reductionist formulations of truth which do not convey life to others.[263] Such was Paul's teaching in his second letter to the Corinthians where he tells them that they had been made competent "ministers of a new covenant, not of letter but of spirit; for the letter kills, but the Spirit gives life."[264] In the three-fold order of events here, first comes the divine enabling, following which comes the divine equipping, which in turn imparts life. As a child Timothy had the first (the gift of eternal life); Paul then encouraged him to use the resources God had equipped him with, in order that he could be a channel of life to others. Words had their place in this trajectory, and certainly were to be carefully used in explaining the content of the faith,[265] but only in the light of their main function, to give "life," otherwise hair-splitting and quarrelling over technicalities and subtleties of the letter would result[266] to the detriment of the hearers.[267] Proclamation of life-imparting truth was to be done in a spirit of gentleness and patience, even if others did not understand and were resistant to the message.[268] As Paul expressed this to the Corinthian church, this ministry of life was to some "a fragrance from death to death," but to others whose hearts were open to receive it, it would prove to be "a fragrance of life to life."[269]

Having a correct knowledge of the truth, therefore, did not *ipso facto* meet the divine requirements for spiritual maturation. Such knowledge was more like Calvin's "surface/outside" metaphor, which could be called "the

263. Paul Janz remarks: "*Aisthesis* enquires 'into things' by giving priority to the senses, *noiesis* by giving priority to the intellect. Idealism (anti-realism) enquires 'into things' based on mind-dependence, realism based on mind-independence, and so on. So now, configuring this in an admittedly oversimplified way (. . .) we can say basically, along with Immanuel Kant, (a) that scepticism is the fate of all philosophical enquires 'into things' that give priority to the senses, and (b) that, likewise, dogmatism is the fate of all philosophical enquiries 'into things' that give priority to the intellect." Janz, *God, the Mind's Desire*, 136–37.

264. 2 Cor 3:6.

265. 2 Tim 2:18.

266. 2 Tim 2:23.

267. 2 Tim 2:14.

268. 2 Tim 2:24–25.

269. 2 Cor 2:16.

form of godliness," rather than his "inmost pith and marrow" metaphor, which could be called "the power of godliness."[270] The treasure was within: the pulsating, energizing "life of God in the soul of man"[271] which was the essential requirement for human growth and development. Words in themselves, even if deemed clever, did not impart life; only "the power of God" could do that.[272] It was the Spirit's ministry to bring life and liberty,[273] and Timothy had received this Spirit of life, which Paul called "the life of Jesus in the [human] body."[274]

When Paul encouraged Timothy to "guard what has been entrusted to you. Avoid the profane chatter and contradictions of what is falsely called knowledge; by professing it some have missed the mark as regards the faith,"[275] the kind of knowledge for which Paul was arguably contending was a knowledge that affected the whole human person. In other words, this was not merely a construal of knowledge which juxtaposed the cognitive and affective faculties of the human person, but was a causality of life which nourished and nurtured the human person in a more fluid, moving, and dynamic sense, involving both the mind and the heart, not in a dualist fashion but together, leading to mature human development. Paul's personal instructions to Timothy to maintain constant vigilance and responsibility for his own life were ultimately for his own good and for the glory of God. Only in maximally engaging in this divine discipline could he become mature in the fullest sense of the word.

In this whole discussion, the language used to describe Timothy as a developing child is positive and encouraging, without negating his need of salvation. The dialectical shape of Timothy's growth in relation to God was not narrowly construed or restricting, but life-invigorating and expansive, providing a means by which Timothy, even as a child, was opened up to the

---

270. 2 Tim 3:5.

271. *The Life of God in the Soul of Man* was the title of a group of letters by Rev. Henry Scougal of Aberdeen published posthumously. Scougal writes: "[T]rue Religion is an Union of the Soul with God, a real participation of the Divine Nature, the very Image of God drawn upon the soul, or, in the Apostle's phrase, *it is Christ formed within us.* Briefly, I know not how the nature of Religion can be more fully expressed than by calling it *a Divine Life.*" Ibid., 4; italics his. He calls this *"a Divine Life"* because of "its permanency and stability": it is "a permanent, and lively principle (. . .) an inward, free, and self-moving principle" (a divine causality) working within the heart of the believer compelling them toward the good and delight in its performance. Ibid., 5.

272. 1 Cor 2:1–5.

273. 2 Cor 3:17.

274. 2 Cor 4:10–11.

275. 1 Tim 6:20–21.

things of God, becoming by this developmental process the person God intended him to be, "ready for every good work."[276]

CONCLUDING REMARKS

As I have looked at these biblical narratives in turn, a picture has emerged which could potentially inform a way of examining what "the divine idea of childhood" is, using biblical terms that describe the beauty of the child in the eyes of the Lord (Moses), the child's growth and development in the presence of the Lord (Samuel), divine knowledge of the child (Jeremiah), and a divine causality of life within the heart of the child (Timothy). Each of these readings has epistemological weight as they present knowledge of children as known by God. At no time in this discourse do we find theologically reductionist language, rather the language is rich and affirmative towards children. Each of the developing children were held within the providential and redemptive purposes of the Lord.

The next task I have deemed requisite is to map out Calvin's dialectical epistemological framework in which such knowledge of children can be placed in relation to God. I seek to show that his framework has the potential to refine such knowledge in an ever more expansive and deepening sense, and that it can bear the epistemological weight of knowledge of children gained not only from the biblical narrative but also from the world of the empirical sciences.

276. 2 Tim 2:21b.

Chapter 2

John Calvin's Theological Methodology

> "So then we must have recourse to this knot of
> God's majesty and man's state together."[1]

BACKGROUND

John Calvin's greatest life work *Institutio Christianae religionis* was a profoundly original way of doing theology for its time, in which he attempted to rebuild a form of Christianity uncontaminated, he contended, by "the subtleties of sophists and (. . .) the squabbles of dialecticians,"[2] namely that of the medieval *scholasticus*,[3] and in particular the "théologiens Sorboniques."[4] Calvin, like his fellow Reformers, did not endorse free inquiry, but held strictly to a hermeneutical methodology of being "ruled by the heavenly oracles [*caelestibus oraculis*]."[5] At the same time, Calvin

1. *Sermons on Timothy & Titus*, no. 27 (1 Tim 3:16), 325.b.39–42 [*CO* 53:315].

2. *Institutes* (1536) "Epistle Dedicatory to Francis," 8 [*OS* 1:29].

3. *Institutes* III.2.2 [*OS* 4:10.1]. Calvin particularly refers to the *Decretals* of Gratian and the *Sentences* of Peter Lombard in this regard, but hardly to the works of Aquinas. The irony is, like many other humanists, Calvin often used Scholastic procedures and modes of thought in which to argue theologically, even if he changed and adapted these for his own purposes, for example, generating conceptual distinctions and categories in his own thinking, evident as early as the first edition of his *Institutes*; cf. Muller, *Unaccommodated Calvin*, chap. 3; Steinmetz, *Calvin in Context*, chap. 18.

4. *Institutes* (1560) IV.19.24 [*CM* 3:436].

5. *Institutes* I.13.21 [*OS* 3:137]. "We must (. . .) keep our minds always enclosed within the confines of the Word, lest we wander from the true God—that is, if we really want to keep him and to follow the religion which pleases him." *Comm. Dan 6:27*,

58

used many of the writings of the Church Fathers to defend his theological position, particularly those of Augustine of Hippo whom he could quote *verbatum et literatum*,[6] as well as the early Church Creeds.[7] Although he had a naturally timid and retiring disposition,[8] Calvin did not baulk from polemical disputation where and when he felt it was appropriate. On the other hand, his "Prefatory Address to King Francis" (first published in the 1536 edition and included in each successive edition) evidences that Calvin was "a lover of peace, and averse from contention"[9] but not at the expense of truth as he envisaged it. Calvin initially published his *magnum opus* in Basle at the age of 27, but incessantly and untiringly continued to work at it with the care of a prodigious lawyer, until its finally much expanded edition was published in 1559,[10] by which time it had grown to four and a half times the length of its original version.[11]

With regard to its architectonic structure, reading the 1559 edition could perhaps be described like entering a vast "cathedral"[12] where the well-

---

COTC 20:274 [*CO* 41:32].

6. Calvin states: "Further, Augustine is so much at one with me that, if I wished to write a confession of my faith, it would abundantly satisfy me to quote wholesale from his writings." *Concerning the Eternal Predestination of God*, 63 [*COR* 3/1:30.23–25].

7. "In some of the later [church] councils also we see shining forth the true zeal for piety, and clear tokens of insight, doctrine, and prudence." *Institutes* IV.9.8 [*OS* 5:156–57].

8. Calvin was "secretly devoted to private study." *Comm. Pss*, "Preface," I:20 [*CO* 31:26]; cf. *CTL* 5:216 [*CO* 13:230]; *CTL* 7:374 [*OS* 2:402.1–5].

9. *CTL* 4:236 [*CO* 11:166].

10. Calvin's constant reworking of the text arguably indicates that he did not perceive his work to be an exhaustive or definitive statement of the Christian faith, reflecting the theological imperative *semper reformanda* ("always reforming"). Calvin affirmed: "Bound as we are with terrestrial and corporeal feathers, we are like a man in prison who sees the sun obliquely through a small window." *Institutes* III.2.19 [*OS* 4:29–30]. At the same time, Calvin did not write at the end of his life, as did Augustine, any kind of *Retractations*. He did, however, admit that there were limitations even in the final edition of his *Institutes*. "I urge my readers not to confine their mental interest within these too narrow limits, but to strive to rise much higher than I can lead them." *Institutes* IV.17.7 [*OS* 5:349]. The implication of this is that Calvin should be respected for his own irreducible particularity, as Barth suggests: "one can fruitfully go *beyond* him only by thinking and speaking *with him* in the direction in which he pointed (. . .)." Barth, "Zum 400. Todestag Calvins," 229; ET in *FragG&G*, 110; italics his.

11. Latin editions published in 1539, 1543, 1550, 1553, 1559; French editions published in 1541, 1545, 1551, and 1560. Barth speaks of Calvin in relation to his *Institutes* as if he had "gradually built it up into a fortress with guns trained in every direction." *TC*, 210; ET, 159.

12. Thomas Parker describes the first edition of Calvin's *Institutes* as "an oratory," and the final edition as "a cathedral." Parker, *John Calvin*, 163.

proportioned sense of both the human (in the proportions and order of the physical space) and the divine (the vastness of the space) intermingle and play off one another. The text comes across as airy and diaphanous, not too dense and suffocating, with the emphasis seemingly more on the mass than on the minute detail, as significant as that may be. We can also see that, as in chiaroscuro, Calvin makes use of an interchange of shadow and light, sin and hope, damnation and salvation, thus generating a certain grace and dialectical tension[13] to the overall structure of his theological masterpiece. His thought throughout is both terse and pointed,[14] revealing a discernable passion for expressing truth in an orderly[15] and persuasive fashion, this being an aim throughout but not at the expense of comprehensiveness, reflecting both his French Renaissance humanistic background[16] as well as his Reformed principles. It is very possible that his training in classical rhetoric, as evidenced by his use of *perspicua brevitas*,[17] freed him from being tied too narrowly to "concerns for logical precision, conceptual clarity, or systematic rigor,"[18] although he was equally adept in all of these intellectual exercises and pursuits. All along, he seems to have resisted writing in an exclamatory style, not allowing his emotive sense to get the better of him, although he was evidently a man of deep passion and sensibility.[19]

13. Hermann Bauke argues that Calvin's thinking revolves around a set of ordering principles, namely rationalism, *complexio oppositorum*, and biblicism. Bauke, *Die Probleme der Theologie Calvinis*, 12.

14. As he said on his deathbed: "[T]hough I might have introduced subtle senses, had I studied subtlety, I cast that temptation under my feet and always aimed at simplicity." *CTL* 7:375 [*CO* 9:893]; cf. Socrates Scholasticus: "Christ and his apostles did not teach us dialectics, art, nor vain subtilties, but simple-mindedness, which is preserved by faith and good works." *Ecclesiastical History* I.8 [*NPNF*[2] 2:9].

15. Calvin writes: "I believe I have so embraced the sum of religion in all its parts, and have arranged it in such an order, that if anyone rightly grasps it, it will not be difficult for him to determine what he ought especially to seek in Scripture, and to what end he ought to relate its contents." *Institutes* "John Calvin to the Reader," 4 [*OS* 3:6].

16. This is in evidence as early as 1532 when Calvin published a commentary on Seneca's *De Clementia*. Cf. Breen, *John Calvin: A Study in French Humanism*.

17. "[L]ucid brevity [*perspicua brevitate*] constituted the particular virtue of an interpreter." *Comm. Rom*, "Dedication to Simon Grynaeus," *CNTC* 8:1 [*COR* II/13:3.8–9]. Further, "Therefore if in the future our Lord gives me means and opportunity to write some commentaries, I will employ the greatest possible succinctness [*brieveté*] because I will not need to make long digressions, since I will have treated here at length practically all the articles which pertain to Christianity." *Institutes* (1541), "Prefatory Argument," 4 [*ad loc.* 1:109–10].

18. Jones, *Calvin and the Rhetoric of Piety*, 159.

19. Calvin testifies: "my mind (. . .) He subdued to teachableness by a sudden conversion. And thus, imbued with some taste of true godliness, I was fired with so vehement a desire to improve in it, that although I did not cast off all other studies, yet I

The fact that Calvin's *Institutes* took the form of an *institutio* indicates that it had a primarily pedagogical, as well as a methodological, purpose. Calvin makes this quite clear as early as the opening paragraph of the Preface: "The book itself witnesses that this was my intention, adapted as it is to a simple and, you may say, elementary form of teaching."[20] He also states one of his avowed aims in writing his *Institutes* was to aid his readers in the formation of a godly character, believing that the theologian's task was both "to equip godly minds"[21] and "to strengthen consciences by teaching things true, safe, and profitable."[22] Moreover, Calvin saw his *Institutes* as providing for both "simple people"[23] and "candidates in sacred theology"[24] a hermeneutical key to a proper understanding of Scripture, so that, equipped with such knowledge, they would, in turn, give themselves fully to God and to the task of spreading God's Word through the divinely appointed channel, the church.

Similar to Nehemiah when he returned to Jerusalem from being exiled in Persia, Calvin surveyed the "fearful ruin" of a rended church[25] and resolved to work toward "restoring the true order of the Church of God"[26] with its proper structural landmarks.[27] This practical intent to his calling, rather than to "empty speculation [which] merely flits in the brain,"[28] energized Calvin for the immense task that lay before him, enabling him not to shirk the many distresses, calamities, and overwhelming odds he faced for the nearly three decades of his ministry in Geneva. During this entire struggle, he made it his firm aim to seek not to please people necessarily but to please God above all things, thus saying, for example, upon being ordered to leave Geneva during his first stay: "If we had served men, we should certainly be ill repaid; but happily for us we serve a greater master, who pays servants even what he does not owe them."[29] Clearly, these are the words of a disciplined and humble man who sincerely believed in the divine

---

pursued them with less warmth." *Comm. Pss*, "Preface," I:18–19 [*CO* 31:22].

20. *Institutes* (1536) "Epistle Dedicatory to Francis," 1 [*OS* 1:21].

21. *Institutes* I.14.19 [*OS* 3:169].

22. *Institutes* I.14.4 [*OS* 3:157].

23. *Institutes* "Subject Matter of the Present Work," 6 [*OS* 3:7].

24. *Institutes* "John Calvin to the Reader," 4 [*OS* 3:6].

25. Fatio, *Confessions et catéchismes de la foi réformée*, 29; ET in *RC* 1:468.

26. *Sermons on 2 Samuel*, no. 16 (2 Sam 6:1–7), 238 [*SC* 1:140.12].

27. "[T]he faithful have still to hold the trowel in one hand and the sword in the other (. . .) because the building of the Church must still be united with many contests." *Comm. Dan 9:25*, CTS 13:220 [*CO* 41:184].

28. *Institutes* I.5.9 [*OS* 3:53].

29. d'Aubigné, 6:351 [*CO* 21:226–27].

origin of his calling, even though at times that call was doubted, indeed lambasted, by others.[30]

The fact that Calvin considered David as his own nearest counterpart in the Bible, and went on to interweave some of his own story in the Preface to his Commentary on the Book of Psalms, is an indicator that Calvin was also a man who was deeply sensitive to "all the griefs, sorrows, fears, misgivings, hopes, cares, anxieties, in short, all the troublesome emotions with which the minds of men are wont to be agitated."[31] With his rich understanding and experience of life, it is no wonder Barth described Calvin as:

> a cataract, a primeval forest, a demonic power, something directly down from Himalaya, absolutely Chinese, strange, mythological; I lack completely the means, the suction cups, even to assimilate this phenomenon, not to speak of presenting it adequately (. . .) I could gladly and profitably set myself down and spend all the rest of my life just with Calvin.[32]

Although Calvin worked hard on his *commentarius, praelectio, tractatus, catechismus,* and *sermo,* it is in his *Institutio* that we find his most comprehensive treatment of theology. Nonetheless, it is important to refer to the wider corpus of Calvin's writings to gain a more complete picture of his maturest thoughts and deepest reflections on how he understood and undertook the theological task.[33] In a sense, writing his *Institutes* to represent the *loci communes* and *disputationes* not of any one book of the Bible but of the whole Bible,[34] then concentrating on the exegesis and exposition of the individual

30. For instance, not long after Calvin had been banished from Geneva, one of his former confidants Louis du Tillet called into question his vocation to the ministry: "I doubt that you have had your vocation there from God, having been called there only by men (. . .), who have driven you away from there, just as they received you by their sole authority." Cottret, *Calvin,* 139 [*COR* 6/1:448–49.32–35]; cf. Calvin's reply, *CTL* 4:94–99 [*CO* 11:269–72].

31. *Comm. Pss,* "Preface," I:16 [*CO* 31:15c].

32. *RT,* 101 [*BTh* II, 80]; cf. Barth: "Calvin and all that is involved with him alone claims me *wholly.*" *RT,* 96; italics his [*BTh* II, 65]. Coleridge declared his "great respect" for Calvin, declaring he was "undoubtedly a man of talent." *TT* II 397.

33. Watson states that on the basis of Calvin's belief in the irreducibility of textuality, "[Calvin's] *Institutes* and his biblical commentaries can be seen as part of a single, coherent theological project." Watson, *Text and Truth,* 135.

34. In this regard, Barth calls Calvin's *Institutes* "a web of exegesis." *TC,* 531; ET, 393. Calvin's theological methodology is perhaps better interpreted as a cluster of *loci communes* combined with biblical exegesis rather than a "central dogma" theology. However, the fact that Calvin did not avoid a dogmatic excursion when it came to lecturing on Hab 2:4 ("The just shall live by (. . .) faith"), for example, indicates that this *locus,* at least, was of paramount importance to his understanding of the Christian faith. *Comm. ad loc. CTS* 15:70–85 [*CO* 43:526–36].

books of the Bible in his Commentaries, gave Calvin the platform to get on with the important task of preaching and applying his understanding of Scripture to the varied congregations who sat under his ministry. There is certainly a clear distinction between each of the literary œuvres which he employed in his writings, which accounts for the varied stylistic and substantive differences amongst them. But the one feature which is impressed upon each and every one of them is Calvin's sense of the *gloria Dei*.[35]

SUMMARIZING CALVIN'S WORK

One of the dangers of seeking to summarize Calvin's work is to make his own distinctions too clean and too rigid, thus over-simplifying as well as obscuring the profound flexibility and dynamic interrelatedness of his theological understanding.[36] Indeed, Torrance argues that many people following Calvin within the Calvinian tradition have succumbed to "a species of Aristotelianism, the very *damnosa hereditas* against which Calvin himself revolted with the full impetus of his mind and soul,"[37] for the simple reason they did not have the intellectual rigor and astuteness of their master, and so "tended to fall back upon an old Aristotelian framework, modified by Renaissance humanism, in order to interpret him."[38] In effect, they imposed a rigid straitjacket upon his thinking.[39]

---

35. "I have written nothing out of hatred to any one, but I have always faithfully propounded what I esteemed to be for the glory of God." *CTL* 7:375 [*CO* 9:893].

36. Calvin's doctrine of the decrees, for example, while it may be seen to be untenably extreme, is a strongly safeguarded formulation written within the context of his overall soteriology. One of the problems, it seems to me, is that Théodore de Bèze and much subsequent Calvinistic orthodoxy have lifted this doctrine of Calvin's out of its context and made more of it than Calvin ever did (cf. his sermons as proof), transmuting it into a rationalistic metaphysic and using it, negatively I would argue, as heavy artillery against unbelievers, rather than as a doctrine which is meant to bring "comfort to godly persons." Article XVII of the Thirty-Nine Articles (1562–63): "Of Predestination and Election" [*RC* 2:760].

37. Torrance, *Calvin's Doctrine of Man*, 7.

38. Torrance, *Theology in Reconstruction*, 76.

39. Torrance argues that this theological distortion came about following the reappropriation of Aquinas, and his form of Aristotelianism, as a champion of the Catholic faith (endorsed by the Counter-Reformation Council of Trent), as well as by later historical movements which swept across Europe during the seventeenth century such as pietism and Cartesianism. As a result, Scripture tended to be viewed "as a fixed corpus of revealed propositional truths which can be arranged logically into rigid systems of belief." Torrance, *Karl Barth, Biblical and Evangelical Theologian*, 227. On this basis, the acrostic TULIP (Total Depravity, Unconditional Election, Limited Atonement, Irresistible Grace, and Perseverance of the Saints) could be described as a "rigid, scholastic system" within

However, Richard Muller argues that this "radical discontinuity" thesis between Calvin and the tradition that followed him is based on "absurd premises," from which "ahistorical conclusions" have been reached by people such as Torrance.[40] Instead, Muller argues that any seeming "discontinuity" should rather be read within its historical context, and that seventeenth-century Protestant scholasticism should be distinguished from rationalism, on the basis that the former used a theological methodology of "dialectic [which] was merged with rhetoric in the service of theology not for the sake of imposing conclusions but in the interest of clarity in argument."[41]

In similar vein, Brian Armstrong suggests that Protestant scholasticism used a "theological approach which asserts religious truth on the basis of deductive ratiocination from given presumptions or principles, thus providing a logically coherent and defensible system of belief."[42] I would argue that a distinction needs to be made between a theological methodology that helps to sharpen truth-claims that are being made (Muller's contention), and a form of theological reductionism in which theological readings of reality are collapsed into black-and-white categories (Torrance's contention) by people like Doherty in relation to their theological construal of children.

By conceptualizing truth in absolute, static, and monolithic terms, the dynamic movement inherent in how Calvin conceived and articulated biblical and theological truth breaks down. So for Serene Jones,

---

the broader Calvinian tradition. Muller, *Calvin and the Reformed Tradition*, 58. Various Scottish writers take this form of critique up in their novels. So for example James Hogg, "The Ettrick Shepherd," records the Laird of Dalcastle's damning assessment of Rev. Wringhim: "You are one, Sir, whose righteousness consists in splitting the doctrines of Calvin into thousands of undistinguishable films, and in setting up a system of justifying-grace against all breaches of all laws, moral or divine." Hogg, *Private Memoirs and Confessions of a Justified Sinner*, 12. MacDonald writes in one of his earliest novels: "For my part, I wish the spiritual engineers who constructed it had, after laying the grandest foundation-stone that truth could afford them, glorified God by going no further. Certainly many a man would have enjoyed Him sooner, if it had not been for their work." *Alec Forbes of Howglen*, 1:41. Vincent Brümmer argues that the Dort theologians (after the Synod of Dort, 1618–19) interpreted salvation in terms of "a state caused in us by God" (i.e., an atomistic soteriology) which for Brümmer did "not provide an adequate account of the complex reciprocal nature of personal relationships in general, and of the personal relationship which we have with God in particular." Brümmer, *Speaking of a Personal God*, 86. According to Brümmer's understanding of the dynamic action of divine grace, "we are personal agents rather than 'stones and blocks.'" Ibid., 120.

40. Muller, *After Calvin*, 66.

41. Ibid., 82; cf. Klauber, "Continuity and Discontinuity in Post-Reformation Reformed Theology," 467–75.

42. Armstrong, *Calvinism and the Amyraut Heresy*, 32.

[Calvin's] *Institutes*, as a literary artefact, has its own integrity: it has a range of appropriate interpretations, with a texture and structure that are capable of resisting irrelevant readings or ideas. The work is also the product of a particular historical era, a fact that reinforces the text's resistance to facile and anachronistic appraisals.[43]

Arguably, linear and propositional readings of Calvin's text fit into Jones' "irrelevant" and "facile" readings. In this regard, Torrance particularly draws attention to what has happened historically to Calvin's pneumatology, especially his doctrine of *testimonium internum Spiritus Sancti*, which was sadly misunderstood by later generations and consequently fell either into disuse or became hardened and fixed, rather than leading to the affective experience to which Calvin pointed.[44]

Perhaps one could also argue the same for Calvin's theological anthropology. Although as we shall see it was pessimistic, natural theology, with reference to God's revelation in nature as read through the spectacles of Scripture, still had an important place within it,[45] something to which Doherty, with his construal of children having "black" hearts, seems oblivious.[46]

CALVIN'S "ORGANIZING PRINCIPLE"

In the past half-century, many Calvinian scholars have attempted to discover how Calvin did his theology, particularly in terms of both the overall structure as well as the content of the various editions of his *Institutes*. So, for example, it has long been recognized that the 1536 edition bears certain resemblances to some of Martin Luther's works, such as his *Small Catechism* (1529) which structures Christian doctrine in terms of Law, Faith, Prayer, and Sacraments, which in Calvin's work are the titles for the first four chapters using

43. Jones, *Calvin and the Rhetoric of Piety*, 186.

44. Torrance, *Theology in Reconstruction*, 96, 103.

45. Calvin did employ the Thomist distinction between "natural" and "supernatural" in his theology, so, for example, he states: "the natural gifts in man were corrupted, but the supernatural taken away." *Institutes* II.2.4 [*OS* 3:245]. See also his references to: human judgment as "natural" or "carnal" [*iuger charnellement*], *Sermons on Galatians*, no. 30 (Gal 4:26–31), 452 [*CO* 50:651]; "fleshly reason" [*raison charnelle*], *Sermons on Timothy & Titus*, no. 52 (1 Tim 6:15–16), 630.a.33–34 [*CO* 53:629]; cf. *PRRD* 1:270–310. Calvin also used the language of "spiritual" and "temporal" to describe the "twofold government in man," that "[t]here are in man, so to speak, two worlds," *Institutes* III.19.15 [*OS* 4:294].

46. See Introduction.

the self-same order.[47] And as for the last two chapters of Calvin's work, *On the False Sacraments* and *Christian Freedom*, Alexandre Ganoczy has traced direct parallels to Luther's *Babylonian Captivity* and *On Christian Liberty*.[48]

Brian Gerrish discerns a three-fold thread running through the *Institutes*, namely "human nature as created, fallen, and redeemed," within God's ultimate purposes for humanity.[49] Others have surveyed the *Institutes* by tracing a downward movement from God to humanity (what God does for humanity) in Books I-II, and then an upward movement from humanity to God (what God does in and with humanity) in Books III-IV. Certainly, Calvin's doctrine of humanity ("as created, fallen, and redeemed") is discussed within his doctrine of God (as Creator and Redeemer)[50] contained in the main in Books I-III. One can also see a chiastic principle in Calvin's bipolar epistemology, namely knowledge of God and of humanity (Book I.1.1); knowledge of God as Creator and of humanity as created (Book I); and knowledge of God as Redeemer and of humanity as fallen/redeemed (Book II).[51]

What could safely be said, however, of the *Institutes* right from the first edition is that Calvin determined and intentionally placed his theologizing within the ancient catholic tradition of the church, thus distancing himself from the charge of being either an inventor or a perpetrator of theological novelties and esoteric doctrines.[52] So, for example, Parker argues that Calvin used the Apostles' Creed as a literary device by which to arrange his theological reflections in the 1559 edition,[53] hence the quadruplicate division of his material under four heads and into four books,[54] namely: Book I, *On*

47. Cf. Lang, "The Sources of Calvin's *Institutes* of 1536," 130–41; Neuser, "The Development of the *Institutes* 1536 to 1559," 36–39.

48. Ganoczy, *The Young Calvin*, 137–45.

49. Gerrish, *The Old Protestantism and the New*, 159.

50. Cf. Muller, "'*Duplex cognitio Dei*' in the Theology of Early Reformed Orthodoxy," 51–61; Dowey, *Knowledge of God in Calvin's Theology*.

51. Not that there are two knowledges of God, one as Creator, the other as Redeemer, but one knowledge compromising of two elements available to the community of the faithful.

52. So, for example, Calvin defended the conciliar definitions drafted in the patristic period such as the Apostles' Creed, and those of the Councils of Nicaea, Constantinople, Ephesus I, and Chalcedon. *Institutes* IV.9.8 [OS 5:156.30–32]. One of his earliest works *Psychopannychia* indicates that Calvin was not attracted to anything he perceived to be exoteric, arbitrary, or aberrant such as the mystical doctrine of soul sleep (*pannychia*, "a night festival") upheld, as he understood it, by the Anabaptists, which he believed led its adherents to indolence, sleepiness, and intoxication.

53. Parker, *John Calvin*, 161–62.

54. It was in the 1536 edition that Calvin first divided the Apostles' Creed into four parts.

the Knowledge of God the Creator (the Creed—"I believe in God, the Father almighty"); Book II, *On the Knowledge of God the Redeemer* ("I believe in Jesus Christ, his only Son, our Lord"); Book III, *On the Mode of Obtaining the Grace of Christ* ("I believe in the Holy Spirit"); and Book IV, *On the External Means or Helps by which God invites us into Fellowship with Christ and keeps us in it* ("I believe in (. . .) the Holy Catholic Church").

For Edward Dowey, however, the really significant "organizing principle" of the 1559 edition (and indeed of all of Calvin's theologizing) was the *duplex cognitio Domini*, the twofold knowledge of God as Creator and Redeemer, around which Dowey goes on to structure his reading of Calvin.[55] Parker refutes Dowey's thesis by suggesting that his insight is too narrow and restrictive and hence does not allow enough scope to the wide range of Calvin's thinking.[56] Certainly, Dowey only uses the 1559 *Institutes* to support his thesis, and not the overall corpus of Calvin's writings.

Taking a somewhat more synthetic position between Dowey and Parker, Cornelis Venema argues that the *ordo docendi* to Calvin's theologizing, based on a Pauline pattern of *loci* that Calvin incorporated into his 1539 *Institutes* as he worked on his Romans commentary (published 1540), was to persuade his readers by a step-by-step process to a salvific knowledge of God.[57] So, for example, Calvin in rather summary fashion writes:

> First in order came that kind of knowledge [of God the Creator] by which one is permitted to grasp who that God is who founded and governs the universe. Then that other inner knowledge was added [of God the Redeemer], which alone quickens dead souls, whereby God is known not only as the Founder of the universe and the sole Author and Ruler of all that is made, but also in the person of the Mediator as the Redeemer.[58]

Here Calvin, as a master-builder, lays the foundation to his systematics by beginning with the doctrine of God the Creator before moving on to the doctrine of God the Redeemer (following Dowey), but within an overall trinitarian framework (following Parker), with the conscious end of leading his readers "to the point of ascribing the praise of salvation to the grace of God alone"[59] (following Venema). Venema's argument thus offers valuable

---

55. Dowey, *Knowledge of God in Calvin's Theology*, 42n4.

56. Parker, *Calvin's Doctrine of the Knowledge of God*, 7.

57. Venema, "The "Twofold Knowledge of God" and the Structure of Calvin's Theology," 156–82.

58. *Institutes* I.6.1 [*OS* 3:61].

59. *Comm. Rom.* 1:18, *CNTC* 8:30 [*COR* 2/13:30.5]. Calvin comments that the apostle Paul "regulated his teaching as the occasion demanded." *Comm. Acts* 18:4,

correctives to both Parker and Dowey without eliminating either of their findings from the overall picture. John Thomas also points out that there was apostolic precedence for Calvin's missiological trajectory, if it could be called that, starting from a more "natural theology" and leading to "revealed theology,"[60] mirroring the apostolic endeavors (of starting where the people were) of Paul and Barnabas in Lystra,[61] and later of Paul when he preached on Mars Hill in Athens.[62]

Another way of reading the 1559 text on the basis of the large themes mentioned above is to note how they can be found throughout the whole text, sometimes dominating it, other times less so, yet always ready to appear again, like islands protruding from the sea which one knows are joined together by a subterranean land mass even though the juncture can often times appear invisible. One could also compare the text analogously to an intricately woven tapestry made up of many various colored threads, or to a vast symphony where various leitmotifs and themes rise and fall throughout the various movements, the whole being greater than the parts.

CALVIN'S EPISTEMOLOGICAL FRAMEWORK

On this basis, I would like to suggest that what gives Calvin's thought its mysterious depth and profundity is the deeply engaging dialectical epistemology he employs.[63] This is suggested by the opening sentence of the 1559 edition: "Nearly all the wisdom we possess, that is to say, true and sound wisdom, consists of two parts: the knowledge of God and of ourselves."[64]

CNTC 7:130 [*COR* 2/12/2:136.2–3].

60. Thomas, "The Place of Natural Theology in the Thought of John Calvin," 107–36.

61. "We know that in teaching the right order requires a beginning to be made from things that are better known. Since Paul and Barnabas were preaching to Gentiles, it would have been useless for them to attempt to bring them to Christ at once. Therefore they had to begin from some other point, not so remote from common understanding, so that, when assent was given to that, they could then pass over to Christ." *Comm. Acts* 14:15, *CNTC* 7:10–11 [*COR* 2/12/2:13.27–31].

62. Cf. *Comm. Acts* 17:22–31, *CNTC* 7:109–126 [*COR* 2/12/2:114–131].

63. Although I use the term 'epistemology' in relation to Calvin's exploration of knowledge, it would be fair to say that Calvin is not really interested in knowledge per se (as in more modern "abstractive," "technical," "speculative" epistemologies), but in what knowledge points towards, namely God in relation to humanity and vice versa ("intuitive," "experiential," "practical," "useful," "existential," "pietistic" knowledge); cf. Harbison, *Christianity and History*, 249–69; Partee, *Calvin and Classical Philosophy*, 29–41; Torrance, *Theology in Reconstruction*, 76–98; Torrance, *Hermeneutics of John Calvin*, Part I.

64. *Institutes* I.1.1 [*OS* 3:31]. This opening sentence of the *Institutes* reflects Cicero's

Originally, in the 1536 edition, Calvin opened with the words "Nearly the whole of sacred doctrine consists in these two parts: knowledge of God and of ourselves,"[65] which he expanded in the 1539 edition by adding, "The whole sum of our wisdom, which is worth calling true and certain wisdom,"[66] a clear indication that the search for wisdom, not knowledge for knowledge's sake (Calvin's contention with medieval scholastic *scientia*), was at the heart of his theological enterprise.

Parker perceives that it was "a stroke of brilliance" when Calvin took this opening sentence of the 1536 edition and made it into two chapters, *On the Knowledge of God* and *On the Knowledge of Man* in the 1539 edition.[67] In the French 1560 edition, Calvin goes even further in binding the two forms of knowledge more tightly together by including the words: "[I]t is in knowing God, each of us knows himself."[68] The subordination of self-knowledge to the knowledge of God in the 1559 edition is indicated by the fact that chapter 2 of the earlier editions (from 1539 to 1554) *On the Knowledge of Man* is not given a book of its own, unlike *On the Knowledge of God* which is divided into two books *De cognitione Dei creatoris* and *De cognitione Dei redemptoris*. Knowledge of humanity is, however, found in both these books, particularly in chapter 15 of Book I and in chapters 1–5 of Book II where it is given its most systematic treatment and analysis. At the same time, Calvin gave the introductory chapter of the 1559 edition the title, *The Knowledge of God and of Ourselves mutually Connected, and the Nature of this Connection.*

Jones argues that Calvin's aim in using such an epistemological methodology right at the start of his *Institutes* was to attract and hold the attention of a humanist readership. However, according to Jones, Calvin used a rhetorical device in the opening sentence in which to set forth the dialectical relationship between the two forms of knowledge but then went on to dismantle it before reconstructing it again, and by this process subverted the whole humanist enterprise which tended to self-glorification rather than the glory of God, Calvin's controlling theological axiom. Thus Calvin played a

---

definition of philosophy: "Wisdom, moreover, as the word has been defined by the philosophers of old, is 'the knowledge of things human and divine and of the causes by which those things are controlled.'" *De Officiis* II.2.5.

65. *Institutes* (1536) I.1 [*OS* 1:37].

66. *Institutes* (1539) I.1.1–2.

67. Parker, *John Calvin*, 98. Parker calls the opening sentence in *Institutes* (1536) a concentration of Calvin's "complete approach to theology." Ibid., 56. Further, Parker argues against Dowey that the initial and most basic twofold knowledge in the *Institutes* is not the twofold knowledge of God but the knowledge of God and of ourselves. Parker, *Calvin's Doctrine of the Knowledge of God*, 119.

68. *Institutes* (1560) I.1.1 [*CM* 1:3].

rhetorical trick on his audience, bending the minds of his readers to his way of thinking, the net result being that God could gain his rightful place in the mind and heart of humanity once more. Calvin also used this destabilizing method, claims Jones, because he wanted to make clear that truth was not to be found straightforwardly in propositional forms, but rather that it was "embedded in a rhetorical play of disrupted claims and displaced images."[69]

Pointing also to chapter 3 of Book I as further evidence of this playful rhetorical device, Jones notes that after setting out his affirmation of a universal *sensus divinitatis*,[70] Calvin went on to deconstruct and fracture this claim by "the play of images, metaphors, rhythms and discursive breaks that are far from propositional or formally systematic in character," out of which he then delineated what he understood to be the identity of the true *pietas*. Jones thus argues that "because Calvin does not always seek referential closure or a tightly logical structure of terms, the chaotic play induced by his inversions does not finally count as a loss but as a gain."[71] I would further argue, as we shall see, that it was Calvin's aim to open up a dynamic epistemological space[72] in which he could lead his readers to engage and explore at the deepest possible level, both in an intellective and affective sense, the nature of true wisdom, namely the knowledge of God and humanity, which for him were intimately related, something which Jones's "rhetorical" thesis may be limited in teasing out.

Arguably then the introductory words of the *Institutes*, both in their comprehensiveness and in their terseness, are to be understood as one of Calvin's basic epistemological propositions, one which he never violated and from which he never departed. They are not, however, a systematic postulate, but an *a posteriori* principle true to how Calvin understood the biblical picture of the relationship between God and humanity. To put this in mechanical terms, this principle could be seen as the hinge on which the whole of Calvin's theological thinking subsequently swung. As Calvin commented: "We cannot know God without knowing ourselves. These two things are connected."[73] Thus according to Ford Lewis Battles, although "[i]nitially mentioned in the 1536 edition, they became by 1559 almost an organizing principle of his thought."[74] Further:

---

69. Jones, *Calvin and the Rhetoric of Piety*, 195.

70. Cf. Helm, *John Calvin's Ideas*, chap. 8.

71. Jones, *Calvin and the Rhetoric of Piety*, 197.

72. Marijn de Kroon argues persuasively: "Calvin's theology is contained in a dynamically charged framework." *Honour of God and Human Salvation*, 171.

73. *Comm. Jer* 9:23–24, CTS 9:500 [COR 6/1:378.1152–53].

74. *Institutes* (1536) "Introduction," xxvii.

These two movements of the human mind lead to the knowledge of God and knowledge of ourselves [*duplex cognitio*], set in antithesis to one another: the gulf between the all-holy God and the fallen sinner which only the incarnate Son of God can bridge. Calvin felt this deeply in his conversion and sought to express it in concentrated form in these first few pages of his critical chapter on the law, with which he begins the first edition of the *Institutio*. Successive editions of the *Institutio* were to see these thoughts dispersed to the growing bulk of the work, ultimately offering for it a kind of organizing principle. But here, and here alone, they stand in a coherent brief theological summary of Calvin's religious experience.[75]

Here Battles acknowledges a sharp dialectical relationship between the two forms of knowledge which he believed mirrored something of Calvin's own religious experience of Christian truth. However, I would argue Battles's image of the fixed gulf can tend toward static understandings of God in relation to humanity which foreclose the dialectical epistemology which Calvin arguably opens up. On the other hand, Barth discerns a unity in Calvin's epistemology, from which the two-fold knowledge of God and humanity was opened up rather than closed down, thus writing:

It is plain that in both cases the knowledge rests on an unstated presupposition, a "cognition" that contains the other two "cognitions" in itself and unfolds them. We *do* know God and God *does* know us: that is the unstated, primary, synthetic knowledge of God and ourselves with which Calvin begins and in the light of which he has to say all the rest. This original cognition is full, sufficient, and beyond emulation. Everything else that has to be said is simply a development, expansion, and elucidation of this original knowledge. It is simply an expression and naming of it. It is not something new and additional, a further step.[76]

Barth intimates here that the synthesis is to be found *a priori*[77] rather than *a posteriori*, although he also does express himself in terms similar to Battles as well, where the thesis and antithesis is only overcome in *a posteriori* synthetic Christology. It seems to me that both of these readings can be

75. Battles, *Interpreting John Calvin*, 149–50.

76. *TC*, 217; ET, 163; italics his. Further: "As remarkable as it may sound when I say this about Calvin, he thinks initially not from God but from the human person and his situation. Yet the situation of *humanity* cannot be considered with any seriousness at all without thinking immediately of *God*. For what purpose is the human created?" *RB*, 148; ET, 94; italics his.

77. As if it were some form of a Platonic Idea.

found in Calvin, but that Barth's interpretation in this context fits more with how Calvin begins his *Institutes*, and Battles's interpretation (to which Barth also would have agreed as we shall see) with how Calvin argues in the end.

Perhaps the dichotomy in interpretation merely reflects a hidden tension in Calvin himself, in which he held together his humanism (with its emphasis more on a natural theology) with his biblicism, particularly his soteriology which in the end, for him, would always gain the upper hand. If so, for Calvin this was not a case of either-or but both-and, thus substantiating the claim of Barth that Calvin had the innate "synthetic power that distinguishes the born systematician."[78] In any case, Calvin did understand that knowledge of God and humanity was always to be found in a dynamic, and not a static, relationship, hence the continuing possibilities which Calvin's epistemological framework offers to my book.

For Calvin then knowledge of God and of humanity were inter-related (*multis inter se vinculis connexae sunt*), but each was to be treated as a distinct form of knowledge, and not different aspects of the same knowledge, as in some form of Sabellianism.[79] Instead, each was to be held in its own right, yet at the same time, they were also to be seen as emphatically going hand-in-hand from the very beginning in a certain kind of dialectical tension,[80] so that one could not be treated without the other being taken into consideration. Hence Calvin wrote: "[W]e cannot have a clear and complete knowledge of God unless it is accompanied by a corresponding knowledge of ourselves."[81] Both are particularized forms of knowledge and stand on their own feet, but in dialectical relationship. Calvin's focus was to discover knowledge of God but always in relation to humanity, never knowledge of God as he was in his own essence, which for Calvin would only be a vain and "incomprehensible"[82] exercise. Arguably, the construction of this dialectical relationship rested upon a delicately balanced "*immediately reciprocal*"[83]

78. *TC*, 215; *ET*, 161.

79. Cf. Bohatec, *Budé und Calvin*, 242–43.

80. Dowey takes dialectic to mean: "the interrelationships of elements of thought belonging to the same universe of discourse that can neither be stated in a continuous logical sequence, nor be systematically related to one another in a rationally consequent system—and yet, cannot be separated from one another or asserted as independently true propositions, without losing their proper meaning." Dowey, *Knowledge of God in Calvin's Theology*, 247.

81. *Institutes* I.15.1 [*OS* 3:173].

82. *Institutes* I.5.1 [*OS* 3:45]; cf. Question 25, *The Geneva Catechism* (1545): "Our mind cannot comprehend His essence." *RC* 1:471 [*OS* 2:77.25]. God "only accommodates" himself to human understanding in revelation. *Comm. 1 Cor* 2:7, *CNTC* 9:53 [*CO* 49:337].

83. Helm, *Calvin*, 24; italics his.

"back-and-forth movement"[84] between God and the world, the creator and his creation.[85]

True self-knowledge, as the Delphic Oracle advised,[86] could only be discovered within knowledge of God if it was going to be based on a solid foundation. So for Calvin, according to Dowey:

> God is never an abstraction to be related to an abstractly conceived humanity, but the God of man, whose face is turned "toward us" and whose name and person and will are known. And correspondingly, man is always decided in terms of his relation to this known God: as created by God, separated from God, or redeemed by him. Thus, every theological statement has an anthropological correlate, and every anthropological statement, a theological correlate.[87]

It was in the "helical"[88] space opened up by the interwovenness of this dialectical relationship, with its constantly shifting perspectives, that both distinct yet related *foci* of knowledge, the theological and the anthropological, could be explored in an ever-deepening and expansive manner, each in reciprocal conversation with the other, each with an integrity of its

---

84. De Kroon, *Honour of God and Human Salvation*, 186.

85. The dialectical opposition of the human and the divine is "one of the principle characteristics of Calvin's entire theology." Ganoczy, *Young Calvin*, 95.

86. Calvin: "With good reason the ancient proverb strongly recommended knowledge of self to man. For if it is considered disgraceful for us not to know all that pertains to the business of human life, even more detestable is our ignorance of ourselves, by which, when making decisions in necessary matters, we miserably deceive and even blind ourselves." *Institutes* II.1.1 [*OS* 3:228]. Alexander Pope's dictum, "Know then thyself, presume not God to scan, The proper study of mankind is man," assumes a concept of God which would have baffled Calvin. *Essay on Man* II.1-2. For Barth, any self-assertive notion such as Pope's "failed to hear the warning of the Reformed confession precisely at this point and has thought fit to exchange the mediæval conception of the world as geocentric for the much more naïve conception of the world as anthropocentric." Barth, *Knowledge of God and the Service of God*, 17. Calvin would also have been critical of the more recent reductionist tendency in Douglas Hofstadter's claim (omission of "upon" revealing a certain form of self-determination in his personalistic thinking) that "[t]he self comes into being the moment it has the power to reflect itself." Hofstadter, *Gödel, Escher, Bach*, 709. In biblical contradiction see, for example, Prov 20:27. On this basis, Loder states: "To stay transcendent, it [the self] must remain in that which transcends it." Loder and Neidhardt, *Knight's Move*, 48. It is no wonder that those who follow Pope's dictum, and understand God to be an accessory to autonomous human life, tend to push God out of the public arena.

87. Dowey, *Knowledge of God in Calvin's Theology*, 20.

88. As opposed to a "linear" space, either horizontally or vertically conceived; cf. Williams, "Logic of Genre," 679–707. For more on what could be described as a hermeneutical "spiral," see Thiselton, *Two Horizons*, 104; Osborne, *Hermeneutical Spiral*, 6.

own,[89] thus avoiding a *reductio ad absurdum* or apotheotic tendency in which knowledge of the human was impoverished or erased by some form of incipient monism or pantheistic absorption into the divine.[90] Making clear this distinction between the Creator and the created, Calvin states: "Meanwhile, to tear apart the essence of the Creator so that everyone may possess a part of it is utter folly. Therefore we must take it to be a fact that souls, although the image of God be engraved upon them, are just as much created as angels are." He concludes: "[C]reation is not inpouring, but the beginning of essence out of nothing."[91] Properly understood, Calvin's theological anthropology relativizes human finitude rather than dissolves it.

For Todd Billings: "Calvin is clear that he does not advocate a union in which humanity is 'swallowed up' or completely assimilated into divinity."[92] Indeed, it could be said that Calvin's literary dialectical epistemology

> ask[s] the reader to live with a certain level of unresolved tension in order to expand upon the ways of describing what is essentially indescribable (. . .) The result is not ideational chaos, but a depth and vibrancy of tone comparable to what a painter achieves by laying color on color.[93]

It is in this context that Barth writes (and Battles, as we have already seen, would have concurred): "Here is the synthesis in which more or less clearly all the theses and antitheses of [Calvin's] theology unfold in their dialectic of opposition and relationship, and to which, when rightly understood, they all seek to point."[94] Taking this one step further, one cannot say that this dialectic can be resolved within a *complexio oppositorum* grand

---

89. Cf. Buber, *I and Thou*, 83–95. One could draw here on the analogy of Jacob's ladder (Gen 28:12; John 1:51) where angels appear "ascending and descending," i.e., from below upwards then downwards again; cf. Barth's comment: CD 1/1:419 [KD 1/1:440].

90. As Calvin said: "we must not imagine as the fantastical sort do, who think that the very substance of God's spirit is in them: for there is not a more abominable heresy than that is." *Sermons on Job*, no. 97 (Job 27:3), 458.a.40–44 [CO 34:454]. For Barth: "Our differentiation before God is a serious thing, and it is only in this differentiation that we can and will love Him." CD 1/2:376 [KD 1/2:414]. MacDonald makes a similar point: "We must not forget, however, that between creator and poet lies the one unpassable gulf which distinguishes—far be it from us to say *divides*—all that is God's from all that is man's." *Dish of Orts*, 2; italics his.

91. *Institutes* I.15.5 [OS 3:181].

92. Billings, "John Calvin," 211. As Calvin comments: "there are fanatics who imagine that we cross over into God's nature so that His nature absorbs ours." *Comm. 2 Pet* 1:4, CNTC 12:330 [COR 2/20:328].

93. Williams, "Logic of Genre," 704.

94. TC, 215; ET, 162.

system such as that found in Georg Hegel,[95] but only in an epistemology which lies in the transcendent, namely God, and which can only be apprehended by faith, such as Reinhold Niebuhr suggests: "To understand himself truly means to begin with a faith that he is understood from beyond himself, that he is known and loved of God and must find himself in terms of obedience to the divine will."[96]

Arguably then the tension created by this dialectic of the human-divine encounter has the potential to support a higher synthetic framework, as one form of knowledge raised the other form of knowledge to a higher level of meaning. Mary Engel suggests: "Rather than a circle with a center of *theos*, Calvin's theology is an ellipse with two foci, *theos* and *anthropos*."[97] It was in the restlessly oscillating movement between these two foci that true knowledge of either could be discovered in an ever-expansive and deepening sense. Calvin himself encouraged Christian believers to enter into the relationality of this dynamic movement: "[I]t certainly is the part of a Christian man to ascend higher than merely to seek and secure the salvation of his own soul,"[98] this being a real indication of God's elective grace.

Paul Tillich, on the other hand, interprets Calvin's dialectical epistemology in relation to a "method of correlation," writing for example:

> When Calvin in the opening sentences of the *Institutes* correlates our knowledge of God with our knowledge of man, he does not speak of the doctrine of man as such and of the doctrine of God as such. He speaks of man's misery, which gives the existential basis for his understanding of God's glory, and of God's glory, which gives the essential basis for man's understanding of his misery. Man as existing, representing existence generally and asking the question implied in his existence, is one side of the cognitive correlation to which Calvin points, the other side being the divine majesty. In the initial sentences of his theological system Calvin expresses the essence of the method of correlation.[99]

95. Where the thesis and antithesis move systematically into a synthesis of a higher order, which not only includes but also transcends both the foregoing thesis and antithesis. The dialectical pattern or model of "thesis, anti-thesis, synthesis," instituted by Johann Fichte, was the typical hallmark of Hegelian Idealism. Kierkegaard contended that the smooth transition to a higher-order synthesis was both a violation of a true understanding of human nature and fundamentally contrary to Christianity, in that it foreclosed information by either nullifying or doing away with contradiction altogether, i.e., by flattening the dialectic. *KW* XI.

96. Niebuhr, *Nature and Destiny of Man*, 1:16.

97. Engel, *John Calvin's Perspectival Anthropology*, 191.

98. *CTL* 1:34 [*CO* 5:391–92].

99. Tillich, *Systematic Theology*, 1:70–71; cf. the whole section, 1:67–73. Again, I

And further: "For [Calvin] human misery and divine majesty are correlated. Only out of human misery can we understand the divine majesty,
and only in light of the divine majesty can we understand human misery."[100]
Dowey also shares Tillich's correlation methodology for understanding
Calvin's dialectical epistemology. He views the opening statement of the
Institutes as an epistemological principle from which, he believed, Calvin
did not depart.[101] Dowey underscores what he believed to be the biblical
character of such an insight, namely, humanity and God are not be seen
abstractly, but rather in their concrete encounter, in which humanity, as
creatures of God, are now being redeemed from their alienation from God.
He quotes Torrance's insight: "Calvin's doctrine of the fall of man and of sin
is a corollary of the doctrine of grace in forgiveness and salvation."[102] Egil
Grislis would also go along with this, stating: "Calvin's introductory and
thus overarching definition of the knowledge of God and man as correlative,
suggests an existential, vertical, and continuous dialectic."[103]

It seems to me, however, that there is a danger in understanding
Calvin's dialectic in terms of a correlation principle: it does not seem to
indicate extensively or intensively enough the dynamic movement and relational depth which can be detected in Calvin's arguably more personalistic
theological epistemological framework.[104] In this context, John Robinson's
critique of how the human-divine relationship has been construed traditionally (in an extremely limited and impersonalistic way, he would suggest)
seems relevant:

---

would argue this understanding, like that of Battles as we have seen earlier, has a tendency to foreclose rather than open up true knowledge of God in relation to humanity.

100. Tillich, *History of Christian Thought*, 263.

101. Dowey, *Knowledge of God in Calvin's Theology*, 19–20.

102. Torrance, *Calvin's Doctrine of Man*, 19.

103. Grislis, "Calvin's Use of Cicero in the *Institutes* I:1–5—A Case Study in Theological Method," 33.

104. Indeed Torrance argues: "The movement of Tillich's thought appears to suffer
from the same kind of inversion in relation to God as that of Schleiermacher." Torrance,
Theological Science, 32n2. This suggests that Tillich's "answering theology" is more an
answer to humanity than an answer to God; cf. Tillich's comment: "Knowing is a form
of union. In every act of knowledge the knower and the known are united; the gap
between subject and object is overcome. The subject 'grasps' the object, adapts it to
itself, and, at the same time, adapts itself to the object. But the union of knowledge is a
peculiar one, it is a union through separation. Detachment is the condition of cognitive
union." *Systematic Theology*, 1:105. An epistemology such as this does not fully posit the
object in relation to the subject (treating them as more equal partners, thus flattening
the dialectical relationship) as arguably Calvin's dialectical bipolar epistemology does.

It is just a correlation—a mere statement that one cannot be spoken of in isolation from the other, in the same way as one term in a pair of correlatives, such as subject and object, cannot be treated as existing *per se* (by itself). Such a relation need be no more than a logical or epistemological connection.[105]

I would argue that Calvin's theological epistemology posits that reality (God in this instance) is refracted or broken back down upon the subject (humanity), and it thus goes below the surface to explore the depth and breadth of both forms of knowledge, making them both more personalistic and intimate in their actions, or to put it in Calvin's terms, consisting "more in living experience than in vain and high-flown speculation."[106] Knowledge is therefore the outcome of a reciprocal flow, movement, process, and interaction of response, refraction, and critical reflection which creates a new relationship, a new level of participation, and a deepened form of knowledge, awareness, and understanding.[107]

Putting this in terms of the development of the human self, "which can be done only through the relationship to God," Kierkegaard writes: "Consequently, the progress of the becoming must be an infinite moving away from itself in the infinitizing of the self, and an infinite coming back to itself in the finitizing process."[108] The boundary for this dynamic movement of the self, "by relating itself to itself and by willing to be itself, [was that] the self is grounded transparently in the Power which posited it,"[109] that is in the love of God in Christ who posits the self in its integrity as a pure gift, otherwise infinite regression could occur.[110]

---

105. Robinson, *Thou Who Art*, 30.

106. *Institutes* I.10.2 [*OS* 3:86].

107. Taking the reading of Scripture to be analogous to an encounter with God, Susannah Ticciati writes: "The more fully I inhabit the biblical world, therefore, the stranger it becomes, leading me to more and more fundamental dispossession; or more positively, to the deeper and deeper reception of myself from beyond myself." Ticciati, "Scriptural Reasoning and the Formation of Identity," 434. Or as Oliver Davies puts it with regards to how one may "read" Moses's personal encounter with God at the burning bush: "the act of reading Exodus 3 draws us by means of the indexicality of the text into a new awareness of our own here and now." "Reading the Burning Bush," 444. Ultimately, this is to know God as God knows the individual, thus establishing "the human spirit in its total depth and uniqueness," Niebuhr, *Nature and Destiny of Man*, 1:61; "Man does not know himself truly except as he knows himself confronted by God." Ibid., 1:140.

108. *KW* 19:30.

109. Ibid., 14.

110. Cf. Jonathan Edwards's ontological sliding-scale. See below, chap. 4.

For Calvin, knowledge of God was the vital touchstone in how humanity could measure or discover itself as it really was. To treat these forms of knowledge as either objective or subjective was to set up a false antithesis. Rather, they were to be seen as forming a hermeneutical circle or dynamic bipolarity in which a cumulative, reflexive awareness and disclosure of divine and human knowledge was unveiled as each reciprocally threw light upon the other. In the words of Niebuhr, this had "a capacity for horizontal perspectives over the wide world, made possible by the height at which the human spirit [was] able to survey the scene."[111] Calvin's dialectic could therefore be seen as potentially opening up dynamic and relational (not static and reductionist) theological and anthropological truth-claims.

Without one of the dialectical polarities, Calvin's whole epistemological framework collapses, and the mysterious depth of both forms of knowledge remains hidden or veiled. Both forms are needed in order to make the essentially and unceasingly dialogical journey of exploration, mutuality not obliterating but intensifying the polarities.[112] So for Torrance: "Without knowledge of ourselves knowledge of God does not take place, but without knowledge of God there is no clear knowledge of ourselves."[113] Calvin believed that the classical humanist tradition was always in danger of putting the emphasis more on the knowledge of humanity rather than on the knowledge of God, an order Jones, as we have seen, argued that Calvin deliberately subverted. Calvin put the emphasis more on the a priori knowledge of God as foundational to the whole pursuit of knowledge and wisdom. For Calvin, humanity could not become properly self-aware unless it placed itself in relation to God.[114] So Calvin writes: "Again, it is certain that man never

111. Niebuhr, *Nature and Destiny of Man*, 1:168. By way of an analogy, see Isa 54:2.

112. In 1956 Barth offered a corrective to his earlier notion of the "wholly other" God (in both editions of *Römerbrief*) when he wrote: "We viewed this 'wholly other' in isolation, abstracted and absolutised, and set it over against man (. . .) in such a fashion that it continually showed greater similarity to the deity of the God of the philosophers than to the deity of the God of Abraham, Isaac, and Jacob (. . .) It is a matter, however, of God's togetherness with man." *Humanity of God*, 44–45. Contrast this with Ludwig Feuerbach's belief that "the divine is constituted only at the expense of the human." Willis, *Theism, Atheism and the Doctrine of the Trinity*, 3.

113. Torrance, *Hermeneutics of John Calvin*, 162. Again Torrance: "We are unable to speak of knowledge of God cut off from the fact that He has addressed us and we have come to know Him, so that our knowledge of God must include the proper place given by God to the human subject." *Theological Science*, xiv. Likewise for Barth, "self-knowledge unaffected by knowledge of God can never achieve true freedom, but can only create *new* ideologies, new idols." *Theology and Church*, 234. Further, "[Man] knows, as he is known by God." *CD* 1/1:244 [*KD* 1/1:257].

114. Cf. St. Augustine's dictum: "You arouse us so that praising you may bring us joy, because you have made us and drawn us to yourself, and our heart is unquiet until

achieves a clear knowledge of himself unless he has first looked upon God's face, and then descends from contemplating him to scrutinize himself."[115]

Calvin believed that "there is none but [God] alone that may be a competent judge to know what we may be, nor that has authority to say it: which thing we ought to mark well (. . .) there is none but only God that knows us, and can truly tell what we be."[116] In other words, if humanity was to consider itself outside of the context of the knowledge of God, then it would end up sadly deluded.[117] The primary movement was therefore from God to humanity and not *vice versa*. Torrance calls this "the supreme *principle of objectivity* that was to govern all Calvin's thought in content and method alike."[118] And further:

> Knowledge of God does not take place without an anthropological coefficient, yet within the bipolarity between man and God that it entails the priority belongs to the divine side, for God alone is the sole standard (*unica regula*) in the formation of our judgments and the straightedge to which (*ad cuius amussim*) our understanding must be shaped.[119]

Because "our very being is nothing but subsistence in the one God,"[120] Calvin believed that knowledge of God had logically to come first in the scheme of things.[121] Calvin therefore concludes the first chapter of the *Institutes* by saying: "Yet, however the knowledge of God and of ourselves may be mutually connected, the order of right teaching [*ordo recte docendi*] requires that we discuss the former first, then proceed afterward to treat the latter."[122] There was obviously a real issue here for Calvin which he perhaps did not fully resolve in his own mind. Knowing that the content of both

---

it rests in you." *Confessions* I.1.1 [*WSA* 1/1:39].

115. *Institutes* I.1.2 [*OS* III:32]; cf. *Institutes* (1539) I.1.25–27. "[F]or, whenever I descended into myself, or raised my mind to thee (. . .)." *CTL* 1:62 [*CO* 5:411]. As an implication of how he understood Calvin's form of 'spirituality,' underpinned by Calvin's hermeneutical doctrine of the dialectical relationship between Word and Spirit, Lucien Richard states: "Knowledge of God enhances the person's moral sensitivity and his own self-understanding." Richard, *Spirituality of John Calvin*, 191.

116. *Sermons on Job*, no. 43 (Job 11:7–12), 203.b.38–40, 60–61 [*CO* 33:541–42].

117. Cf. 2 Cor 10:12b.

118. Torrance, *Hermeneutics of John Calvin*, 64; italics his.

119. Ibid., 162–63; cf. *Institutes* I.1.2 [*OS* 3:33].

120. *Institutes* I.1.1 [*OS* 3:31].

121. "[N]o one can look upon himself without immediately turning his thoughts to the contemplation of God, in whom he 'lives and moves' [Acts 17:28]." *Institutes* I.1.1 [*OS* 3:31].

122. *Institutes* I.1.3 [*OS* 3:33–34].

forms of knowledge was so closely related, one being "the knowledge of the infinite wisdom and goodness of God," and the other, as Calvin put it contrastingly, the "knowledge of our own nothingness," this made it difficult for Calvin to rank one form of knowledge above the other, believing that true wisdom was to be found in holding both together. The perplexing question for him was where to begin this journey of discovery when both had equal weight and importance.[123]

Perhaps the only way he could find to resolve this dilemma was to use a certain form of linear logic,[124] in which, because, as he held, knowledge of humanity was encompassed by knowledge of God, and not *vice versa*, knowledge of God should consequently come first to enable the journey to get started on sure methodological grounds. In this Calvin would have agreed with Robinson when he wrote: "Man is only one pole of a relationship, and that not the primal determinative pole. The principle of his being

---

123. Barth poses this dilemma as follows: "Calvin begins [*Institutio* I, 1] by insisting that the essence of all wisdom (*sapientia*) lies in the twofold *cognitio Dei et nostri*—this raises the question which of the two precedes the other, which is the basis of the other. *Non facile est discernere!* Calvin concedes at once that knowledge of God seems to be wholly based on self-knowledge, indeed on the knowledge of our *tenuitas*. It is the *miserabilis ruina*, to which the Fall has reduced us, which compels us to lift our eyes upwards. It is the sight of that whole world of wretchedness (*mundus omnium miseriarum*) which we now discover in man, the feeling of our own ignorance, fatuity, indigence, weakness, even perversity and corruption, which makes us realise that power, goodness, righteousness and truth have their *locus* solely *in Domino*. Before we begin to be dissatisfied with ourselves, we cannot long for Him. The self-satisfied man rests upon himself and has no need of God. Therefore it is *cognitio sui* which impels us to seek God and sets us on the way to find Him. But how do we achieve a real self-knowledge? Only in the presence of God, condescending *ex illius intuitu ad se ipsum inspiciendum* (. . .) Our knowledge of God may be limited by our corresponding knowledge of self, but in this conditioning relationship the first place decidedly belongs to the knowledge of God." *CD* 1/2:263 [*KD* 1/2:286–87]. Benjamin Warfield has also waxed eloquent on this subject: "The knowledge of God is given in the very same act by which we know self. For when we know self, we must know it as it is: and that means we must know it as dependent, derived, imperfect, and responsible being. To know self implies, therefore, the co-knowledge with self of that on which it is dependent, from which it derives, by the standard of which its imperfection is revealed, to which it is responsible. Of course, such a knowledge of self postulates a knowledge of God, in contrast with whom alone do we ever truly know self: but this only more emphasises the fact that we know God in knowing self, and the relative priority of our knowledge of two objects of knowledge which we are conscious only of knowing together may for the moment be left undetermined." *WBBW* 5:31. It was a straightforward matter for Aquinas: "Holy teaching does not pronounce on God and creatures as though they were counterbalancing, but on God as principal and on creatures in relation to him, who are their origin and end." *ST* Ia.1.3.

124. *TC*, 107–8; ET, 80.

lies outside him: he is essentially one who is called into being by Another, and whose life from beginning to end is a responsive existence."[125]

The knowledge of God in turn acted as a mirror reflecting back knowledge of the rest of the created order, and in particular, humanity. It was thus the mystery of the divine which opened up vistas and provided clues into what humanity in itself really was like, which, according to Calvin, was so often misunderstood, misconstrued, and misappropriated by past theologians, even by many of the early Church Fathers. So Calvin writes: "First of all let us have an eye unto God, and secondly let every [one] of us enter into himself, and examine himself well. For that is the true wisdom, and therein it consists."[126] True self-knowledge could only be obtained in turning to God, and when this happened, humanity could begin to see itself as in a mirror.[127] And so Parker writes: "It is not the task of theology to concern itself with God outside his relationship to man, nor with man outside his relationship to God."[128]

With reference to the relational personalism in Calvin's thought and its continuing relevance for today, Torrance concludes:

> In our personal relations with God and in the very act of faith we engage in a movement of mind in which we presume everything of God and nothing of ourselves, so that from beginning to end it involves us in a reshaping of the self and a reconstructing of our prior understanding. Thus one of the outstanding marks of Calvin's theology is that he is able to hold *objectivity* and *personalism* closely together, whereas in much modern theology they tend to fall apart with disastrous consequences.[129]

This holding of "*objectivity* and *personalism* closely together" was vital in Calvin's framework not only for the discovery of knowledge itself ("we cannot have a clear and complete knowledge of God unless it is accompanied by a corresponding knowledge of ourselves"),[130] but also in providing safe parameters along which the journey could proceed. Clearly there was a grave danger in giving self-knowledge top priority for it could potentially lead to unhealthy forms of self-introspection and morbidity (the extreme of "personalism"), which was why the other pole of "objectivity" was so vital.

125. Robinson, *Thou Who Art*, 137. Loder argues that a Chalcedonian christological framework might hold the tension better. Loder and Neidhardt, *Knight's Move*, chap. 5.

126. *Sermons on Job*, no. 18 (Job 5:3–7), 81.b.21–24 [*CO* 33:227].

127. Cf. 1 Cor 13:12; Jas 1:23.

128. Parker, *John Calvin*, 56.

129. Torrance, *Theology in Reconstruction*, 98; italics his.

130. *Institutes* I.15.1 [*OS* 3:173].

On the other hand, the danger in giving "objectivity" top priority was that it could lead to abstractive impersonalistic thought. This again emphasizes why both forms of knowledge were needed, otherwise the whole thing could end up in contradictions and confusion.

At the same time, Calvin did stress the primacy of the knowledge of God over and above the knowledge of humanity, thus reflecting his reading, for example, of 1 John chapter 1, where fellowship with "one another" is made possible only within the context of fellowship with God. This is also expressed by Cornelis van der Kooi when he writes: "In knowing God, the person who knows is taken up into a relationship, defined by the proximity of God."[131] In other words, it is only when the *a priori* knowledge of God was acknowledged that humanity could truly find the inner dynamic and logic of relationality, in terms of its relationship with God, self and others, for only in God do "we live and move and have our being."[132] On this point, David Willis writes:

> God and man are seen together in a continual story of the one's effort persuasively to relate himself to the other and of the other's growing self-knowledge and maturity as the subject of his persuasive history. God remains God; and man's being really human depends on God's remaining God in relation to him. But God is God for man by his self-accommodation to human capacity.[133]

The movement then from humanity to God was encompassed within the movement from God to humanity. Without this one-inside-the-other relationship, the discovery of true self-knowledge was impossible. It was knowledge of God that enabled humanity to rise from the "horrible pit" that the fall had put it in and from the "miry clay" that dragged it down into further depravity.[134] By the prevenient grace of God,[135] it could gain true knowledge of itself as both fallen and redeemed, such that Calvin writes:

> First, We bid a man begin by examining himself, and this not in a superficial and perfunctory manner, but to assist his conscience before the tribunal of God, and when sufficiently convinced of his iniquity, to reflect on the strictness of the sentence pronounced upon all sinners (. . .) Then we show that the only

---

131. Van der Kooi, *As in a Mirror*, 9.

132. Acts 17:28; cf. *Comm. Acts* 17:28, *CNTC* 7:119–21 [*COR* 2/12/2:124–26].

133. Willis, "Rhetoric and Responsibility in Calvin's Theology," 57–58; italics his.

134. Cf. Ps 40:2.

135. Cf. Ps 63:8.

haven of safety is in the mercy of God, as manifested in Christ, in whom every part of our salvation is complete.[136]

It was only God who remained immutable throughout the whole salvific process, although God would become bigger in humanity's eyes, not for his own sake, but only in order that humanity could begin to perceive (albeit dimly in this life)[137] what God's true size was like all along (true divine knowledge).[138]

In relation to this insight, Hardy has highlighted the danger of what happens when the theological and cultural meanings of life and reality are collapsed into a single human construct.[139] Perceiving this form of reductionism occurring in western culture (both in the USA and in the UK), Hardy warned that the transcendent meaning to life would be lost. For him, it was the transcendent which gave true meaning to human reality. Hardy thus wrote:

> Insofar as anything is distinct from this God,[140] God—as the ultimately defining reality—is the source by which it and all other reality is established, and its value constituted. Its differentiation as "other" from God is one constituted by God, and the nature of its independence is established by God. For example, "creation" is constituted as distinct, but even this distinctness is one maintained as the expression of God's positive valuation.[141] The same applies to the distinctions which are brought about in creation by God. The existence and nature of the otherness of things from each other is constituted by God, and they are

136. *CTL* 1:41–42 [*CO* 5:397]; cf. *Institutes* III.12.2 [*OS* 4:209–10].

137. Cf. 1 Cor 13:12.

138. Cf. "In whatever way or state you understand Mister God, so you diminish his size. He becomes an understandable entity among other understandable entities. So Mister God keeps on shedding bits all the way through your life until the time comes when you admit freely and honestly that you don't understand Mister God at all. At this point you have let Mister God be his proper size and wham, there he is laughing at you." Fynn, *Mister God*, 118.

139. Hardy, *God's Ways with the World*, 292–310; cf. Luther: "[the heart] is so curved in on itself [*cor curvum in se*] that no man (. . .) can understand it." *Comm. Rom* 5:4, *LW* 25:291 [*WA* 56:305].

140. Hardy defined God in terms of the classic Transcendentals: "unity, truth, goodness and beauty". Hardy, *God's Ways with the World*, 308.

141. Hardy adds here in a footnote: "Alternatively, if creation takes possession of its distinctness, a possibility which inheres in it by virtue of the fact that it is given genuine distinctness by God, it may bring divine judgment upon itself." Ibid., 309n31.

thereby proportioned to achieve their fullest, while not over-reaching themselves.[142]

In his Inaugural Lecture before the University of Berlin in 1930, Dietrich Bonhoeffer made a similar point to that of Hardy when he said:

> the human being experiences his foundation not through himself, but through God. Whomever God summons is in essence a human being. The point of unity from which the human being understands himself thus resides with God (. . .) If the human being is to get an answer to the question about the human, to the question he not only raises but is himself, then he must be torn completely out of his inversion into himself and be directed to that which is absolutely exterior to his own existence. Only from beyond himself can he perceive the answer as God's answer (. . .) The human being understands himself only by his act-of-relating [Aktbezug] to God, which only God can establish.[143]

Taking up this "transcendental" point of view, Émile Doumergue suggests, in rather an experimental fashion but to make a more serious point, that the opening passages of Calvin's *Institutes* represent two theological methods, one a deductive and *a priori* method which proceeded from God to humanity; the other, an apologetic method which proceeded from humanity to God. But he then goes on to dismiss both possibilities as foreign to Calvin's whole mentality, because, he claims, Calvin did not seek to live in the realm of pure dialectical abstraction, postulation, and deduction, but rather in the realm of "two realities, two beings, two persons, in the intimate rapport of Creator and creature, of Father and child."[144] In other words, Doumergue argues, Calvin only rationalizes the whole process as a means to a noble end, in order that his readers would be enabled to discover and enter into an intimate relationship with the Creator of heaven and earth, which was God's ultimate desire and purpose for his most excellent creation, humanity itself. So here again we discover, to repeat Torrance, Calvin's objectivity coexists with his personalism, the chief end being the *gloria Dei*. Through this whole process, the journey of self-discovery only proceeded as God first sought humanity. This, for Calvin, was the reason why humanity had been created in the first place, to reflect God's glory.

142. Ibid., 309.

143. *DBWE* 10:400, 401–2, 405.

144. Doumergue, 4:26.

However, as Parker has pointed out, there was "a religious discontinuity"[145] between God and humanity and their respective forms of knowledge in Calvin's framework. This was because God and humanity were so drastically different in both nature and essence, as different as night was from day, that it took a different "kind" of knowing on the part of finite humanity to gain access to either form of knowledge. This could only come about by an act of divine enlightenment, a work of the Spirit of God, in which an analogous likeness or continuity between God and humanity could be effectively actualized, thus opening up the possibility for humanity to gain a true knowledge of God, not as God was in himself (his essence) but as he had revealed or disclosed himself in his works of creation and redemption.

As we have already seen, the investigation into the knowledge of humanity was not for Calvin an end in itself, that is, having an independent status, but it had the essential function of enabling humanity to reach toward a better spiritual understanding and appreciation of the glory of God. How that glory was revealed and what the appropriate human response to that glory should be was pivotal to how Calvin thought out the whole of his theology and anthropology,[146] as he suggests in a prayer: "Assuredly, the thing at which I chiefly aimed, and for which I most diligently laboured, was, that the glory of thy goodness and justice after dispersing the mists by which it was formerly obscured, might shine forth conspicuous, that the virtue and blessings of thy Christ (all glosses being wiped away) might be fully displayed."[147]

Indeed, he believed that in the life of prayer, "we are allowed to ask only unto the Lord's glory that which we seek for our own advantage."[148] Thus Wilhelm Niesel claims (following Hermann Weber) that the whole of Calvin's theology rested upon a certain fundamental premise: "[T]he honour of God."[149] As Calvin himself put it: "[W]e call the worship of God

---

145. Parker, *Calvin's Doctrine of the Knowledge of God*, 136. Otherwise known as the Reformed non-analogical view of the dichotomy between nature and grace. Contra Aquinas's view: "[G]race does not scrap nature but brings it to perfection." *ST* Ia.1.8; and Bonaventure: "[G]race does not destroy nature itself nor any part therof, but only the defects surrounding the nature." *M. Trin.*, q.1, a.2, rep. obj. 5.6 (V, 50).

146. *Institutes* I.14.15 [*OS* 3:165–66].

147. *CTL* 1:58 [*CO* 5:409].

148. Article 24, "Calvin's Catechism," *RC* 1:433 [*COR* 3/2:76.16–17]; cf. the French version of Calvin's Catechism (1537): "[I]t is not legitimate to ask (. . .) the things useful to us, except in view of the glory of God." *RC* 1:380 [*COR* 3/2:77.18–20].

149. Niesel, *The Theology of Calvin*, 13.

the beginning and foundation of righteousness."[150] To live a life of gratitude and thanksgiving to God for all good things was therefore the ultimate expression of true virtue and holiness on the part of humanity. It was to this that the whole enterprise of Calvin's theology tended: "Thus, steeped in the knowledge of him [God], they may aspire to contemplate, fear, and worship, his majesty; to participate in his blessings; to seek his help at all times; to recognize and by praises to celebrate, the greatness of his works—as the only goal of all the activities of this life."[151]

It is only when humanity knew itself to be a creature utterly dependent on the grace and goodness of God that it could then begin to live a life of gratitude and worship, knowing that, apart from God, it was nothing and could do nothing that was of any eternal significance in the sight of God.[152] Humanity's inspiration, motivation, and energy was thus secured by its knowledge of God and the downward movement of grace which came to meet it in its poverty and need, thus lifting it to a life of true felicity and happiness, all to God's praise and glory.[153]

CONCLUDING REMARKS

In light of my overall study, the way Calvin opens his magnum opus arguably provides an epistemological framework in which knowledge of children in relation to God can be explored. As Calvin does refer to children in his corpus, as we shall see in the next chapter, his framework can be used to critique his use of language in relation to children by comparing it to that of the biblical narratives I have already explored, the latter deemed theologically normative. His framework also allows critical attention to be given to empirical discoveries in relation to children from the world of empirical science. Potentially Calvin's theological framework can carry a lot of epistemological weight.

---

150. *Institutes* II.8.11 [*OS* 3:352].

151. *Institutes* II.8.16 [*OS* 3:358].

152. Cf. John 15:5.

153. The first question of the *Westminster Shorter Catechism* (1647), "*What is the chief end of man?*" is answered in a short, terse statement: "Man's chief end is to glorify God, and to enjoy him for ever." *RC* 4:353; italics in the original.

Chapter 3

Calvin's Theological Anthropology

"[Hezekiah] rather was willing himself to be confounded with shame,
that God might be glorified."[1]

HUMANITY IN RELATION TO GOD

One becomes distinctly conscious of Calvin's awareness of the frailty
and vulnerability of humanity in its fallen condition, particularly
when he places humanity in diametrical opposition to the overwhelming
grandeur and awesomeness of the Creator and Redeemer of the world.
According to Torrance's understanding, Calvin only did this placing
within the context of God's grand redemptive purposes for humanity.[2] In
other words, although Calvin treated his hamartiology and soteriology
separately in "the right order of teaching," he did not isolate them from
each other. Instead, his biblical understanding of salvation provided the
over-arching framework within which he discussed his doctrine of humanity as created, fallen, and redeemed, such that Billings remarks: "Calvin is concerned, along with key patristic writers, to affirm the goodness

1. *Sermons on Hezekiah's Song*, no. 1 (Isa 38:9–12a), 10 [*SC* 3:413.29].

2. Torrance, *Calvin's Doctrine of Man*, 14. Thus, Towner misconstrues what the
Confessio Scotiana Prior (1560) is attempting to say when it uses totalizing categories in
its theological anthropological statements such as in Article 3: "By which transgression
(. . .) was the image of God utterly defaced in man." *RC* 2:189. Arguably, this statement
should only be read within its Calvinian soteric context. Towner, "Children and the
Image of God," 319. Cf. Barth: "the image of God is not just (. . .) destroyed apart from
a few relics: it is totally annihilated (. . .) man has completely lost the capacity for God."
CD 1/1:238 [*KD* 1/1:251].

of creation and that redemption is a fulfilment rather than a disruption of the originally good human nature."[3]

Without this one-inside-the-other relationship (again more than a relationship of simply being "correlated"), humanity was liable to fall into the trap of either despondency under an overwhelming sense of sin and shame (arguably a sharp vertical dialectic) or presumption having little or no sense of repentance (arguably a more flat horizontal dialectic). So, for example, after referring to the twofold knowledge of God as Creator and Redeemer in chapter 6 of Book I, Calvin noted: "But because we have not yet come to the fall of the world and the corruption of nature, I shall now forgo discussion of the remedy."[4] When he did go on to explore the Fall and its damage to human nature, Calvin never in the process lost sight of the remedy: "Therefore, since we have fallen from life into death, the whole knowledge of God the Creator that we have discussed would be useless unless faith also followed, setting forth for us God our Father in Christ."[5]

Although his argument may be deemed systematic, it would be simplistic to describe it as linear or sequential. Calvin's thought pattern was much too nuanced and multi-layered for this, not because he desired to make things more complex than they actually were, but rather because this was nearer to his understanding and reading of truth and reality. Calvin thus reveals his control of the subject matter at hand, being mastered as he was by his knowledge of God, always showing himself to be aware of the bigger picture, hardly being liable to fall into the trap of missing the wood for the trees. Calvin also reveals somewhat his pastoral sensitivity to the complexity of the issues involved, especially as they related to the fallen human condition.

On this basis, I would also argue that one of the dangers that Calvin seems to have avoided in his preaching was that of impressing on the forefront of the minds of his listeners an image of an angry judgmental God without a vital underlying sense of what God had done in Christ for humanity's redemption and reconciliation. Removing the soteriological background would have been highly disturbing, leaving his listeners to wallow in their own miseries without any necessary sense of a remedy. His theologically-balanced approach (albeit terse) understood that the downward motion of grace came to meet humanity in the midst of its misery and need, thus preventing a collapse of human self-understanding into a state of utter hopelessness.

3. Billings, *Calvin, Participation, and the Gift*, 196.
4. *Institutes* I.6.1 [*OS* 3:61].
5. *Institutes* II.6.1 [*OS* 3:320].

Evidently, Calvin did not take delight in leaving the convicted sinner in a grovelling, miserable state, but saw this as only a means to an end, namely that humanity would accept the grace of God offered in the gospel, all redounding to God's praise and glory.[6] As Henry Chadwick has put it: "The submission of faith is not grovelling servility but spontaneous love and gratitude."[7] The grace of God as well as the glory of God were thus held together in order to both humble humanity to acknowledge that it was sinful, but, at the same time, to lead it to exult in the One who bestowed salvation on the unworthy.[8] Thus Calvin writes:

> Scripture attributed nothing else to him [Adam] than that he had been created in the image of God [Gen 1:27], thus suggesting that man was blessed, not because of his own good actions, but by participation in God. What, therefore, now remains for man, bare and destitute of all glory, but to recognize God for whose beneficence he could not be grateful when he abounded with the riches of his grace; and at least, by confessing his own poverty, to glorify him in whom he did not previously glory in recognition of his own blessings?[9]

It could be said that Calvin's notion of dialectic, in terms of a radical discontinuity between God who is holy and humanity which has fallen into sin, was of a particular kind, derived from theological considerations, for it was only when humanity understood its pitiable condition before God that it could be "sharply aroused from [its] inactivity,"[10] from its sinful slumber and sleep, in order to seek God's mercy and grace. Calvin was deeply persuaded that the initiative of this soteriological act lay decisively with God. From such a "supernatural" perspective there were thus two points of emphasis: human wretchedness before God (knowledge of humanity) and the divinely-given fullness of saving grace (knowledge of God).

It was only those who recognized their sinfulness before God who could truly appreciate what God had done for them. God in Christ had stooped down to those who knew they were unworthy of him in order to lift them out of their sin and misery. As Calvin preached: "Since then there is in us nothing but spiritual infection and leprosy and that we are corrupt in our iniquities, what shall we do? What remedy is there? Shall we go seek

6. Barth: "It was God who went into the far country, and it is man who returns home." *CD* 4/2:21 [*KD* 4/2:21].

7. Chadwick, *Early Christian Thought and Classical Tradition*, 52.

8. Cf. Rom 11:22.

9. *Institutes* II.2.1 [*OS* 3:241–42].

10. Ibid.

help from the Angels in Paradise? Alas! they can do nothing for us. No, we must come to our Lord Jesus Christ (. . .)."[11]

It was Calvin's contention that humanity necessarily needed this kind of knowledge in order to strip it of all confidence in any ability or merit it may think it possessed in itself, thus depriving it of any opportunity to boast in anything apart from what Christ had done for it.[12] Only by this means could the blind self-love and self-assertion innate to humanity be negated, for naturally speaking humanity was vain and full of pride. The gospel, according to Calvin, completely undermined this corrupt disposition in humanity. For humanity to boast in any natural capacity it was born with was to take away something from the glory of God, and thus to make God smaller rather than larger in humanity's eyes. So Calvin writes:

> For we always seem to ourselves righteous and upright and wise and holy—this pride is innate in all of us—unless by clear proofs we stand convinced of our own unrighteousness, foulness, folly, and impurity (. . .) As long as we do not look beyond the earth, being quite content with our own righteousness, wisdom, and virtue, we flatter ourselves most sweetly, and fancy ourselves all but demigods.[13]

For Calvin, the purest self was theocentric, not anthropocentric, being in subordination to God's sovereign rule and authority, characterized by a distinct form of self-abasement and humility, yet holding this in tension with a natural, though fragile, nobility, reflecting albeit dimly the *imago Dei*. By this reconstruction of humanity in relation to God, Calvin managed to maintain both a humanist high regard for humanity's natural capacities in the practical and in the intellectual spheres with, at the same time (holding them in antithesis), an anti-humanist denial of the spiritual or moral regeneration of humanity by its own efforts, stating: "We have nothing of the Spirit (. . .) except through regeneration."[14]

Even though the *imago Dei* had in a certain sense been lost, this did not necessarily mean a loss in "substance" or "essence" of the being of humanity in sin, but rather a radical disorientation from God, hence its bewilderment and state of confusion. So Calvin writes: "[God] is hostile toward the corruption of his work rather than toward the work itself."[15] In

---

11. *Sermons on Isaiah's Prophecy of the Death and Passion of Christ*, no. 3 (Isa 53:4–6), 75 [CO 35:628A].

12. Cf. Rom 3:27; Eph 2:8–10; 1 Cor 1:28–31.

13. *Institutes* I.1.2 [OS 3:32].

14. *Institutes* II.3.1 [OS 3:272].

15. *Institutes* II.1.11 [OS 3:240].

other words, God was not necessarily against the work of his own hands, but rather against the corruption into which humanity had fallen. That was why humanity in sin was under the wrath of God according to Calvin's understanding of Scripture. Reorientation to God and humanity's spiritual development could only come about by a dynamic dependence on the saving grace of God, mediated through Word and sacrament, resulting in a life of loving and faithful obedience in relation to God and service towards others.

Charles Partee compares Calvin's thinking on this matter analogically to a house with "a heavenly attic and a hellish cellar" with humanity stuck between the two in the living-room.[16] It was God, the estate agent and thus in control of the house, who either raised or lowered humanity at its own whim and discretion.[17] For those in the ascendancy, the proper human attitude and response was humility and gratitude, with no sense of superiority over those who may be going in the opposite direction, instead only one of sadness and pity, recognizing that "there but for the grace of God go I."[18] An *a priori* freedom for humanity in terms of free will was therefore nonexistent, leaving no room for any meritorious cause in humanity.[19]

Humanity was thus created in a dynamic state of response, either one of obedience or one of disobedience, to the eternal act of God's creating, redeeming, and sustaining love, which could either bring it closer or push it further away, in a salvific sense, in relation to God. Only by being lifted higher and deeper into the inexhaustible salvific knowledge of God could humanity come to a better knowledge of itself, confessing its sins and depravity in the process, and that only by the grace and goodness of God.[20] The converse of this was true as well, humanity being unable to prevent itself from falling deeper into sin and depravity, having little or no sense of the salvific knowl-

16. Partee, "Predestination in Aquinas and Calvin," 21.

17. The determinism in this statement may be too arbitrary for Calvin.

18. Cf. 1 Cor 4:7.

19. Just as Luther taught in The *Bondage of the Will* (1525), Calvin believed that the choice God gives to obey or disobey his commandments and exhortations did not in any manner reflect any ability or capacity in human nature to obey them; rather these exhortations merely revealed how incapacitated and impotent fallen human nature really was, and that only by a work of God's free grace (free will in humanity being nonexistent) could humanity respond in obedience. This ability was therefore unnatural to human nature but could be given by God as a supernatural gift. So, for example, following Augustine's argument in On *Rebuke and Grace* III.5, Calvin writes: "God does not measure the precepts of his law according to human powers, but where he has commanded what is right, he freely gives his elect the capacity to fulfil it." *Institutes* II.5.4 [OS III:301]. Cf. Augustine's remark: "You command continence: give what you command, and then command whatever you will." *Confessions* X.29.40 [WSA 1/1:263].

20. Cf. Augustine: "The house of my soul is too small for you to enter: make it more spacious by your coming. It lies in ruins: rebuild it." *Confessions* I.5.6 [WSA 1/1:42].

edge of God, and so losing the right to any sense of true self-knowledge. Thus Calvin writes: "[I]t is clear that all those who do not direct every thought and action in their lives to this goal [of knowing God] degenerate from the law of their creation."[21] It is quite evident here that Calvin's dynamic conception of humanity in relation to God (like a sliding-scale rule)[22] is quite different to the more static, reductionist anthropologies being articulated within certain Protestant fundamentalist circles in vogue today.[23]

THE FUNCTION OF THE LAW OF GOD

Calvin believed that it was the function of God's law to reveal to humanity what it was really like in its fallen condition before God, a condition sharply delineated by Paul in Rom 3:10–20.[24] So Calvin writes:

> But he who scrutinizes and examines himself according to the standard of divine judgment finds nothing to lift his heart to self-confidence. And the more deeply he examines himself, the more dejected he becomes, until, utterly deprived of all such assurance, he leaves nothing to himself with which to direct his life aright.[25]

Calvin held that the convicting power of the law (which in itself was holy and just and good)[26] revealed a real discord in the human condition. Thus those who came under the effects of its sword would be led to a high sense of displeasure and loathing in their own eyes, feeling unworthy in the sight of God. In his argument here, Calvin tended to magnify the law in humanity's eyes so that its maximum effect was reached, humbling and crushing it to the dust, so that it saw "that [its] whole brightness is as nothing in God's presence,"[27] that it "can bring nothing but that is nought,"[28] that it was nothing in and of itself apart from the grace of God.[29] Calvin then went further by declaring that humanity was no better, indeed lower than, or at least

---

21. *Institutes* I.3.3 [*OS* 3:40].

22. Cf. Edwards's sliding-scale of being and beauty; see below in chap. 4.

23. See Introduction.

24. *Institutes* II.3.2 [*OS* 3:273–74].

25. *Institutes* II.1.3 [*OS* 3:230].

26. Cf. Rom 7:12.

27. *Comm. 1 Pet* 1:24, *CNTC* 12:253 [*COR* 2/20:48].

28. *Sermons on Timothy & Titus*, no. 14 (1 Tim 2:5–6), 170.b.4–5 [*CO* 53:169].

29. *Institutes* II.2.1.3 [*OS* 3:3.25]; cf. *Comm. 1 Cor* 1:31, *CNTC* 9:47 [*CO* 49:332]; *Comm. Dan* 4:34–35, *COTC* 20:194–99 [*CO* 41:684–89].

could be likened to, "wretched worms,"[30] "wretched beasts,"[31] "vermin,"[32] "the common herd,"[33] "a snail,"[34] "grubs crawling upon the earth,"[35] that humanity was "made of dust and ashes, and full of rottenness and decay."[36] As if these epithets were not enough, Calvin proceeded to paint one image of humiliation upon another as he set forth his portrait of humanity:

> If a man, then, is considered in himself and in his own nature, what shall he be able to say? See, a creature cursed of God and worthy to be refused acceptance in the common range of all other creatures, even of worms, flies, lice and vermin. For there is more worth in all the world's vermin than there is in man. For man is a creature in which God's image is effaced, and the good he put into it corrupted. There is nothing in it but sin, so much so that we turned over to the devil, and he not only rules us, but also possesses us and is our prince.[37]

In a later address in the same Ephesians sermon series, Calvin once again graphically depicted fallen human nature using startling anthropological epithets:

> But when our father Adam was once fallen, and had become alienated from the fountain of life, he was soon stripped stark

30. *Sermons on Ephesians*, no. 13 (Eph 2:13–15), 188 [*CO* 51:402]. Other references to worms include: "a five-foot worm," *Institutes* I.5.4 [*OS* 3:47–48]; "The majesty of God is too high to be scaled up to by mortals, who creep like worms upon the earth," *Institutes* II.6.4 [*OS* 3:325]; "a worm of the earth," *Sermons on Genesis*, no. 67 (Gen 15:4–6), 320 [*SC* 11/2:747.25]; "We are miserable earthworms, creatures full of vanity, and liars into the bargain," *Four Sermons*, no. 2 (Heb 13:13), 36 [*CO* 8:399]; "mere worms of the earth," *Sermons on Isaiah's Prophecy*, no. 1 (Isa 52:13—53:1), 32 [*CO* 35:597]. Cf. Calvin's quotations from the book of Job: "And what can man do, who is rottenness itself [Job 13:28] and a worm [Job 7:7; Ps 22:6]," *Institutes* I.1.3 [*OS* 3:33]; "Man is far from being justified before God, man who is rottenness and a worm" [Job 25:6; cf. Vg], "abominable and empty, who drinks iniquity like water [Job 15:16]," *Institutes* III.12.5 [*OS* 4:212]; "Alas, I am but a worm, there is nothing in me but vanity," *Sermons on Job*, no. 28 (Job 7:7–15), 128.a.2–4 [*CO* 33:346]; "They be but worms and rottenness," ibid., no. 94 (Job 24:1–6), 443.b.56 [*CO* 34:416].

31. *Sermons on Job*, no. 80 (Job 21:13–15), 375.b.30 [*CO* 34:231]; cf. "man is likened to the brute beasts," ibid., no. 28 (Job 7:7–15), 128.b.5 [*CO* 33:348].

32. *Sermons on Genesis*, no. 29 (Gen 5.1–25), 490, 493 [*SC* 11/1:327.1, 328.31]; *Sermons on 2 Samuel*, no. 24 (2 Sam 7:18–21), 357 [*SC* 1:208.28]; *Sermons on Job*, no.72 (Job 19:26), 337.a.39 [*CO* 34:129].

33. *Sermons on Eph*, no. 9 (Eph 2:1–5), 130 [*CO* 51:351].

34. *Sermons on Job*, no. 143 (Job 36:25–33), 671.b.4 [*CO* 35:305].

35. *Institutes* II.6.4 [*OS* 3:325].

36. *Sermons on Galatians*, no. 20 (Gal 3:15–18), 303 [*CO* 50:526].

37. *Sermons on Ephesians*, no. 9 (Eph 2:1–5), 133 [*CO* 51:355].

naked of all good. For being separated from God, what could he be but utterly lost and hopeless? Can we find either life, or righteousness, or holiness, or soundness, or uprightness out of God? You see then that Adam was, as it were, cut off from the company of creatures. He was not worthy to be reckoned even among the frogs and the vermin of the earth. Boast as much as we please, that is our nature. We bear a greater curse from God than is upon all the lice and fleas, and in all the worms of the earth.[38]

The preparatory role of the law was "in order to humble men, having convinced them of their own condemnation."[39] This legal humiliation was essential in order for humanity to gain proper knowledge of itself, for "he who is most deeply abased and alarmed by the consciousness of his disgrace, nakedness, want and misery has made the greatest progress in the knowledge of himself."[40] The law thus acted like a mirror,[41] in which humanity could discover what it was really like in the sight of God. Or, to change the metaphor, it was like a balance in which humanity would be found wanting.

It was quite wrong for humanity to think that it deserved anything from the hand of God apart from the righteous wrath and judgment of God. Thus it was vital that it should be struck dumb, its mouth shut,[42] that it knew itself to be a guilty, lost, hell-deserving sinner. It needed to be reduced in its own eyes in order that God would be glorified in its dependence, as Calvin states: "Let all be little ones, and let all the world be guilty before God."[43] Calvin thus likened the effects of the law to "horrible threats [which] hang over us, constraining and entangling not a few of us only, but all of us to a man. They hang over us, I say, and pursue us with inexorable harshness, so that we discern in the law only the most immediate death."[44]

Only by being abased or humiliated could humanity discover what it really was like, and hence be led outside of itself to receive something that was not native to it, a righteousness which was imputed to it by God and accepted by faith. Or as Calvin puts it: "[T]hat, naked and empty-handed, [man might] flee to his mercy, repose entirely in it, hide deeply within it,

---

38. Ibid., no. 30 (Eph 4:23–26), 436 [CO 51:620–21].

39. *Institutes* II.7.2 [OS 3:328].

40. *Institutes* II.2.10 [OS 3:252].

41. *Institutes* II.7.7 [OS 3:333].

42. *Institutes* II.7.8 [OS 3:334]; cf. *Comm. Rom* 3:19, CNTC 8:68 [COR 2/13:66].

43. *Institutes* II.7.9 [OS 3:335]; cf. Edwards: "that I might become as a little child," *WJE* 16:796.

44. *Institutes* II.7.3 [OS 3:329]; cf. *WJE* 22:404–18.

and seize upon it alone for righteousness and merit."[45] The function of the law was therefore "in order to strike humanity more effectively with fear of the wrath of God, and whet its desire for obtaining grace through Christ."[46] Parker summarizes Calvin's position thus:

> It is precisely at this point of complete hopelessness that the Law, no less, proves itself in God's saving work. It presses its demands and threats to the extremity where man, defenceless, can only admit that God is righteous and true and he himself completely wrong and false. At this depth of humiliation and despair, knowing himself as he is in reality, in the eyes of God, nothing is left but to surrender and beg for mercy. Then the judge reveals himself as the Father, "good-natured, merciful, kind, and lenient."[47]

In other words, this legal humiliation and despair was truly health-giving for those who would receive it, because it brought humanity, to use Luther's words, "near to grace,"[48] for "only those afflicted and wounded by the awareness of sins can sincerely call upon God's mercy."[49] This mercy and grace was offered in the gospel, but could not be appreciated unless humanity had a sense of its spiritual neediness and poverty. "But that knowledge begins with a sense of our poverty. For to desire a remedy one must first be conscious of one's ills."[50] And "no one is permitted to receive God's blessings unless he is consumed with the awareness of his poverty."[51] That need could only be met if humanity was prepared to empty itself of anything which it knew alienated it from God. So Calvin writes: "[T]hey are not fit to receive Christ's grace unless they first be emptied. Therefore, through the recognition of their own misery, the law brings them down to humility in order thus to prepare them to seek what previously they did not realize they lacked."[52]

The gospel was only good news for those who felt their burden of sin and came to Christ the divine Physician to relieve them from that burden and restore them to spiritual life and vigor, for ultimately "man needs a physician, not an advocate."[53] Commenting on Jesus's invitation to weary burdened sinners as recorded by Matthew, Calvin writes: "Christ means by

45. *Institutes* II.7.8 [*OS* 3:334].

46. *Comm. Rom* 2:8, *CNTC* 8:45 [*COR* 2/13:44.7–8].

47. Parker, *John Calvin*, 57.

48. *LW* 33:190 [*WA* 18:718].

49. *Institutes* (1536) V.18 [*OS* 1:200].

50. *Comm. John* 4:10, *CNTC* 4:91 [*COR* 2/11/1:120.32–34].

51. *Institutes* II.2.10 [*OS* 3:336].

52. *Institutes* II.7.11 [*OS* 3:337].

53. *Institutes* II.5.18 [*OS* 3:318].

'ye that labour and are heavy laden' those whose consciences are afflicted by the guiltiness of eternal death and are inwardly so moved by their wretchedness that they faint. For this failure makes us fit to receive His grace (. . .) Our ills drive us to desiring Christ."[54]

In humanity's fallen state, God could only be known as a God of wrath and judgment, for his justice had been violated by the disorder in humanity and its sinful life on earth. God as a righteous judge had the right to face humanity with the terrors of the broken law whose penalty was the death sentence. The gospel for Calvin, however, was that God, even though just and holy (and his justice had always to be upheld) still loved humanity in spite of its fallen condition, and so in his grace and mercy provided a means by which humanity could be saved and his wrath turned away at the same time. That means was the sacrificial death of Christ on the cross. By the blood of Christ, humanity's sins could be cleansed, and humanity reconciled to God once more. So Calvin writes:

> God, apart from Christ, is always angry with us, and (. . .) we
> are reconciled to Him when we are accepted by His righteousness. God does not hate in us His own workmanship, that is, the
> fact that He has created us as living beings, but He hates our uncleanness, which has extinguished the light of His image. When
> the washing of Christ has removed this, He loves and embraces
> us as His own pure workmanship.[55]

Calvin insisted that although God treated sinners as his enemies, he always loved and willed the good of all that he had created.[56] But that love could only be known by humanity if and when it turned from its sin and received the cleansing, liberating redemptive power of Christ. For Calvin, the sense of utter wretchedness and helplessness on the part of humanity was sure evidence of the Spirit of God at work in the human heart applying the law of God, because it was the work of the Holy Spirit to bring about a true conviction of sin and a sense of need, causing in turn the convicted and condemned sinner to plead for mercy and seek grace for forgiveness and cleansing. "Scripture lays down that the right way to seek God is that a man prostrate, smitten with the accusation of eternal death, and despairing of himself, should fly to Christ as the only refuge for salvation."[57]

As suggested earlier, Calvin did not take particular delight in leaving the sinner in a grovelling, miserable, prostrate state before Almighty God. It was,

---

54. *Comm. Matt* 11:28, *CNTC* 2:25 [*CO* 45:320–21].

55. *Comm. Rom* 3:25, *CNTC* 8:76 [*COR* 2/13:73.15–20].

56. *Institutes* III.23.8 [*OS* 4:402].

57. *Comm. Heb* 11:6, *CNTC* 12.163 [*COR* 2/19:28–31].

however, absolutely essential for the sinner to come before God in a spirit of fear and trembling, rather than a spirit of pride and arrogance. The gospel he believed destroyed any lingering hope in humanity of retaining any sense of satisfaction in the works of its own hand.[58] It was to the penitent sinner that God gave saving faith, "whose office it [was] to raise up the hearts which were cast down with fear, and to encourage them to pray for forgiveness."[59] Showing his sensitivity to the plight of the self-condemned sinner, Calvin hardly advocated a protracted process whereby the sinner, after confessing their need for mercy, unduly did not find it until sometime later.[60] As he comments:

> God, when he has cast down his people, immediately raises up and restores them. (. . .) Let not men therefore faint or be discouraged by the knowledge of their nakedness and emptiness; for the eternal word is exhibited to them by which they may be abundantly supported and upheld.[61]

The sinner's confession was thus encompassed within God's redemptive purposes, so that the sinner could soon discover "a firm assurance as to [their] salvation."[62] And this mercy, as Calvin prayed, was "daily offered to us in the Gospel, through Christ Jesus our Lord,"[63] something which Calvin kept to the forefront both in his preaching and his pastoral ministry. By the grace of the gospel humanity was enabled to keep and obey God's moral commandments. God's laws and precepts did not reveal any innate capacity or power in humanity to obey them; rather their function was ultimately to lead humanity to depend on God's grace and mercy to enable it, in turn, to follow, obey, and honor God in everything, for "[t]he greater our desire for righteousness, the more fervent we become to seek God's grace."[64]

In all this, Calvin made no distinction amongst those who heard this message, whether they be young or old, rich or poor. All needed to hear the

---

58. So Luther: "[W]e can do nothing of ourselves, and (. . .) whatever we do, God works it in us." *De servo arbitrio, LW* 33:149 [*WA* 18:690].

59. *Comm. Ps* 130:4, *CTS* 6:131 [*CO* 32:335].

60. A doctrine of preparation for conversion [*preparatio ad conversionem*] became typical in seventeenth-century Puritanism. Cf. *MTP* 9:531.

61. *Comm. Isa* 40:8, *CTS* 8:212 [*CO* 36:12]; cf. "God does not cast down his own to leave them lying on the earth but immediately raises them up." *Comm. Ezek* 2:1, *COTC* 18:58 [*CO* 40:61]; "For God abases us, not to abandon us, but to lift us up to himself, so that we will know that [it is] he alone [who] is all powerful." *Sermons on Genesis*, no. 88 (Gen 18:24–33), 715 [*SC* 11/2:998.7–8].

62. *Comm. Mic* 7:9, *CTS* 28:377 [*CO* 43:414].

63. *Comm. Jer* 31:21, *CTS* 20:111 [*COR* 6/2:1177.1544–45].

64. *Institutes* II.5.10 [*OS* 3:308].

gospel no matter their age or station in life for all were equally fallen, and apart from the grace of God, had no hope or source of comfort to which to turn.

SIN IN RELATION TO THE IMAGO DEI WITH PARTICULAR REFERENCE TO CHILDREN

Taking for granted the theological precept that true self-knowledge is to know oneself in relation to God, one of the key issues with which Calvin grappled in his theological anthropology was to delineate the extent to which original sin had corrupted the *imago Dei* in humanity. In this discussion, it is important to recall the historical context in which Calvin was writing. His argument was not only theological but also polemical. He himself felt that "the most ancient doctors of the church" who had referred to this subject had either been too ambiguous in their deliberations, not expressing themselves sufficiently enough ("they explained it less clearly than was fitting"), or had simply ignored the question altogether.[65] Calvin even contended with Chrysostom and Jerome, claiming that their discussion of the freedom of the will had gone too far in crediting humanity "with more zeal for virtue than [it] deserved."[66] Although Augustine had admirably done much work in this area and, as it were, set the parameters for the overall debate, still, for Calvin, he had not gone far enough in some of the finer details.

Calvin also deliberately took to task various medieval scholastics such as Peter Lombard and Duns Scotus, believing that their theological anthropologies did not emphasize clearly enough the devastating effects of the Fall upon human nature. Lombard, for instance, affirmed that the flesh is polluted and corrupted, but corruption occurs in the soul solely by derivation through contact with the flesh;[67] and Duns Scotus stated that humanity had been corrupted only in its sensual part, leaving its reason and will largely unblemished.[68] In Calvin's estimation, these ideas were not based on the simple, genuine testimony of Scripture. Thus Calvin hit hard on medieval natural theology, and consequently emphasized in his estimation a more 'revealed' theology. By doing so, he effectively distanced himself from his

---

65. *Institutes* II.1.5 [*OS* 3:233]. Calvin believed that "the ancient teachers" had "confused earthly things with heavenly" in their attempt "to appease the wise of this world." *Concerning Scandals*, 23 [*Des Scandales*, 76–77].

66. *Institutes* II.2.4 [*OS* 3:245].

67. *Sententiarum Libri quatuor* II.30.7–8; II.31.2–4 [MPL CLXCII:722, 724].

68. *In Sententias* II.29.1 [Wadding, 13:267–68].

nearer contemporaries, and came up with a theological anthropology which was uniquely his own, albeit grounded in his interpretation of Scripture.[69]

Calvin took it upon himself to state as clearly and accurately as possible what he believed had happened to human nature after the Fall and the extent to which the *imago Dei* in humanity had been damaged. However, before he turned to this, Calvin began his theological anthropology by exploring the state of "original integrity"[70] when humanity was first made in the image and likeness of God:

> the integrity with which Adam was endowed is expressed by this word, when he had possession of right understanding, when he had his affections kept within the bounds of reason, all his senses tempered in right order, and he truly referred his excellence to exceptional gifts bestowed upon him by his Maker. And although the primary seat of the divine image was in the mind and heart, or in the soul and its powers, yet there was no part of man, not even the body itself, in which some sparks did not glow (. . .) to begin with, God's image was visible in the light of the mind, in the uprightness of the heart, and in the soundness of all the parts.[71]

Humanity in its original integrity and uprightness mirrored the divine glory, and would have been a dazzling sight. Although this would have been reflected in humanity's outward appearance, essentially the proper seat of the image of God was in humanity's soul, thus making humanity essentially a spiritual being.[72] By living a life "in utter and thankful dependence on the kindness of God alone,"[73] humanity would have continued to reflect God's glory. The downward movement of grace was thus recapitulated by humanity in its created intelligent life back to the glory of God, such that Torrance writes:

> [M]an has been created an intelligent being in order to know God in such a way that in the act of knowing (*acknowledgment*, as Calvin would say) man is brought to re-live consciously and in a qualitatively new fashion (*celestial* is Calvin's word) the very movement of grace in which he is created and maintained in being, so as to be carried beyond himself in responsible union

---

69. Cf. Cairns, *Image of God in Man*, 128–45.

70. *Institutes* I.15.1 [*OS* 3:173].

71. *Institutes* I.15.3–4 [*OS* 3:178–79].

72. *Institutes* I.15.3 [*OS* 3:173].

73. Torrance, *Calvin's Doctrine of Man*, 25; cf. *Institutes* I.14.22 [*OS* 3:172]; *Comm. Acts* 17:26–29, CNTC 7:116–23 [COR 2/12/2:121–27].

with God, in whom he finds his true life and felicity, *i.e.*, in the image of God.[74]

It was the proper rectitude of humanity's mind to live in this thankful fashion which characterized how God first fashioned humanity. Only by refusing to acknowledge that grace in its life would humanity distort and deface the image of God in which it was made, thus putting itself in a disorientated and discontinuous relation to God.

God also intended humanity to discern objectively something of his glory in the "magnificent theater of heaven and earth, crammed with innumerable miracles."[75] So, for example, Calvin comments on Ps 104:1:

> although God is invisible, yet his glory is conspicuous enough. In respect of his essence, God undoubtedly dwells in light that is inaccessible; but as he irradiates the whole world by his splendour, this is the garment in which He, who is hidden in himself, appears in a manner visible to us.[76]

The very fact that humanity had been created physically upright in posture was a sure indication to Calvin that, quoting Ovid: "By nature men are formed in such a manner as to make it evident that they were born to contemplate the heavens, and thus to learn their Author."[77] Although the Creator's handiwork could be discerned in the beauty of both the heavens and the earth, it was the heavens wherein his glory could principally be seen. Calvin commented on Ps 19:1:

> There is certainly nothing so obscure or contemptible, even in the smallest corners of the earth, in which some marks of the power and wisdom of God may not be seen; but as a more distinct image of him is engraven on the heavens, David has particularly selected them for contemplation, that their splendour might lead us to contemplate all parts of the world.[78]

Originally, God had given humanity the necessary sensory faculties by which it could discern and appreciate his glory in the beauty and splendor of creation, in all its rich variety.

---

74. Torrance, *Calvin's Doctrine of Man*, 32; italics his; cf. *Institutes* I.15.3 [*OS* 3:176–79]; *Sermons on Deuteronomy*, no. 46 (Deut 6:4–7), 271–77 [*CO* 27:432–44].

75. *Institutes* II.6.1 [*OS* 3:320]; cf. I.5.8 [*OS* 3:52]; I.6.2 [*OS* 3:62]; I.14.20 [*OS* 3:170]. See also Schreiner, *The Theater of His Glory*; Kaiser, "Calvin's Understanding of Aristotelian Natural Philosophy," 77–92.

76. *Comm. Ps* 104:1, *CTS* 6:145 [*CO* 32:85].

77. *Comm. Isa* 40:26, *CTS* 8:231 [*CO* 37:25]; cf. *Institutes* I.15.3 [*OS* 3:177].

78. *Comm. Ps* 19:1, *CTS* 4:308 [*CO* 31:194].

In grasses, trees, and fruits, apart from their various uses, there is the beauty of appearance and pleasantness of odor [cf. Gen 2:9]. For if this were not true, the prophet would not have reckoned them among the benefits of God, "that wine gladdens the heart of man, that oil makes his face shine" [Ps 104:15p.]. (. . .) Has the Lord clothed the flowers with the great beauty that greets our eyes, the sweetness of smell that is wafted upon our nostrils, and yet will it be unlawful for our eyes to be affected by that beauty, or our sense of smell by the sweetness of that odor? What? Did he not so distinguish colors as to make some more lovely than others? What? Did he not endow gold and silver, ivory and marble, with a loveliness that renders them more precious than other metals or stones? Did he not, in short, render many things attractive to us, apart from their necessary use?[79]

However, this appreciation for beauty in the created order was only meant to be a means to an end, namely the honoring of God for all his works. Due to the contaminating effects of original sin on humanity's sensory faculties, this order had been severely distorted, to the extent that humanity was now unable to see beyond the visible and reach toward the invisible. Invariably, this disorder in humanity could only lead to a false idolization of creation, thus subverting God's original intention. This ghastly state of affairs was what made Calvin rather skeptical of those who held to a more natural theology, when they used such terms as innate wisdom, virtue, or worthiness. It was Calvin's belief that this sort of language only tended to give more glory to humanity than was theologically warranted, and consequently deprived God the gratitude and praise that was his by right. So Calvin states:

Here, however, the foul ungratefulness of men is disclosed. They have within themselves a workshop graced with God's unnumbered works and, at the same time, a storehouse overflowing with inestimable riches. They ought, then, to break forth into praises of him but are actually puffed up and swollen with all the more pride. They feel in many wonderful ways that God works in them; they are also taught, by the very use of these things, what a great variety of gifts they possess from his liberality. They are compelled to know—whether they will or not—that these are the signs of divinity; yet they conceal them within. Indeed, there is no need to go outside themselves, provided they do not, by claiming for themselves what has been given them from

---

79. *Institutes* III.10.2 [*OS* 4:178]; cf. *Comm. Gen* 4:20, *CTS* 1:217–19 [*CO* 23:99–100].

heaven, bury in the earth that which enlightens their minds to see God clearly.[80]

This is not to say that Calvin had no room for a natural theology in his overall argument, but for him the chief emphasis had to be more on humanity's fallenness in order that God and not humanity should be honored and glorified. Concentrating on any natural gifts that remained in humanity after the Fall, he believed, would only pander to humanity's innate pride. Hence he wrote:

> Therefore, in nearly every age, when anyone publicly extolled human nature in most favourable terms, he was listened to with applause. But however great such commendation of human excellence is that teaches man to be satisfied with himself, it does nothing but delight in its own sweetness; indeed, it so deceives as to drive those who assent to it into utter ruin. For what do we accomplish when, relying upon every vain assurance, we consider, plan, try, and undertake what we think is fitting; then—while in our very first efforts we are actually forsaken by and destitute of sane understanding as well as true virtue—we nonetheless rashly press on until we hurtle to destruction? Yet for those confident they can do anything by their own power, things cannot happen otherwise. Whoever, then, heeds such teachers as hold us back with thought only of our good traits will not advance in self-knowledge, but will be plunged into the worst ignorance.[81]

Calvin believed that humanity was now in such a low and grovelling state that it was unable by its own efforts to come to any sense of awe and wonder of the Maker of heaven and earth. Consequently, humanity displayed an ungrateful and haughty spirit, not realizing that the natural talents or abilities it may still possess were merely gifts from the hand of its Creator and not its own in the first place. Humanity had no basis in itself for such self-glorification, but due to the damaging effects of original sin, this had become a natural disposition in it,[82] to the extent that it had, in its stupidity and ignorance, even turned its back on God and gone its own way, a disorientation in which all of humanity participated.[83]

Calvin went on to discuss in greater depth the cause of this severe dislocation, namely the "hereditary corruption, which the ancients called original sin." Calvin defined original sin as "a hereditary depravity and

80. *Institutes* I.5.4 [*OS* 3:47].
81. *Institutes* II.1.2 [*OS* 3:230].
82. *Institutes* I.5.4 [*OS* 3:47–48].
83. *Institutes* I.5.11 [*OS* 3:45].

corruption of our nature, diffused into all parts of the soul, which first makes us liable to God's wrath, then also brings forth in us those works which Scripture calls 'works of the flesh' [Gal 5:19]."[84] From his reading of Ps 51:7, Calvin believed: "The teaching of Scripture about the corruption of the nature is that, because we bear an innate corruption and badness from the womb, it is accordingly impossible to produce anything from a bad tree but bad fruit (. . .)."[85] Calvin made frequent reference to the beginnings of depravity within human nature coming from "our mother's womb," not justifying this position in relation to the efficacy of Christ's redemption but more on his reading of human nature. Thus Calvin comments on the *locus classicus* of the doctrine of original sin: "The natural depravity which we bring from our mother's womb, although it does not produce its fruits immediately, is still sin before God, and deserves His punishment. This is what is called original sin (. . .) We have, therefore, all sinned, because we are all imbued with natural corruption, and for this reason are wicked and perverse."[86]

Here we see Calvin indicating, like his great forebear Augustine, that no one is exempt from God's punishment, and that this is because human nature is so fallen that even a babe in the womb can be or do nothing to merit God's grace or favor. Calvin explains: "When I say that the whole human race is convicted of pollution, I mean that we take nothing from the womb except genuine filth, and that there is no uprightness in our nature which may procure the favour of God for us."[87] Thus Calvin interpreted Paul's statement "by nature all are children of wrath"[88] to mean that "[it] had already been cursed in the womb itself."[89] That all are sinners even in the womb was for Calvin an *ipso facto* state of affairs. New-born babies were just as deserving of God's damnation to eternal death as fully-developed adults were as Calvin indicates in his first Catechism:

> We are, therefore, sinners from the womb, born all of us for God's wrath and vengeance; grown up, we subsequently heap upon ourselves a heavier judgment; at last we proceed through our whole life to death. For if there is no doubt that all iniquity is hateful to God's righteousness, what do we poor folk expect from his sight save the surest confusion, such as his indignation bears

84. *Institutes* II.1.8 [*OS* 3:236–37].

85. *Concerning Scandals*, 50 [*Des Scandales*, 119–20].

86. *Comm. Rom* 5:12, CNTC 8:111–12 [COR 2/13:108.28–31, 35–37].

87. *Comm. Acts* 15:9, CNTC 7:35 [COR 2/12/2:38.28–31].

88. Eph 2:3.

89. *Institutes* II.1.6 [*OS* 3:234].

toward us who are both pressed down under a huge weight of sins and befouled with limitless dregs? This knowledge, though it strikes man with terror and overwhelms him with despair, is nevertheless necessary for us in order that, stripped of our own righteousness, cast down from confidence in our own power, deprived of all expectation of life, we may learn through the knowledge of our own poverty, misery, and disgrace to prostrate ourselves before the Lord, and by the awareness of our own wickedness, powerlessness, and ruin may give all credit for holiness, power, and salvation to him.[90]

How it was that children who have not yet done good or evil were just as culpable as adults of such a judgment Calvin answered as follows: "Although sin does not appear immediately and produce its fruits, that accursed seed is still in them [little children] and they are small serpents filled with poison, which they show with time."[91] Calvin refers to this poison in babies and consequently describes them as "serpents" in a further sermon:

It is true that the heathen will think it strange that young babes which are not able to discern between good and evil, nor have any discretion or will, should already be sinners and damned before God, according to St. Paul's saying; he calls them the children of wrath, but yet, we must be brought to judgment whether we like it or not. As soon as babes are able to give any indication, it is certain that they will show enough and too much that they are froward and perverse, that there is a secret poison lurking in them, and that although they do not show it at first, yet they are like a brood of serpents.[92]

Here Calvin begins to spell out just what he thought that "poison" consisted of which made even babies culpable of God's judgment: evidently they were "froward and perverse."[93] Pertinently, in a passage reminiscent of Augustine's observations concerning a child breast-feeding,[94] Calvin spells out even more clearly just what he thought that culpability of children was:

90. *RC* 1:412 [*COR* 3/2:9.23–36].

91. *Sermons on Genesis*, no. 14 (Gen 3:4–6), 246 [*SC* 11/1:172.30–33].

92. *Sermons on Ephesians*, no. 10 (Eph 2:3–6), 143 [*CO* 51:363].

93. One wonders if this was an observation made by Calvin himself, or based on his theological reasoning.

94. Cf. "I have watched and experienced for myself the jealousy of a small child; he could not even speak, yet he glared with livid fury at his fellow-nursling." *Confessions* I.7.11 [*WSA* 1/1:46].

Now it is quite true that as soon as a child distinguishes between good and evil, he is already showing he is a little serpent which descended from Adam's accursed race, which is completely corrupt and preserved in sin. That is clear and you do not have to go to school to learn about evil, for everyone is very well learned in that subject. And even infants at their mother's breast already give indications of their perversity. All you have to do is look at that simple nature and you will find they are centred upon themselves, wanting to be respected and served. Think about them. There is ambition. There is envy. They are vindictive. They will scratch their mother if she does not immediately do what they demand. When we observe that, it is clear they do not distinguish between good and evil so that we can say there is sin, but it is certain that, in the eyes of God, that disposition is accursed and merits condemnation for the children.[95]

Consequently, for Calvin children were just as deserving of God's punishment as adults are. In effect, there was only one theological anthropology for the whole of humanity: all share in the "miserable ruin" into which their common ancestor Adam has cast them, a calamity that has brought upon them their own "*ignorantiae, vanitatis, inopiae, infirmitatis, pravitatis denique et corruptionis.*"[96] As he further states: "[W]e are all cursed in Adam, and bring nothing but damnation with us out of our mother's womb."[97] The fact that Adam's sin had such devastating effects on his offspring, entangling them in the same miseries that Adam himself suffered, came as no surprise to Calvin, believing as he did that as rotten branches originate from a rotten root, so "were the children corrupted in the parent, so that they brought disease upon their children's children."[98] Adam's disobedience had directly led to the blotting out or obliterating of "the heavenly image"[99] in which Adam had been created in the beginning, and, consequently, all of his posterity suffered in the same plight and calamity. In other words, Adam was the fountainhead from which the corrupting stream had flowed throughout human history to all of Adam's descendants, with the direct consequence that "in place of wisdom, virtue, holiness, truth, and justice, with which adornments he had been clad, there came forth the most filthy plagues, blindness, impotence, impurity, vanity, and injustice."[100] All were made guilty by the

95. *Sermons on Genesis*, no. 33 (Gen 6:5–8), 562 [*SC* 11/1:372.28–38].

96. *Institutes* I.1.1 [*OS* 3.31].

97. *Sermons on Job*, no. 100 (Job 27:13–19), 469.a.53–55 [*CO* 34:484].

98. *Institutes* II.1.7 [*OS* 3:236].

99. *Institutes* II.1.5 [*OS* 3:232–33].

100. *Institutes* II.1.5 [*OS* 3:233].

guilt of one and thus sin had become common to all.[101] Calvin summarizes his position on this particular *locus*, copied almost verbatim in each version of his *Institutes*, as follows:

> [W]e are so vitiated and perverted in every part of our nature that by this great corruption we stand justly condemned and convicted before God, to whom nothing is acceptable but righteousness, innocence, and purity. And this is not liability for another's transgression. For, since it is said that we became subject to God's judgment through Adam's sin, we are to understand it not as if we, guiltless and undeserving, bore the guilt of his offence but in the sense that, since we through his transgression have become entangled in the curse, he is said to have made us guilty. Yet not only has a punishment fallen upon us from Adam, but a contagion imparted by him resides in us, which justly deserves punishment (...) For that reason, even infants themselves, while they carry their condemnation along with them from the mother's womb, are guilty not of another's fault but of their own. For, even though the fruits of their iniquity have not yet come forth, they have the seed enclosed within them. Indeed, their whole nature is a seed of sin; hence it can be only hateful and abhorrent to God.[102]

As to the human faculties, this corruption of human nature affected the mind or understanding in its soundness, the heart in its uprightness, and the will in its freedom, each faculty being both weakened and impaired by sin, so that consequently human nature was no longer capable of thinking, desiring, or willing after "heavenly things" such as "the pure knowledge of God, the nature of true righteousness, and the mysteries of the Heavenly Kingdom."[103] Yet in all this, Calvin believed that "[s]ome seed of religion is sown in all: and also, the distinction between good and evil is engraven in their consciences,"[104] indicating that he did have a natural theology to which I shall shortly draw attention.

What stands out in Calvin's understanding of human sinfulness in relation to children is its comprehensiveness, particularly in terms of the range of its effect. It included both actual sinning and the proclivity to sin, sinfulness being a condition which could potentially give birth to any and every

---

101. *Comm. Rom* 5:12, *CNTC* 8:111–12 [*COR* 2/13:108–9].

102. *Institutes* II.1.8 [*OS* 3:237]; cf. *Institutes* (1536) IV:17 [*OS* 1:131].

103. *Institutes* II.2.13 [*OS* 3:256].

104. *Comm. John* 1:5, *CNTC* 4:12 [*COR* 2/11/1:19.34–36].

conceivable sinful act that was humanly possible. This affected every stage of life including infancy, as he put it in one of his sermons on Deuteronomy:

> [E]ven infants are sinners aforehand: they be condemned before GOD being yet in their mothers wombs. The evil is not yet perceived: but yet for all that their nature is sinful and froward, they have a secret seed within them, and they be already in condemnation, because of the original sin that is come from Adam upon all mankind. Now seeing that the little babes are not exempted from the wrath and curse of GOD, in so much that if he punish them it is not without cause, (. . .) for there is fault to be found even in them also.[105]

Calvin realized that this claim would offend many people naturally speaking, but he remained adamant that this was what Scripture testified, what his great mentor Augustine had taught, and what his own experience of life verified. Human nature therefore in its guilty, vitiated, perverted, defiled, rotten, miserable, foul, and dishonorable condition after the Fall was like "a burning furnace [which] gives forth flame and sparks, or water [which] ceaselessly bubbles up from a spring," a spring which Calvin described as being contaminated or polluted. This contamination affected every part of humanity's being, such that "the whole man [was] nothing but concupiscence."[106] Calvin commented on Ps 51:5:

> [Man's] nature was entirely depraved (. . .) he was born in iniquity, and was absolutely destitute of all spiritual good (. . .) we are cherished in sin from the first moment that we are in the womb (. . .) [sin] exists within us as a disease fixed in our nature (. . .) We have no adequate idea of the dominion of sin, unless we conceive of it as extending to every part of the soul, and acknowledge that both the mind and heart of man have become utterly corrupt (. . .) that from his [David's] very infancy he was an heir of eternal death.[107]

Calvin claimed that it was necessary to assume *a priori* that all were born into a miserable state of sin in order that no one would have any grounds for boasting in themselves before God, that God would hence be

---

105. *Sermons on Deuteronomy*, no. 32 (Deut 5:8–10), 189.b.52–63, 190.a.5–7 [*CO* 26:262]; cf. *Institutes* IV.15.10 [*OS* 5:292]. Unlike Augustine, Calvin refused to speculate on how Adam's sin was transmitted to his offspring, not desiring to enter "upon such mysterious discussions." *Comm. Ps* 51:5, CTS 5:291 [*CO* 31:510].

106. *Institutes* II.1.8 [*OS* 3:238].

107. *Comm. Ps* 51:5–6, CTS 5:290–92 [*CO* 31:510].

exalted in humanity's eyes. Calvin did not see any other way by which these desirable results could occur. Hence he preached:

> God is never exalted of us as he deserves, unless we ourselves be utterly confounded, and cast down to the bottomless pit of hell. For as long as man reserves the least iota that may be to himself, God is spoiled of his right which he ought to have (. . .) So then, until men be come to a reckoning, to condemn themselves wholly, and confess that they have nothing in them, but only curse, and only wretchedness, and that they are creatures cast away, and worse than nought, until they become thus far, the glory of GOD is not known, as need is it should be known (. . .) when we know that we are but worms, and that there is nothing in our nature but wretchedness and misery, that there is neither life nor strength, nor else whatsoever, and come to this infinite highness, which is God: this ought to move us much more to set forth his praises.[108]

By seeing his fallenness and nothingness in the sight of God, humanity would then be in the best position, low and humble in its own eyes, to enter into all that God had for it. It was confidence in itself that had prevented it from entering into that salvific blessing in the first place, such that Calvin states in his first catechism:

> From this knowledge of ourselves, which shows us our nothingness if it seriously lodges in our hearts, is provided a ready access also to a truer knowledge of God. Indeed, it has already opened the first door into his kingdom, when it has overthrown those two most harmful plagues of all, carefree disregard of his vengeance and false confidence in our own capacity. For we then begin to lift our eyes, formerly glued to earth, heavenward; and we who were resting secure in ourselves now long for the Lord.[109]

Calvin spoke of the condition of fallen humanity in "total" categories of which the following can be taken as typical: "[T]he whole of man's nature is condemned;"[110] "[f]or we are poor dust of the earth. We are nothing but powder and corruption. In addition, within our souls there is nothing but filth, and we are so alienated from God that we do not merit being allowed

---

108. *Sermons on Timothy & Titus*, no. 7 (1 Tim 1:14–15), 81.b.12–19, 29–39; ibid., no. 8 (1 Tim 1:17–19), 89.b.7–15 [CO 53:83, 91]; capitals his.

109. *RC* 1:413 [*COR* 3/2:10.1–8].

110. *Comm. John* 3:6, *CNTC* 4:66 [*COR* 2/11/1:90.56–57]; cf. *Institutes* II.1.9 [*OS* 3:239].

among his creatures;"[111] "[t]here is nothing but rottenness and infection in us (. . .) There is not one drop of life in us that deserves the name of life (. . .) our souls are altogether sinful (. . .) there is nothing in us but faults, sins and offences;"[112] "we are so completely held in bondage to sin that we can do nothing but sin;"[113] "men have none other stuff in them but sin: all is corrupted (. . .) all our whole life is given to evil: and as a fish feeds upon the water, so men do nothing else but feed upon sin;"[114] "[o]ur Lord created us after his own image and likeness. It is true: but that was wholly defaced and wiped out in us by the sin of Adam: we are accursed, we are by nature shut out from all hope of life;"[115] "man, after he had been deceived by Satan, revolted from his Maker, became entirely changed, and so degenerate, that the image of God, in which he had been formed, was obliterated."[116]

In contrast to Lombard who, as we have noted, held that only a part of human nature had been wounded by original sin and that sin lay in the flesh and was not intrinsic to it, Calvin in no uncertain terms stated: "[O]ur nature is not only destitute and empty of good, but so fertile and fruitful in every evil that it cannot be idle (. . .) the whole man is of himself nothing but concupiscence";[117] "the whole man is overwhelmed—as by a deluge—from head to foot, so that no part is immune from sin and all that proceeds from him is to be imputed to sin."[118] The implication of this state of affairs was that only a "full reformation"[119] of all parts of human nature would be sufficient to restore any semblance of order and true dignity to human nature, making humanity thus once more fit enough to stand before God. Calvin believed that "man's power [needed to be] rooted out from its very foundations [in order] that God's power may be built up in man,"[120] a salvific act and process only the power of God could accomplish.

111. *Sermons on 2 Samuel*, no. 24 (2 Sam 7:18–23), 357 [*SC* 1:208.9–12].

112. *Sermons on Ephesians*, no. 9 (Eph 2:1–5), 129 [*CO* 51:351].

113. *Comm. Rom* 6:6, *CNTC* 8:125 [*COR* 2/13:121.30].

114. *Sermons on Job*, no. 58 (Job 15:11–16), 274.a.24–25, b.15–17 [*CO* 33:728, 730].

115. *Sermons on Deuteronomy*, no. 141 (Deut 24:19–22), 869.a.2–6 [*CO* 28:205]; cf. "Thus you see what the spiritual life of man is and where it lies (. . .) according to the image that was lost and utterly defaced in us by Adam's sin." *Sermons on Ephesians*, no. 9 (Eph 2:1–5), 129 [*CO* 51:350].

116. *Comm. Gen* 3:1, *CTS* 1:139 [*CO* 23:52]; cf. Calvin on an Augustinian understanding of original sin: *Comm. Gen* 3:6, *CTS* 1:154–57 [*CO* 23:61–63].

117. *Institutes* II.1.8 [*OS* 3:238].

118. *Institutes* II.1.9 [*OS* 3:239].

119. Ibid.

120. *Institutes* II.2.1 [*OS* 3:242].

Calvin understood this to be "both fundamental in religion and most profitable for us,"[121] because it was the only way whereby the radical breach between God and humanity caused originally by Adam's disobedience could effectively be dealt with. Such was the seriousness of the situation that humanity found itself in, that it needed to be radically confronted with the problem of its condition before the remedy could begin to take effect. Consequently, Calvin set up an absolute contrast between what humanity was like before the Fall and what it was like after it, in order to extenuate humanity's need and cause it to cry out for help.

> But that primal worthiness cannot come to mind without the sorry spectacle of our foulness and dishonour presenting itself by way of contrast, since in the person of the first man we have fallen from our original condition. From this source arise abhorrence and displeasure with ourselves, as well as true humility, and thence is kindled a new zeal to seek God, in whom each of us may recover those good things which we have utterly and completely lost.[122]

However, Calvin's 'totalizing' language must be understood and interpreted in its soteriological context and not on its own for, as Engel suggests, his "insistence on the total corruption of the self allow[ed] him to highlight simultaneously the insufficiency of all human merit and the sufficient, gratuitous character of God's redeeming grace."[123] As Calvin put it:

> Now we see that men ought to have a double knowledge of themselves. For on the one side it behoves them to know how there is nothing but rottenness and corruption in them, to the intent they may obtain favour of God, and move him to use mercy and pity towards us.[124]

In this context, Torrance writes:

> [I]t is just because faith must speak of salvation and forgiveness in total terms that it must also speak of sin and depravity in total terms. But it is only within the context of grace, and on the ground of grace, that we have any right to make such a total judgment upon man as he is (...).[125]

---

121. Ibid.
122. *Institutes* II.1.2 [*OS* 3:229].
123. Engel, *John Calvin's Perspectival Anthropology*, 57.
124. *Sermons on Job*, no. 28 (Job 7:12–15), 131.a.12–18 [*CO* 33:354].
125. Torrance, *Theology in Reconstruction*, 106.

As has already been suggested, this contextualization of Calvin's anthropology within his soteriology offers a corrective to those who take many of his theological statements, such as that humanity needs to be "brought to nothing in its own estimation" in order that God may be all,[126] out of the context of his theological methodology. Indeed, Barth was scathing of this form of reductionism, remarking: "It is apparent at once that the formula 'God everything and man nothing' as a description of grace is not merely a 'shocking simplification' but complete nonsense."[127] Ontologically speaking, this fundamental error of Calvinian interpretation can lead to a form of "self-emptying"[128] whereby the person feels completely worthless and consequently loses any sense of identity, going from a state of being to one of nothingness, which I have argued Calvin's dialectical epistemology was careful to protect against (humanity never loses its state of being, always being in relation to God—part of the *imago Dei*—whether that be continuous or discontinuous). Perhaps this is why Torrance distanced himself from such a train of thought and demarcated what he understood to represent best Calvin's thought in this regards of sin in relation to humanity when he wrote:

> Total depravity does not entail on the Reformed view any ontological break in man's relation with God, but it does mean that the essential relation in which true human nature is grounded has been utterly perverted and turned into its opposite. Thus, it views "sin as properly of the mind" [*peccatum proprie animi est*], and thinks of it as an active perversity which drags the whole man into pollution and inverts the whole order of creation.[129]

Calvin did claim "that men are not so stripped of all glory, that they may lie down in disgrace; but that they may seek a better glory, for God delights not in the degradation of men,"[130] thus indicating that although he believed humanity needed to be humbled, it was only with the intent to raise it up again, not because God wanted to annihilate humanity altogether. In the Calvinian salvific process, humanity was identified with Christ in his

126. Cf. Edwards: "By the creature's being thus wholly and universally dependent on God, it appears that the creature is nothing, and that God is all." *WJE* 17:211.

127. *CD* 4/1:89 [*KD* 4/1:88].

128. Cf. Edwards: "I felt withal, an ardency to be (. . .) emptied and annihilated; to lie in the dust, and to be full of Christ alone (. . .)." *WJE* 16:801. Calvin did say: "Men need not empty themselves to be of no value (. . .)." *Deity of Jesus Christ and Other Sermons*, no. 2 (Luke 2:1–14), 36 [*COR* 5/8:7.69–70].

129. Torrance, *Theology in Reconstruction*, 107; cf. *Comm. Rom* 2:1, *CNTC* 8:40 [*COR* 2/13:39.20].

130. *Comm. Jer* 9:23–24, *CTS* 9:498 [*COR* 6/1:377.1099–1101]; cf. *Institutes* II.2.15 [*OS* 3:258]; III.2.25 [*OS* 4:35].

death and resurrection, in order that it may become a new person in Christ, thus showing that God still had a plan and purpose for humanity who was his special creation in the first place. Indeed, Calvin suggested: "Although we are nothing in our hearts, perhaps something of us may lurk in the heart of God."[131] There was something about humanity which God had respect toward, namely a dignity which, though damaged by original sin, still remained intact in humanity.

Engel argues that the dichotomy or tension in these anthropological statements of Calvin arises from the fact that Calvin seems to be writing from two different perspectives, namely one which could be described from a "natural" or relative perspective, and the other from a "supernatural" or absolute perspective.[132] Although many of Calvin's anthropological claims appear on the surface to be logically contradictory, when placed side-by-side, Engel contends that they should be read as complementary,[133] one offering a corrective to the other, thus giving a more full and complex picture of Calvin's understanding of humanity in relation to God, rather than one which concentrates only on one perspective, subsequently forcing or twisting the other to conform to it.[134] In this regard, Paul Pruyser is near the mark when he writes: "[M]an is for Calvin a being in a state of tension, a dynamic system in an unstable equilibrium."[135]

So, for example, from Calvin's soteriological point of view (Engel's "supernatural" perspective), "the image of God, in which [humanity] had been formed, was obliterated (. . .) and (. . .), in this way, much of its native excellence was destroyed."[136] However, Calvin qualified this (Engel's "natu-

131. *Institutes* III.2.25 [*OS* 4:36].

132. Engel points out that although Torrance presents plenty of examples of the Thomist distinction of "natural" and "supernatural" from the Calvinian corpus, he offers no clear discussion of different definitions "to compare relative human judgments with the absolute judgment of God on sinful human beings." Engel, *John Calvin's Perspectival Anthropology*, 12n48; 17n78.

133. Loder's thesis of "complementarity" is similar in many ways to Engel's thesis of "perspectivalism" (seeing things from different viewing-points) and also Torrance's thesis of "kinetic thinking," helping to make better sense of more Calvin texts, with their disparate, dynamic, shifting, both-and, contradictory yet complementary, earthly and heavenly anthropological statements, than other theses (e.g., pessimism and its counter-thesis of optimism, as well as the compromised thesis of contradiction) on their own allow. Loder and Neidhardt, *Knight's Move*, 87; cf. Charles Pierce's "abductionism" and Kierkegaard's "leap of faith" hypotheses. The question arises, how much logical weight can these carry?

134. Engel reads Torrance's interpretation of Calvin's anthropology as "too systematic (in the pejorative sense) a presentation of Calvin's anthropology." *John Calvin's Perspectival Anthropology*, 63n2.

135. Pruyser, "Calvin's View of Man," 53.

136. *Comm. Gen* 3:1, *CTS* 1:139 [*CO* 23:52].

ral" perspective) by affirming the commonly held medieval formulation, based on a claim Augustine had originally made, that "the natural gifts were corrupted in man through sin, but that his supernatural gifts were stripped from him."[137] In other words, it was only the supernatural gifts in human nature that had been totally destroyed and wiped out, and not humanity's natural gifts. And these natural gifts were not defiled in and of themselves but only by the person who possessed them.[138] This distinction can be found, for example, in Calvin's comment on Jas 3:9:

> If it is objected, that the image of God in human nature was removed by the sin of Adam, we must admit that it was sadly deformed, yet in such a way that certain lineaments of it still appear. Righteousness, equity, the freedom to seek after good, these things have gone; but many gifts are left to us, by which we are superior to beasts. The man who has a true respect and reverence towards God will beware of being insulting towards people.[139]

So for Calvin, although humanity had lost much of the dignity which God had originally bestowed upon it, humanity yet remained unique in God's creation, even to the extent that it "towers over all the kinds of living creatures."[140] It was only humanity who had been made in the image of God, and although that image had become corrupted, there was still something left of it including certain "notable endowments"[141] that nothing else in creation possessed, hence the reason why humanity should be eternally grateful and give honor to God for continuing mercies so completely undeserved. Indeed, humanity still had within itself "a workshop graced with God's unnumbered works and, at the same time, a storehouse overflowing with inestimable riches."[142] That there were "some remaining traces of the image of God in man"[143] was a sure indication that God had not quite given up on humanity, but had bestowed a certain "general" or *specialis Dei gratia* upon it.[144] If God had not granted this mercy, humanity would be in an even worse condition than it was already in, for this "would have entailed the destruction of [his] whole nature,"[145] a collapse into utter depravity and

137. *Institutes* II.2.12 [*OS* 3:254.30–32].

138. *Institutes* II.2.16 [*OS* 3:259].

139. *Comm. Jas* 3:9, *CNTC* 3:292 [*COR* 2/20:287–88].

140. *Institutes* I.15.3 [*OS* 3:179].

141. *Institutes* III.14.2 [*OS* 3:222].

142. *Institutes* I.5.4 [*OS* 3:47].

143. *Institutes* II.2.17 [*OS* 3:260].

144. Ibid. Later known in the Reformed tradition as the doctrine of common grace.

145. Ibid.

a state of nothingness, which of course was non-existence. But though this worst-case scenario had been avoided, humanity was still in a calamitous state as Calvin intimated:

> [E]ven though we grant that God's image was not totally annihilated and destroyed in him, yet it was so corrupted that whatever remains is frightful deformity (. . .) God's image is the perfect excellence of human nature which shone in Adam before his defection, but was subsequently so vitiated and almost blotted out that nothing remains after the ruin except what is confused, mutilated, and disease-ridden.[146]

Calvin delineated where vestiges of the *imago Dei* could still be traced, namely in humanity's understanding and will: "If, therefore, God has imprinted his image in men, if he has given them sense and discretion, if they are prudent—and indeed, many of them are very sharp, possessing wise and able counsel—it is certain that God has shown himself to have been most generous to them in having bestowed such a wonderful gift upon them."[147] For Calvin it was primarily "the mind of man," rather than the will, which "is the true image."[148] This image Calvin spoke of in terms of rationality or understanding, such that, "in man's perverted and degenerate nature some sparks still gleam. These show him to be a rational being, differing from brute beasts, because he is endowed with understanding."[149] However, as children lack such understanding, Calvin claimed "our childhood is such, that they which are in it, differ little or nothing from brute beasts, saving that there is more [e]ncumbrance and trouble with them: but as for understanding or reason, there is small or none in little ones."[150] Even so, although the mind had been perverted from its original wholeness, nonetheless it was "clothed and ornamented with God's excellent gifts."[151] However, "this light was choked with dense ignorance, so that it cannot come forth effectively."[152]

When it came to "earthly things," the mind, though fallen, was still capable of such things as "government, household management, all mechanical skills, and the liberal arts,"[153] "even after it was despoiled of its true good."[154]

---

146. *Institutes* I.15.4 [*OS* 3:179–80].

147. *Sermons on 2 Samuel*, no. 41 (2 Sam 13:1–14), 618–19 [*SC* 1:359.29–32].

148. *Comm. Acts* 17:22, *CNTC* 7:110 [*COR* 2/12/2:114.19–20].

149. *Institutes* II.2.12 [*OS* 3:255].

150. *Sermons on Job*, no. 17 (Job 4:20—5:2), 75.b.21–25 [*CO* 33:211].

151. *Institutes* II.2.15 [*OS* 3:258].

152. *Institutes* II.2.12 [*OS* 3:255].

153. *Institutes* II.2.13 [*OS* 3:256].

154. *Institutes* II.2.15 [*OS* 3:258].

Calvin thus granted limited natural gifts and powers to the mind, allowing it some knowledge in earthly matters, though not in heavenly wisdom or true knowledge of God. But these natural gifts had been distorted by sin, so that even the greatest geniuses that the world had ever known were "blinder than moles."[155] This fact did not, however, prevent Calvin from speaking of the excellent qualities which could still be attributed to humanity, thus revealing it as the crown jewel of God's creation.

After his fairly robust analysis of the corruption of the mind by sin, Calvin went on to defend his understanding of the bondage of the will. With regards to the will, Dewey Hoitenga argues that Calvin understood sin not only to wound and corrupt it but nearly to destroy it altogether, for in its fallen state it could only be inclined toward evil.[156] Calvin, like Luther, believed that the will in fallen humanity was not free, rather completely bound by original sin.[157] However, following Augustine, Calvin did state that the will in fallen humanity remained substantively intact. It was just that it was, naturally speaking, only inclined to evil, and it was only the restraining common grace of God that prevented humanity from falling into complete degradation and depravity. Salvific grace redirected the will to seek righteousness and holiness of living to the glory of God, the only reason why it could be described as "a new will," not because it had been substantively changed. Thus Calvin writes:

> [T]he beginning of our regeneration is to wipe out what is ours (. . .) Meanwhile, we do not deny that what Augustine says is very true: "Grace does not destroy the will but rather restores it." The two ideas are in substantial agreement: the will of man is said to be restored when, with its corruption and depravity corrected, it is directed to the true rule of righteousness. At the same time a new will is said to be created in man, because the natural will has become so vitiated and corrupted that he considers it necessary to put a new nature within.[158]

Evidently Calvin held to the traditional faculty psychology,[159] thus stating: "[T]he human soul consists of two faculties, understanding and

155. *Institutes* II.2.18 [*OS* 3:260].

156. Hoitenga, *John Calvin and the Will*, 69–91.

157. Calvin held that to believe in the freedom of the will robbed God of the honor he was due.

158. *Institutes* II.5.15 [*OS* 3:315]; cf. Peter van Mastricht: "[S]ince by regeneration spiritual life is bestowed upon the will of man, which was before dead, it is so far from being destroyed that it is restored to its proper life and perfection." *A Treatise on Regeneration*, 39.

159. Cf. Plato, *Republic* IV.439a–440d.

will."[160] Both these faculties had been corrupted by original sin and thus no longer functioned as God originally intended.[161] At the same time, Calvin did give a more detailed account of the fallen mind's capacity to good in comparison to his account of the will's capacity toward good.[162] One could conclude therefore on this basis that Calvin was not so pessimistic on his understanding of the fallenness of the mind compared to that of the will, but this would be a simplistic reading of the text. Calvin does say that the mind "has not only been wounded, but so corrupted that it needs to be healed and put on a new nature as well."[163] Further: "[M]an is so much corrupted in all parts of him through the sin of Adam, that there is neither understanding nor will but it tends wholly to evil, and is utterly steeped in it."[164] That he goes into more detail on the sinful condition of the will in comparison to the sinful condition of the mind simply echoed the theological tradition. By exploring both the radical corruption of the mind[165] as well as that of the will,[166] Calvin went further than any of his theological predecessors whom he understood to be too optimistic in their assessment of fallen human nature. Consequently Calvin has become in many senses the fountainhead of a deeply intensified pessimistic understanding of human nature and its possibilities. At the end of his discussion of humanity's natural condition in relation to God, Calvin concludes:

> Therefore let us hold this as an undoubted truth which no siege engines can shake: the mind of man has been so completely es-tranged from God's righteousness that it conceives, desires, and undertakes, only that which is impious, perverted, foul, impure, and infamous. The heart is so steeped in the poison of sin, that

160. *Institutes* I.15.7. Further: "Scripture is accustomed to divide the soul of man, as to its faculties, into two parts, the mind and the heart. The mind means the understand-ing, while the heart denotes all the dispositions or wills. These two terms, therefore, include the entire soul (. . .)." *Comm. Phil* 4:7, *CNTC* 11:290 [*COR* 2/16:374.62–65].

161. *Institutes* II.1.8–9 [*OS* III:236–39]; cf. *Comm. Ps* 119:37, *CTS* 6:427–28 [*CO* 32:220]. Barbara Pitkin contends that Calvin gave greater prominence in his discussion to the noetic capacity of human nature in relation to sin, rather than the volitional, in contrast to the earlier theological tradition which tended to treat the volitional more than the noetic, not that Calvin himself failed to discuss the role of the will in relation to sin as well. Pitkin, "Nothing But Concupiscence," 347–69.

162. In his analysis of the volitional capacity of human nature, he did state that there was still some place for a natural morality which he attributed to God's special grace. *Institutes* II.3.3–4 [*OS* 3:274–76].

163. *Institutes* II.1.9 [*OS* 3:238].

164. *Sermons on Ephesians*, no. 28 (Eph 4:17–19), 416 [*CO* 51:591].

165. *Institutes* II.2.12–25 [*OS* 3:254–68].

166. *Institutes* II.2.26–27; II.5.19 [*OS* 3:269–71; 3:318–20].

it can breathe out nothing but a loathsome stench. But if some men occasionally make a show of good, their minds nevertheless remain enveloped in hypocrisy and deceitful craft, and their hearts bound by inner perversity.[167]

THE OVERALL SHAPE OF CALVIN'S EPISTEMOLOGICAL FRAMEWORK

The question can now be asked: what shape did Calvin's epistemological framework take as he developed his understanding of the knowledge of humanity, including children, in relation to God? As has already been indicated in the last chapter, a profound bipolarity and dualism in Calvin's epistemology marks his thinking from at least the time of writing his 1536 *Institutes*. It is very likely that the dialectical thought of Luther would have had some sort of influence on Calvin, including Luther's use of hyperbole and paradox in his theological writings. Arguably Calvin used two forms of dialectic: the art of reasoning according to the demands of formal logic; and the habit of systematically placing divine and human knowledge in opposition to each other. So how does this pan out in his theology?

As has been argued, Calvin gave some space in his thinking to what may be called natural theology only in order to present a fuller picture of humanity, but this was not his main emphasis. Rather, what really mattered to him was humanity's salvific relation to God. The natures of God and humanity were diametrically opposed to each other, in a state of complete estrangement. It was the law of God that revealed the discontinuity between the two, a "gulf" unbridgeable from humanity's side. But although the problem was with humanity, God in his grace had taken the initiative to deal with the situation. This was necessary because a radical reorientation in humanity had to take place before it could be truly reconciled to God.

It was the simultaneous understanding of humanity and of God that Calvin called a "quickening,"[168] what could be described as "a supernaturally-heightened consciousness,"[169] which was the only way by which humanity could begin to perceive something of the mystery of the glory of God,[170] invariably preceded by the apprehension and experience of the nothingness

---

167. *Institutes* II.5.19 [*OS* 3:319–20].

168. *Institutes* III.3.3 [*OS* 3:57].

169. Miles, "Theology, Anthropology, and the Human Body in Calvin's *Institutes of the Christian Religion*," 305.

170. Cf. Otto, *Idea of the Holy*.

of all human endeavour: "We cannot (. . .) rise to our feet unless we are first laid low";[171] "we must be mortally wounded in our hearts and sense God's judgment, which terrifies us and reduces us to a state of complete despair."[172] Gratitude as well as faith was one of the pivotal elements of this quickening consciousness.

Consequently, the true nature, in Calvin's opinion, of the bipolar divine-human relation was patently clear: God was holy and humanity was sinful,[173] and the only solution to this state of affairs was the mediation of Christ, with the direct intention to magnify the glory of God. The net result of this bipolar dialectic was to quicken or energize humanity to seek God's face with an all-pervading earnestness, even vehemence. This is what effectively "forced him to order his exposition in terms of sin and grace,"[174] with little room for anything else, leading him to an arguably narrow conception of God[175] as well as narrow conception of humanity (including children). By a rhetorical method he "heightened" the original condition of human being as the good creation of God and then sequentially, after the Fall, its miserable condition. Consequently, there is a certain rigidity and verticality to the overall shape of Calvin's epistemological framework as it worked out.

However, it could be suggested that Calvin's epistemological claims exaggerated the helplessness of humanity, including children, in order to demonstrate, maintain, heighten, dramatize and display the glory of God in humanity's eyes,[176] that in effect, Calvin used humanity as a foil, as he states

171. *Songs of the Nativity*, no. 24 (Luke 2:9–14), 139 [*CO* 46:287]; cf. *Institutes* III.3.3 [*OS* 3:57].

172. *Sermons on Genesis*, no. 68 (Gen 15:6), 333 [*SC* 11/2:756.13–15]. Rob Roy McGregor notes: "That experience [of despair] never appears as intense in the Reformer's dogmatic and exegetical writings." I would argue that it is implicit in the latter. Ibid., n1.

173. Cf. Barth: "In the very act of acknowledgment and confession we must always acknowledge and confess together both the distance of the world from God and the distance of God from the world, both the majesty of God and the misery of man." *CD* 1/2:173 [*KD* 1/2:189].

174. Williams, *Revelation and Reconciliation*, 173.

175. MacDonald: "How terribly, then, have the theologians misrepresented God in the measures of the low and showy, not the lofty and simple humanities! Nearly all of them represent him as a great King on a grand throne, thinking how grand he is, and making it the business of his being and the end of his universe to keep up his glory, wielding the bolts of a Jupiter against them that take his name in vain. They would not allow this, but follow out what they say, and it comes much to this. Brothers, have you found our King? There he is, kissing little children and saying they are like God. (. . .) The simplest peasant who loves his children and his sheep were—no, not a truer, for the other is false, but—a true type of our God beside that monstrosity of a monarch." "The Child in the Midst," *Unspoken Sermons First Series*, 22–23.

176. For a summary of the claims concerning the "sharp separation" of God and

explicitly: "[O]ur insignificance is his exaltation."[177] Other examples of this rhetoric could be given: "How is it that God (. . .) stoops down to us, poor worms of the earth, if it is not to magnify and to give a more illustrious manifestation of his goodness?"[178] And: "Therefore Saint Paul, to set forth the goodness and mercy of God more clearly, shows here the most pitiful state wherein he [Paul] was, he was over the ears and drowned, before that Christ had pity upon him, and drew him out."[179] On this basis, it could be claimed that Calvin got carried away by the current of his own rhetoric (even though the end for him may have justified the means) by using hyperbolic language in how he described each dialectical pole.[180]

But the question remains, is Calvin completely justified in using such language of children for example?[181] Clearly there is a contrast in his use of language in relation to children to that of the biblical material to which I have drawn attention. Admittedly, Calvin would be the first to concede that the biblical mandate for usage of language in relation to children must take precedence over how he actually spoke of children, regardless of how he developed his systematics, as Barth suggests:

> [W]e shall be doing Calvin the most fitting honour if we go the way that he went and start where he started. And according to his own most earnest protestations, he did not start with himself, nor with his system, but with Holy Scripture as interpreted in his system (. . .) And it is to Scripture alone that we must ultimately be responsible.[182]

---

humanity in Calvin, see Butin, *Revelation, Redemption and Purpose*, chapter 1.

177. *Institutes* II.2.11 [*OS* 3:254].

178. *Comm. Ps* 8:3–4, CTS 4:101 [*CO* 31:91].

179. *Sermons on Timothy & Titus*, no. 6 (1 Tim 1:12–13), 64.b.20–27 [*CO* 53:66].

180. As Gerrish comments in a footnote on Calvin's "worms, flies, lice and vermin" text in *Sermons on Ephesians*, no. 9 (Eph 2:1–5), 133 [*CO* 51:355]: "It is important to recognize that it is a judgment on man 'considered in himself,' but for all that it still smacks of hyperbole." *Old Protestantism and the New*, 346n9. Gerrish, following Cairns, wrongly cross-references this text to Calvin's sermons on Job.

181. As noted earlier, it is important not to lose sight of Calvin's interest in the "glory of God" when approaching his anthropological statements about humanity, including children, otherwise they could be misinterpreted and misappropriated. To literally compare children, for example, to "worms, flies, lice and vermin" would be epistemologically inappropriate and dangerous.

182. *CD* 2/2:36 [*KD* 2/2:38].

CONCLUDING REMARKS

Calvin's methodology has some fluidity and movement to it even though he holds a form of binary thinking in terms of total categories of nature and grace. The question for him though is, does his dialectical pattern of worthiness and foulness stimulate something else, i.e., a seeking after God who can lift humanity out of a pit rather than a static moment of decision of asking God to make a "black" heart "white"? I would argue the former.

At the same time, by comparing Calvin's use of language in relation to children with the biblical narratives looked at earlier in chapter 1, we have to conclude that something has gone seriously wrong. The question arises, can Calvin be rescued from this theological conundrum without jettisoning his biblically-based *loci* of sin and grace? It is my contention he can, but not necessarily from resources which Calvin provides.

This is where Jonathan Edwards arguably can bring something to the proceedings. Edwards works within a Calvinian epistemological framework as we shall see, and also uses language in relation to children in a similar fashion to Calvin. But what Edwards offers, unlike Calvin, is an aesthetic ontological sliding-scale where existence is determined by "excellence." Edwards understands simple equalities as the lowest form of beauty, while complex beauty is mental and spiritual and therefore "infinitely the greatest." The complexity of this beauty involves a complex nexus of relations, some of which are irregular ("deformities"). Since God is "infinitely the most excellent being," his beauty consists of the greatest complexity and would (theoretically) give place for the ontological existence of even the reprobate. Given the placing of children on Edwards's theoretical sliding-scale of being and existence, they can arguably be construed in terms more in keeping with the biblical narrative, particularly of Moses as a child, without necessarily infringing upon the Godness of God (both Calvin's and Edwards's[183] doxological aim) or upon the creatureliness of the creature.[184]

---

183. "[T]he great and last end of God's works (. . .) is most properly and comprehensively called, 'the glory of God.'" *WJE* 8:530.

184. In his debate with Brunner, Barth states: "Even as a sinner man is man and not a tortoise." *NT*, 79 [*DT*, 218]. Further, as Torrance argues: "Barth insists that the total otherness of God does not diminish the intelligibility, the worth of the significance of the creature, for it is in his total otherness that God is infinitely free to love the creature and to bestow upon him and preserve his natural significance. God is in no way exalted by the suppression of the creature, or by the belittling of his rational nature." Torrance, "The Transitive Significance of Beauty in Science and Theology," 406. This suggests a different dialectical shape (i.e., the creature is not "flattened") from what Calvin offers. It is in how to ground this kind of language in relation to children theologically and biblically I am particularly interested.

Chapter 4

Jonathan Edwards's Theological Proposal

"My heart as it were panted after this, to lie low before GOD, and in the dust;
that I might be nothing, and that God might be all;
that I might become as a little child."[1]

EDWARDS'S LANGUAGE OF CHILDREN

In his polemical treatise *The Great Doctrine of Original Sin Defended* (1758), Jonathan Edwards (1703–1758) sets out a Calvinian[2] understanding of the "innate sinful depravity of the heart"[3] of every person born into the world, an inheritance from the Fall, as a theological antidote to Dr John Taylor of Norwich's *The Scripture-Doctrine of Original Sin Proposed to Free and Candid Examination* (1738). Taylor argued that sin was the product of bad example, not of hereditary depravity, and posed the conundrum: "And pray, consider seriously what a God he must be, who can be displeased with, and curse his innocent Creatures, even before they have a Being. *Is this thy God, O Christian?*"[4]

Writing earlier than Edwards but working within a similar Calvinian framework, Thomas Boston of Ettrick (1676–1732) also painted a very

---

1. *WJE* 16:796.

2. Edwards records: "I should not take it at all amiss, to be called a Calvinist, for distinction's sake: though I utterly disclaim a dependence on Calvin, or believing the doctrines which I hold, because he believed and taught them; and cannot justly be charged with believing in everything just as he taught." *WJE* 1:131.

3. *WJE* 3:107.

4. *First edition* (1740), 151; italics his. Further editions in 1741, 1750, and 1767.

pessimistic picture of fallen human nature in his *Human Nature in its Four-fold State* (1720).[5] Both Edwards and Boston believed that children were born wicked and innately depraved even though their volitional and cognitive faculties were not yet properly functional.[6] Using language comparable to Calvin's "worms, flies, lice, and vermin" and "brood of serpents" texts, Boston writes:

> [T]he Scriptures hold out the natural man (. . .) as a compound of the evil qualities of the worst of the creatures; in whom the fierceness of the lion, the craft of the fox, the unteachableness of the wild ass, the filthiness of the dog and swine, the poison of the asp, and such like, meet. Truth itself calls them "serpents, a generation of vipers;" yea, more, even "children of the devil" (. . .) Surely, then, man's nature is miserably corrupted.[7]

Like Calvin, in describing wherein children are culpable to God's judgment, Boston recommends: "Observe how early this corruption of nature begins to appear in young ones (. . .) What a vast deal of little pride, ambition, sinful curiosity, vanity, wilfulness, and averseness to good, appears in them?"[8] Moreover, when asked what sin caused the death of infants, Boston answered that although infants had committed no actual sin, they were still culpable because of their innate depravity: "But as men do with serpents, which they kill at first sight, before they have done any hurt, because of their venomous nature, so it is in this case."[9] In reference to original sin and the extent of its corrupting effect upon human nature (described in terms of the understanding, the will, the affections, the memory, the conscience, and the body), Boston claims: "It goes through the whole man, and spoils all. Other sins mar particular parts of the image of God, but this at once defaces the whole (. . .) The corruption of nature is the poison of the old serpent cast into the fountain of action, which infects every action, and every breathing of the soul."[10] Because of their ruined, miserable state before God, infants need to be born again in order to enter into an evangelical state of grace, but their innate corruption would still linger. Only in the eternal state of glory

5. Edwards: "I have read [Boston's] Fourfold State of Man, and liked it exceeding well. I think he therein shows himself to be a truly great divine." *WJE* 16:235.

6. Dr. John ("Rabbi") Duncan: "[B]etween Boston and Edwards there is no contradiction, and they are important to each other." *In the Pulpit and at the Communion Table*, 34.

7. Boston, *Fourfold State*, 67.

8. Ibid., 68.

9. Ibid., 140.

10. Ibid., 144. "Thus was the image of God defaced all at once." Ibid., 133; quoted in *WJE* 20:461.

after this life would that corruption be completely removed and the *imago Dei* restored to its full glory.

Edwards also held to Calvin's doctrine of total depravity.[11] Using similar language to both Calvin and Boston, he contends: "[W]e are but worms and insects, less than insects, nothing at all, yea, less than nothing (. . .) What miserable creatures are we all, what nothings, what worms";[12] "is it a heinous thing for God to slight you, a little, wretched, despicable creature; a worm, a mere nothing, and less than nothing; a vile insect, that has risen up in contempt against the Majesty of heaven and earth?"[13] In several places he uses the "serpent" metaphor when referring to children: "Wicked children are in God's sight like young serpents. We hate young snakes. They are the children of the devil (. . .) The devil is the old serpent and wicked children are his children."[14] Like Calvin he also heaps up the epithets:

> As innocent as children seem to be to us, yet if they are out of Christ, they are not so in God's sight, but are young vipers, and are infinitely more hateful than vipers, and are in a most miserable condition, as well as grown persons; and they are naturally very senseless and stupid, being "born as the wild ass's colt" [Job 11:12], and need much to awaken them.[15]

In his treatise *Religious Affections* (1746), Edwards writes: "[I]nfants become sinners by that one act and offense of Adam"; "infants are not looked upon by God as sinless, but (. . .) are by nature children of wrath," even if they are "to a lesser degree guilty of sin"; they are "totally corrupt and utterly ruined, as they are in themselves," "wicked by nature (. . .) and

---

11. Both Edwards and Boston used the language of "total" or "entire depravity," a doctrine upheld by the Synod of Dort, but it does not seem that Calvin himself used such nomenclature; cf. Cairns, *Image of God*, 138n1. At the same time, like Calvin, Edwards "sought to give full weight to our logical and noetic capacities without destroying the depth of sin's effects on our abilities." Oliphint, "Jonathan Edwards on Apologetics," 146.

12. *WJE* 10:417, 420.

13. *WJE* 19:354.

14. #592. Sermon on 2 Kings 2:23–24, "To the children at a private meeting" (February 1740–41), published as "God is Very Angry at the Sins of Children," in Edwards, *Seeking God*, 432.

15. *WJE* 4:394. George Marsden partly (and incorrectly) quotes this passage, but offers no critique of Edwards's use of language in reference to children; indeed he seems to exonerate him by accepting that Edwards used it as a means to an end, namely to awaken children to a sense of need. Marsden, *Jonathan Edwards*, 321. My contention with Edwards in this instance is that the end does not necessarily justify the means. Both means and end must be construed in a biblically appropriate manner if they are to bear the proper epistemological weight due them.

born exceedingly depraved."[16] Further, they are born into a "natural, blind, wicked, miserable condition."[17] The way children are born signified this woeful condition: "Children's coming into the world naked and filthy, and in their blood, and crying and impotent, is to signify the spiritual naked-ness, pollution of nature and wretchedness of condition with which they are born."[18] In Edwards's eyes, God was therefore justified to condemn children forever: "[I]t is most just, exceeding just, that God should take the soul of a new-born infant and cast it into eternal torments."[19] Showing some deli-cacy of feeling on behalf of the abject suffering of these hell-bound infants, Edwards reflects:

> To think of poor little infants bearing such torments for Adam's sin, as they sometimes do in this world, and these torments end-ing in death and annihilation, may sit easier on the imagination, than to conceive of their suffering eternal misery for it. But it does not at all relieve one's *reason*.[20]

Because of this dire state of affairs, infants needed to be converted, but there was still some hope for the elect child at least: "[A]s to the Time of bestowm[en]t of Conv[ersion] when G[od] hath a design of mercy he sometimes bestows it on Persons when young & even in their Childhood & sometimes not till they are old."[21] Indeed, children had some advantages over adults in this regard "because they have less guilt, less hardness of heart. Infants hadn't provoked God and hardened their hearts by sinning against light and rejecting offered mercy, despising counsels and warnings, and resisting the Holy Ghost."[22]

Edwards itemized "Growth of children" in the index to his 'Images of Divine Things,'[23] not to present any insights he may have had into child development per se, but rather to present what this could mean in a spiri-tual sense: "The gradual progress we make from childhood to manhood is a type of the gradual progress of the saints in grace."[24] However, he did

---

16. *WJE* 3:343, 215, 114, 283.

17. *WJE* 18:526.

18. *WJE* 11:54.

19. *WJE* 13:169.

20. *WJE* 3:410; italics his.

21. #345. Sermon on John 3:8, *WJEO* 49.

22. *WJE* 20:78.

23. *WJE* 11:138.

24. *WJE* 11:61.

give attention to the cognitive development of children as this pedagogical statement indicates:

> vast the Influence that a Parent may have upon a Child Education is that which next to nature & Grace in forming the tempers & manners of men it is of the Greatest Influence of any means that Can be used. Parents have the advantage of the most tender years of their Children they may begin upon them as soon as Reason begins to Bud forth when the mind is soft and Easily Receives Impressions & like a young twig that is Easily bent hither thither as we Please.[25]

Using his dispositional ontology to construe what may be going on in an infant's heart, Edwards inserted in his private notes on original sin (1743):

> The infant that has a disposition in his heart to believe in Christ—if he had a capacity and opportunity—is looked upon and accepted as if he actually believed in Christ, and so is entitled to eternal life through Christ. So the infant that has a full disposition in his heart to such an act of rebellion as Adam's, is looked upon and treated as though he actually so rebelled, and is actually condemned to eternal death through him.[26]

Still conjecturing whether infants can be truly converted, Edwards asserts that this can only become apparent as the child's reason develops:

> If there ever are any that are regenerated in their infancy that live till they are adult, then doubtless there are some whose first exercise of grace is not such a particular manner of closing with Christ as some think necessary, and as perhaps is commonly the first gracious act in those that have for some time lived in an allowed way of sinning. For such infants without doubt exercise grace gradually as they exercise their reason.[27]

---

25. #136. Sermon on Job 1:5, *WJEO* 44 (Edwards's deletions removed). Edwards evidently took "the deepest interest" in child pedagogy. *WJE* 16:414. One of his lectures is entitled: "The religious education of children is one of the principle means of grace that God has appointed in his church." *WJE* 25:723. Hopkins testifies: "[Edwards] took much pains to instruct [his children] in the principles of religion; in which he made use of the [*Westminster*] *Assembly's Shorter Catechism*: not merely by taking care that they learned it by heart; but by leading them into an understanding of the doctrines therein taught, by asking them questions on each answer, and explaining it to them." Hopkins, *Life and Character of the Late Reverend, Learned, and Pious Mr. Jonathan Edwards*, 58; italics his; cf. *WJE* 16:88.

26. "Controversies Notebook," *WJEO* 27.

27. *WJE* 13:389.

Both Boston and Edwards were pastors of various congregations in southern Scotland and New England, respectively, and thus came into contact with real children. Boston lost two of his own children in their infancy, describing one death scene with much pathos:

> When the child was laid in the coffin, his mother kissed his dust. I only lifted the cloth off his face, looked on it, and covered it again, in confidence of seeing the body rise a glorious body. When the nails were driving, I was moved, for that I had not kissed that precious dust which I believed was united to Jesus Christ, as if I had despised it.[28]

Edwards was also a family-man, coming from a family of eleven children and being the father of eleven children. Moreover, many of those who were converted and admitted to church membership during the 1734–35 Revival were children ("near thirty were to appearance so wrought upon between ten and fourteen years of age, and two between nine and ten, and one of about four years of age").[29] In his account of the Revival, *A Faithful Narrative of the Surprising Work of God* (1737),[30] he gave pride of place to the testimonies of a four-year-old girl called Phoebe Bartlett,[31] as well as a girl called Abigail Hutchinson.[32] Again, perhaps reflective of Edwards's sensitivity toward children, of the extant sermons from the period 1739–42, four were addressed to children, including his first Great Awakening sermon to children,[33] while two sermons were directed to young people, and only one each to middle-aged people and to elderly people.[34]

---

28. Thomson, *Thomas Boston of Ettrick*, 103.

29. *WJE* 4:158. Edwards: "[W]e had the most wonderful work among children that ever was in Northampton." *WJE* 16:119.

30. *WJE* 4:144–211.

31. *WJE* 4:199–205.

32. *WJE* 4:191–99; cf. Scheick, "Family, Conversion, and the Self in Jonathan Edwards's *A Faithful Narrative of the Surprising Work of God*," 40–66.

33. Here Edwards points to occasions when Jesus took special notice of children (Matt 19:13–15; Mark 10:14–16; Luke 18:15–17), then promises: "But Christ is ready to receive little children into communion with him, and that, even the poor children of poor parents. Those that are despised in the world, Christ don't despise them. He don't only offer to give himself to them, but to give 'em his kingdom and to give 'em all that he has, and to give 'em his angels, so that they shall be their angels, though they are glorious creatures." *WJE* 22:175. Edwards's sermons to children are striking for their rigorous theological content and application, particularly their insight concerning youthful sins; cf. Minkema, "Informing of the Child's Understanding, Influencing His Heart, and Directing Its Practice," 163n6.

34. *WJE* 22:168n2.

As recorded in the *Faithful Narrative*, Abigail is alleged to have said: "I am quite willing to live, and quite willing to die; quite willing to be sick, and quite willing to be well; and quite willing for anything that God will bring upon me! And then (. . .) I felt myself perfectly easy, in a full submission to the will of God."[35] What is interesting here is what may be referred to as her voluntary passivity or resignation. But rather than seeing this as a mark of weakness, Edwards understood it to be an act of true humility which came about by an assertion of her will,[36] something she could only exercise properly because she possessed true identity, or genuine selfhood, as constituted by her relationship to God.

According to a Calvinian understanding, by regenerating grace Abigail's will, no longer subjectively deluded by pride, had come into contact with ultimate objective reality, namely God, and thus she had come into possession of "an inward firm persuasion of the reality of divine things," which reflected a perception of reality given to her by sovereign grace which could be called a form of "personal knowledge." The question arises, how could this be if Edwards construed children as "young vipers"? The answer would seem to be that his anthropology, like Calvin's, sat inside his soteriology, and so did not tend to the belittlement of a child's cognitive and affective nature, but rather to a certain recognition of a child's "fullness of life." If so, Edwards's language of children should therefore be read as soteriologically intended. This theological intention in Edwards's (and indeed Calvin's) use of language in relation to children is something theological reductionists such as Doherty have failed to understand in his claim of children having "black" hearts.

Edwards's sensitivity toward children perhaps arose out of his own spiritual struggles and anxieties as a child growing up in church as narrated in his 'Personal Narrative'. However, Edwards possibly read back into and interpreted his actions in childhood in the light of his adult understanding of Christianity, being quick to name sin in his early development whilst giving little regard to his actions which could be deemed good, such as his building a prayer-den in his childhood. But, for Edwards, this kind of "natural" action lacked spiritual permanence and therefore could not be put forward as evidence for persevering grace.[37] In other words, in some ways similar to Augustine, it is possible that Edwards may have painted his pre-conversion

---

35. *WJE* 4:196.

36. Cf. Scheick, *Will and the Word*, 66–76.

37. "I had a variety of concerns and exercises about my soul from my childhood; but had two more remarkable seasons of awakening, before I met with that change, by which I was brought to those new dispositions, and that new sense of things, that I have since had." *WJE* 16:790.

years darker than they really were.[38] On the other hand, central to Edwards's theological enterprise were the redemptive purposes of Christ, which for Edwards only really made sense if humanity, including the new-born child, was truly fallen and consequently in need of salvation.

EDWARDS'S THEOLOGICAL AESTHETICS

It is in this context that I find Roland Delattre's contention that Jonathan Edwards's deepest reflections on the nature of reality, the structure of being, and the perfection of being were conceived primarily in aesthetic rather than in dogmatic or ethical terms to be of pertinent interest.[39] As we shall see, according to Delattre, Edwards seems to have constructed a sliding-scale of relations in which all of creation could be placed in terms of being and beauty. What I intend to do in the following discussion is to describe Delattre's (and briefly Edward Farley's)[40] understanding of Edwards's aesthetic theory, then in the light of this understanding ask the question where children could be located on this ontological sliding-scale. At this point, I would suggest that Edwards's aesthetic theory potentially provides a conceptual tool which could be used to develop a language of children more in keeping with the biblical narrative discussed earlier, in particular that of Moses as "beautiful before God."

Many of Edwards's reflections on being and beauty can be found in his 'Miscellanies,' 'The Mind,' 'Of Being,' 'Beauty of the World,' 'Images of Divine Things,' and 'Personal Narrative,' and in his treatises *Religious Affections, Freedom of the Will, Original Sin,* and posthumous *Two Dissertations,* 'Concerning the End for which God Created the World' and 'The Nature of True Virtue.' Delattre argues that the concepts of beauty and sensibility were formative and characteristic rather than derivative and secondary in respect of Edwards's theophilosophic system of being and understanding of the nature of reality, leading him to label Edwards as an "aesthetic-realist."[41]

38. Paula Fredriksen argues that conversion narratives only reveal "the retrospective moment, and the retrospective self." "Paul and Augustine," 34.

39. Delattre, *Beauty and Sensibility in the Thought of Jonathan Edwards;* Delattre, "Beauty and Theology," 136–50; Delattre, "Aesthetics and Ethics," 277–97.

40. Farley, *Faith and Beauty.*

41. Delattre, *Beauty and Sensibility,* 10. Alexander Baumgarten introduced and defined the term "aesthetic" as "a science which might direct the lower cognitive faculty in knowing things sensately." It originally had more to do with perception than with beauty. *Meditationes Philosophicae de Nonnullis ad Poema Pertinentibus* (1735), §115; ET in *Reflections on Poetry,* 78.

This interpretation of Edwards's life and work has gone some way to readdressing the popular caricature of Edwards as a hell-fire-and-brimstone preacher, a view largely based on a sermon he preached at Enfield.[42] Here he used graphic imagery to describe the horrors of hell, depicting sinners as literally hanging by a slender thread over the pit of hell, "with the flames of divine wrath flashing about it [the thread], and ready every moment to singe it, and burn it asunder."[43] He depicts God as the one who "holds you over the pit of hell, much as one holds a spider, or some loathsome insect, over the fire, [who] abhors you, and is dreadfully provoked."[44] Understandably, such imagery produced a variety of reactions, not least in those who heard the sermon, sparking a religious awakening. However, it would be quite wrong to say that this sermon is representative of Edwards's thought, as even a cursory comparison with his sermon output indicates. So for Delattre: "It was the beauty of God and of all things in God rather than the fires of hell that most moved his [Edwards] mind to dialectics and his tongue to eloquence."[45]

Although Edwards worked within a Calvinian framework,[46] he did not restrict himself solely to texts belonging to that tradition, but applied his mind to engage critically with and draw ideas from the texts of a variety of schools of thought which were available to him principally through the library at Yale College, such as Cambridge Platonism,[47] Newtonian science,[48]

42. *WJE* 22:404–18.

43. *WJE* 22:412.

44. *WJE* 22:411. Contrast this to MacDonald's opinion: "From all copies of Jonathan Edwards's portrait of God, however faded by time, however softened by the use of less glaring pigments, I turn with loathing. Not such a God is he concerning whom was the message John heard from Jesus, *that he is light, and in him is no darkness at all.*" "Justice," *Unspoken Sermons Third Series*, 161–62; italics his. John Piper argues that Edwards, and not MacDonald, was right in his depiction of God in relation to sinners. Piper, *Pleasures of God*, 166–75.

45. Delattre, *Beauty and Sensibility*, 130.

46. Edwards was well acquainted with François Turretin's *Institutio theologiae elencticae* (Geneva, 1679–85) and Peter van Mastricht's *Theoretico-practica theologia* (Amsterdam, 1682–87). *WJE* 16:217.

47. Cf. *WJE* 23:640–713. Daniel Howe states: "Edwards had even more in common with the Cambridge Platonists than he did with Descartes and Malebranche." Howe, "The Cambridge Platonists of Old England and the Cambridge Platonists of New England," 473.

48. In his youthful essay "Of the Rainbow," Edwards thought that his explanation of the rainbow "will be satisfactory to anybody, if they are fully satisfied of Sir Isaac Newton's different reflexibility and refrangibility of the rays of light." *WJE* 6:298; cf. *WJE* 26:132.

Lockean empiricism,[49] Berkeleyan idealism,[50] and Hutchesonian moralism,[51] amongst others.[52] Indeed, Robert Brown goes as far as to say that the sources of Edwards's thought should be better thought of "in terms of milieu rather than direct influences."[53] Although Perry Miller and Douglas Elwood had already drawn attention to some of the features of Edwards's aesthetics prior to Delattre's publication,[54] it was Delattre who developed the argument that

49. Hopkins comments that Edwards, as a thirteen-year-old at Yale, "was as much engaged, and had more satisfaction and pleasure in studying it [Locke's *An Essay concerning Human Understanding*], than the most greedy miser in gathering up handfuls of silver and gold from some new discovered treasure." Hopkins, *Life and Character*, 12. Miller argues that Locke was a major influence on Edwards. Miller, *Jonathan Edwards*, 54–61. So, for example, in a possible allusion to Locke, Edwards compared the new spiritual sense to "what some metaphysicians call a new simple idea." *WJE* 2:205. However, according to Norman Fiering: "Edwards himself was no Lockean." *Jonathan Edwards's Moral Thought*, 37. Further: "[T]he notion that the *Essay* [Locke's] played a key functional role in the development of Edwards's metaphysics is not sustainable." Fiering, "The Rationalist Foundations of Jonathan Edwards's Metaphysics," in Hatch and Stout, eds., Jonathan *Edwards and the American Experience*, 92. However, the underlying premise of Locke's *Essay*, that the mind is actively involved in the knowledge-process, Edwards shared and presumably gained from his reading of Locke.

50. Wallace Anderson argues that Edwards's metaphysics took the form of a "phenomenalistic idealism," similar to that found in George Berkeley's *An Essay towards a New Theory of Vision* (1709), and *A Treatise Concerning the Principles of Human Knowledge* (1710, 1734). *WJE* 6:112; cf. Daniel, "Edwards, Berkeley, and Ramist Logic," 55–72; Daniel, "Edwards as Philosopher," in Stein, ed., *Cambridge Companion to Jonathan Edwards*, 162–80.

51. Miklos Vetö argues that Francis Hutcheson's notion of "moral sense" in his treatises was crucial in the development of Edwards's theory of spiritual knowledge. Vetö, "Spiritual Knowledge According to Jonathan Edwards," 161–81. It is incontestable that Edwards shared with Hutcheson (and others as we shall see) something of the formal analysis of virtue's beauty. *WJE* 26:8, 22, 32.

52. According to Fiering, influential texts in Edwards's intellectual formation were Samuel Clarke's *Discourse Concerning the Unchangeable Obligations of Natural Religion* (1706) and Malebranche's *De la recherche de la vérité* (1674–75). Fiering, *Jonathan Edwards's Moral Thought*, 75–76. So, for example, Edwards's notion that "[t]rue virtue most essentially consists in benevolence to Being in general" [*WJE* 8:540] resembles Malebranche's "inclination toward the good in general." *De la Recherce* 4.2.1. Edwards cites Malebranche, but only second-hand. *WJE* 23:235; 26:180.

53. Brown, *Jonathan Edwards and the Bible*, 64.

54. Thus Miller: "For Edwards, the Puritan in pioneer America, the definition of the ethical is beauty." *Jonathan Edwards*, 290. On the other hand, Elwood argues that the definition of the ontological, rather than the ethical, was central to Edwards's aesthetics. So Edwards states: "In treating of human nature, treat first of being in general." *WJE* 6:388. On this basis, Elwood claims that for Edwards "ontology was to be the foundation of epistemology; the science of knowledge was not to be separated from the problem of being." Elwood, *Philosophical Theology of Jonathan Edwards*, 12. As if to hold a mediating position, Richard Niebuhr holds the ontological and the ethical together,

Edwards's aesthetics was of fundamental importance to Edwards's thinking, indeed that it captured the whole of his imagination.[55] Delattre argues that Edwards did not use his aesthetic concepts haphazardly, but instead treated them in a systematic fashion all the way through his theological project.[56] Further, Edwards did not turn to these aesthetic concepts as a way of escaping any theological or philosophical conundrum that may have confronted him, but rather he began with the aesthetic.[57] The way Edwards reflected on

claiming: "Edwards does not use the word ontology. It is not part of his vocabulary. However, if we employ it, we should say that the foundation of his ontology, the foundation of his philosophy of being, lies in proportionality or in complex, intense beauty. In fact, Edwards's ethics is founded on this conviction as well." Niebuhr, *Streams of Grace*, 23. This is an important caveat in light of my argument as most recent Edwardsean scholars tend to read Edwards purely from an ethical point of view.

55. Similarly, Farley argues: "[I]n Edwards' interpretation of philosophical and religious themes (God, redemption, evil, human psychology and cosmology), is more central and more pervasive than in any other text in the history of Christian theology." Farley, *Faith and Beauty*, 43.

56. Delattre's interpretation has continued to be of importance to Edwardsean scholars such as Terrence Erdt, Sang Lee, Michael McClymond, and Amy Pauw. Lee contends that the coordinate category with beauty in Edwards's metaphysical scheme is a relationally and dynamically conceived "dispositional ontology." For example, Edwards states: "[a soul's] essence consists in powers and habits." *WJE* 13:358. Further, Lee claims: "[T]he universe is the external expression and repetition of God's internal being (. . .) the world is in some sense a further actualization of God's own being." Lee, *Philosophical Theology of Jonathan Edwards*, 81, 201. "[God] is capable of being increased or self-enlarged through the world (. . .) The created world, then, is the framework in and through which God adds to God's own being (. . .) The exercise of the divine disposition in God's creative act is an ontological increase of God's own fullness." Lee, "God's Relation to the World," in Lee, ed., *Princeton Companion to Jonathan Edwards*, 59, 65. However, as Oliver Crisp points out, Edwards held to the traditional doctrines of immutability and divine simplicity which does not sit comfortably with these claims. Crisp, "Jonathan Edwards on the Divine Nature," 175–91; "Jonathan Edwards's God: Trinity, Individuation, and Divine Simplicity," in McCormick, ed., *Engaging the Doctrine of God*, 83–103; "Jonathan Edwards's Ontology: A Critique of Sang Hyun Lee's Dispositional Account of Edwardsian Metaphysics," 1–20. I would argue that it is within Edwards's theological conservatism, and by the way he qualifies himself, is how his "private" notes should be interpreted. For example: "[I]t is [God's] essence to incline to communicate himself." *WJE* 13:277–78. This can be qualified by: "[T]here is something in that disposition in God to communicate goodness which shows him to be independent and self-moved in it, in a manner that is peculiar, and above what is in the beneficence of creatures (. . .) God being all and alone is absolutely self-moved." *WJE* 8:462. There is nothing here to suggest God changes or expands his quiddity, nothing which compromises his *actus purus*; cf. Barth: "[God's] being and activity *ad extra* is merely an overflowing of His inward activity and being, of the inward vitality which He has in Himself." *CD* 2/2:175 [*KD* 2/2:192]. See also Aquinas, *SCG* I.22.

57. Edwards uses aesthetic language when he speaks of his ambitious (unfinished) project, *A History of the Work of Redemption*. *WJE* 16:727–28.

his own conversion experience (which probably happened during his days at Yale College) seems to indicate that the idea of beauty (encapsulated by God) and its interface with the "aesthetic-affectional" self[58] (involving the sensibility) left a deep impression upon him, and consequently proved to be foundational to the rest of his life and work. This is how he narrates this experience in his "Personal Narrative":

> The first that I remember that ever I found anything of that sort of inward, sweet delight in God and divine things, that I have lived much in since, was on reading those words, I Tim. 1:17, "Now unto the King eternal, immortal, invisible, the only wise God, be honor and glory forever and ever, Amen." As I read the words, there came into my soul, and was as it were diffused through it, a sense of the glory of the divine being; a new sense, quite different from anything I ever experienced before (...) From about that time, I began to have a new kind of apprehensions and ideas of Christ, and the work of redemption, and the glorious way of salvation by him. I had an inward, sweet sense of these things, that at times came into my heart; and my soul was led away in pleasant views and contemplations of them. And my mind was greatly engaged, to spend my time in reading and meditating on Christ; and the beauty and excellency of his person, and the lovely way of salvation, by free grace in him.[59]

For Delattre, this experience, and subsequent experiences like it which he also recorded in his 'Personal Narrative,'[60] led Edwards to put beauty or excellency[61] at the heart of his theology. So in the first entry to his notes on "*The Mind*" Edwards wrote: "[excellency] be what we are more concerned with than anything else whatsoever. Yea, we are concerned with nothing else."[62] Delattre further argues that Edwards's ideas of beauty or excellency provided him with the critical-analytical tools with which to engage with other ideologies current in his day, giving him in the process particular

58. Delattre, *Beauty and Sensibility*, 6.

59. *WJE* 16:792–93.

60. See, for example: "Once, as I [rode] out into the woods for my health, *anno* 1737; and having lit from my horse in a retired place, as my manner commonly has been, to walk for divine contemplation and prayer; I had a view, that for me was extraordinary, of the glory of the Son of God (...) I have several times, had views very much of the same nature, and that have had the same effects." *WJE* 16:801.

61. Edwards used the two concepts interchangeably and sometimes in parallel with each other, thus radically identifying them together. For more on this theme, see Delattre, *Beauty and Sensibility*, 58–67. Edwards's further concepts of goodness and holiness were also informed by his governing models of beauty and sensibility.

62. *WJE* 6:332.

insights into the nature of reality and the order of being, and allowing him to expand and deepen the Calvinian framework within which he worked.[63] Elwood acknowledges the radical nature of this way of understanding Edwards by stating:

> his stress on the primacy of the aesthetic element over the moral and legal in our experience of God places the old Calvinism on a very different footing. His [Edwards's] neo-Calvinism [stress on the *neo*] appears most prominently in his fundamental conception of God in terms of absolute *beauty* and not merely absolute *power*, and in his appeal to immediate experience in our knowledge of God.[64]

However, not all Edwardsean scholars would agree with Delattre's contention that beauty for Edwards is "the first principle of being, the inner, structural principle of being-itself," and thus the "measure and objective foundation of the perfection of being—of excellence, goodness, and value."[65] For example, Norman Fiering takes issue with Delattre's notion that in Edwards's metaphysical scheme beauty was the primary transcendental quality of being, suggesting that although this "is attractive and simplifying, (. . .) it erroneously biases Edwards's metaphysics."[66] Further: "[Delattre's] overidentification with this thesis has led in the end to distortions and special pleading."[67] Fiering's frustration with Delattre is perhaps shared by Farley,

---

63. Cf. Daniel Shea: "[I]t is appropriate to consider Edwards's thought, not as a system, but as the expression of a profound experience of the interrelatedness of things." Shea, "Jonathan Edwards: Historian of Consciousness," 180.

64. Elwood, *Philosophical Theology of Jonathan Edwards*, 9; italics his. Calvin, if that is who "old Calvinism" reflects, did not posit God's justice simply and solely in terms of "absolute *power*." Indeed, he did not hold to the medieval distinction between *potentia absoluta* and *potentia ordinata*, for he believed it potentially made God into a tyrant. See, for example, *Sermons on Job*, no. 138 (Job 23:1–7), 415.a.44–46 [*CO* 34:339–40]; cf. Schreiner, "Exegesis and Double Justice in Calvin's Sermons on Job," 322–38; Steinmetz, *Calvin in Context*, chapter 3. Elwood further writes: "Calvin, probably under the influence of Roman Stoicism and the philosophy of Duns Scotus, emphasized absolute power, in terms of legal authority, as the foundation of goodness in God; Edwards, under the inspiration of Neoplatonism, stressed absolute beauty, as excellency, in the Being of God." *Philosophical Theology of Jonathan Edwards*, 30. This juxtaposition of terms, "old" and "neo," arguably leads Elwood to a reductionist, antithetical, and a-historical reading of the Calvinian tradition. Interestingly, Joseph Haroutunian argues that Edwards's followers such as Joseph Bellamy and Samuel Hopkins disposed of Edwards's interest in aesthetics and reverted to "governmental and legalistic conceptions of Calvinism." Haroutunian, *Piety versus Moralism*, xxii.

65. Delattre, *Beauty and Sensibility*, 1–2.

66. Fiering, *Jonathan Edwards's Moral Thought*, 80.

67. Fiering, "Review of Delattre's *Beauty and Sensibility*," 658. As a corollary of this,

who writes: "If his [Delattre's] work has a single thesis, it is probably that Edwards has an objectivist notion of beauty."[68] For Farley, Edwards's understanding of beauty was too sophisticated for any such oversimplification. Because Delattre held to such a thesis (almost like a pretext), according to Farley, inevitably he had to collapse into his objectivist system Edwardsean terms such as heart, consent, and disposition, instead of taking them simply as they were, as subjective terms, so that when Edwards writes: "Pleasedness in perceiving being always arises, either from a perception of consent to being in general, or of consent to that being that perceives,"[69] what Delattre sees him to be doing is enmeshing a subjective element within the structure of beauty, and thus the objective structure of being. As we shall see, Edwards works with a-turn-to-the-subject approach, particularly in his *Religious Affections*, exploring subjective states of the heart, hardly a straightforward "objectivist notion of beauty."

Delattre's all-encompassing understanding of Edwards's aesthetics is rather like the "central dogma" debate in Calvin's theology discussed earlier. William Danaher, for example, offers a variation on the same theme when he states: "[I]f beauty is Edwards's favoured theological *definiens*, the Trinity is the *definiendum* of his theological ethics."[70] But, as Danaher acknowledges, Edwards did believe that the triune relations within the Godhead *ad intra* provided "a certain economy and order of acting" *ad extra* that was "in itself fit, suitable and beautiful."[71] It would be quite wrong, therefore, to say that the concept of beauty was not important to Edwards. At the same time, in light of my book, I want to argue that there is an implicit argument in Edwards's aesthetic theory which could have purchase in terms of describing children in relation to God using language quite different to that which Edwards actually uses.

Delattre draws attention to what Edwards brings to the proceedings:

---

it is noticeable that Delattre hardly refers to Christian doctrines in his thesis, which consequently does not explain why Edwards preached on the doctrines he did. It is almost as if Edwards, as seen through the eyes of Delattre, could be described as a Puritan version of Pseudo-Dionysius.

68. Farley, *Faith and Beauty*, 49.

69. *WJE* 6:336. William Wainwright thinks that these two elements, the objective and the subjective, resemble Locke's ideas of primary and secondary qualities, so that the sense of beauty and beauty itself relate as matter and consciousness are thought to by materialists. Wainwright, "Jonathan Edwards and the Sense of the Heart," 47.

70. Danaher, *Trinitarian Ethics of Jonathan Edwards*, 2–3. Defining everything in relation to God (theocentricism) is hardly a revolutionary idea for a Calvinian theologian. Just as for Calvin, everything in Edwards's scheme tended to "the glory of the blessed Trinity." *WJE* 9:125.

71. *WJE* 20:431.

in his doctrine of the Trinity and of the nature of the Holy Spirit and its place in the Godhead, Edwards carries the intimate correlation of beauty and sensibility in moral beings right to the center of the divine life itself, from which it derives its validity *in the creature*. He shows in this way that the place of beauty and sensibility in the moral life of creatures has an *ontological basis* in the very nature of things and especially in the nature of Him from Whom and in Whom and to Whom all things are.[72]

The first aspect of Edwards's theological anthropology that needs unpacking is his understanding of "mind" or "soul." Like John Locke he notionally made a distinction between the faculties of understanding and will, not that he saw them as working separately but rather together as one, thus asserting: "[N]or can there be a clear distinction made between the two faculties of understanding and will, as acting distinctly and separately, in this matter."[73] He goes on to describe the function of these faculties as follows:

> God has indued the soul with two faculties: one is that by which it is capable of perception and speculation [... which] is called the understanding. The other faculty is that by which the soul (...) is some way inclined with respect to the things it views or considers (...) This faculty is called by various names: it is sometimes called the *inclination*: and, as it has respect to the actions that are determined and governed by it, is called the *will*: and the *mind*, with regard to the exercises of this faculty, is often called the *heart*.[74]

72. Delattre, *Beauty and Sensibility*, 156; italics mine.

73. *WJE* 2:272. Further: "[A]s it is in God, there are no distinctions to be admitted of faculty, habit and act, between will, inclination and love: but that it is all one simple act." *WJE* 21:113; cf. 18:452–66. Locke claims: "the *Understanding* and *Will* are two *Faculties* of the mind." *Essay* II.xxi.6:236; italics his. However, this was not quite the same way in which as Calvin understood "faculty." For Calvin the two faculties were individual entities or parts; for Locke: "*Faculty, Ability*, and *Power*" were "different names of the same things." *Essay* II.xxi.20:244; italics his. Malebranche argues: "It should not be imagined that the soul's different faculties, of which the understanding and the will are the chief ones, are entities different from the soul itself." *De la Recherche, Elucidation* 2. So what Locke and Malebranche (and Edwards follows in this) call faculties really refers to modifications or modes of the soul to be taken as an integrated whole rather than essential divisions within the soul. Richard Steele helpfully suggests that for Edwards "volition and affection are construed as distinct modalities of a single faculty," but mistakenly claims that this marks "a return to the *totus homo* doctrine of the Reformers." Steele, "'*Gracious Affection' and 'True Virtue*,'" 21–22. Edwards's understanding represents a Lockean departure from the traditional (and Calvinian) faculty psychology.

74. *WJE* 2:96; italics his.

Edwards admits his language here to be "somewhat imperfect," his meaning "loose and unfixed," perhaps an indication of his moving away from traditional faculty psychology into unconventional territory. Nevertheless, his account seems to indicate that the first faculty, the understanding, was that by which the mind was made capable of perception and speculation; of discernment and judgment. The second faculty was given different names depending on what the mind apprehended: with respect to the actions it governed, it was called the will; with respect to the affections it produced, it was called the heart. The exercises of the will and heart were therefore not two faculties, for "the affections are not essentially distinct from the will, nor do they differ from the mere actings of the will and inclination of the soul."[75] By identifying the heart with the junction of the will, and the affections as distinct, but not separate, from the understanding, Edwards created a non-dualist, whole-person sensibility.[76] It was only in the degree of inclination or disinclination—"the liveliness and sensibleness of exercise"—that the differences between the two faculties became apparent.[77]

This is where Edwards differed from his near contemporaries Locke and Nicolas Malebranche. For them, virtue was attained by subordinating the will to the understanding. In contrast, for Edwards the affections were the locus for virtuosity such that he claims: "True religion consists in great measure in vigorous and lively actings in the inclination and the will of the soul, or the fervent exercises of the heart."[78]

Although Edwards took the relation between the understanding and the will to correspond to the relation between being and goodness respectively,[79] it was his concept of "sensibility" which provided him with the key to understanding the self's engagement with reality. He related natural sensibility to secondary beauty (harmony and proportion), and spiritual sensibility to primary beauty. By doing so, he identified spiritual understanding with the new spiritual sense or "sense of the heart,"[80] which apprehends the beauty and moral excellence of divine things,[81] and on this

---

75. WJE 2:97.

76. Richard Bushman argues that for Edwards "[w]ill and emotions were organically bound together." Bushman, "Jonathan Edwards and Puritan Consciousness," 385. Arguably, this interpretation is too essentialist.

77. WJE 2:97.

78. WJE 2:99.

79. According to Elwood, the unity of being and good is an axiom of Augustinian mystical realism. Elwood, *Philosophical Theology*, 29.

80. WJE 2:272; cf. Erdt, *Jonathan Edwards*.

81. WJE 2:206–7.

basis gave spiritual sensibility greater weight in his ontological scheme of things than natural sensibility.

As sensibility was always involved in the self's engagement with reality to some degree or other, the state of a "mere notional understanding"[82] which did not involve the spiritual sensibility was always going to be restrictive in terms of true knowledge, but it still had its place in Edwards's overall scheme of things: "[A] speculative, without a spiritual knowledge, is to no purpose, but to make our condemnation the greater. Yet a speculative knowledge is, also, of infinite importance in this respect, that without it we can have no spiritual or practical knowledge."[83] It was the consent of the heart which made all the difference, quickening the powers of the mind, granting it a "taste of the moral beauty of divine things."[84]

Just as the concept of sensibility provided Edwards with the key to exploring the relationship between the understanding and the will in the self's engagement with reality (his subjectivist, emotionalist, and relativist model), even so the concept of "beauty" provided him with the key to exploring the relationship between being and goodness, which for Edwards were one in God (his objectivist, structuralist, and relational model). The priority of excellency over pleasure was a form of the priority of beauty over spiritual sensibility in his thought,[85] although for him both were necessary in the determination of primary (moral and spiritual) beauty in its fullest and truest sense.

Edwards used the concept of beauty creatively and imaginatively in three different ways: as a concept in itself, as a category of interpretation, and as a mode or category of being. He took beauty to be synonymous with both the order of being and the perfection of being, believing that beauty provided the surest clue and deepest penetration into the mystery of being and moral virtue, rather than the concepts of excellency or goodness.[86] Fundamentally, it was his objective, structural, and relational understanding of beauty, in contrast to his nearer contemporaries Shaftesbury, Hutcheson, and Burke's evaluative, moral, and subjective understanding of beauty,[87]

82. *WJE* 2:272.

83. #525. Sermon on Heb 5:12, *WJEO* 54.

84. *WJE* 2:273.

85. Delattre, *Beauty and Sensibility*, 63n5.

86. Delattre discusses the relationship of Edwards's concept of beauty to the concepts of excellency and goodness, and held that beauty was central to this triangulation of concepts in Edwards's thought. Ibid., chap. 4.

87. Shaftesbury, *Characteristicks of Men, Manners, Opinions, Times* (1711, 1714); Hutcheson, *An Inquiry into the Original of our Ideas of Beauty and Virtue in Two Treatises* (1725, 1726); Burke, *A Philosophical Enquiry into the Origin of our Ideas of the Sublime and Beautiful* (1757, 1759).

which helped Edwards to make sense of and articulate his own ontological-moral-theological vision of reality on what he believed to be clear and indisputable first principles.[88]

Beauty was fundamental to Edwards's understanding of being, beauty being inherent to "the very power of being,"[89] and also determining being's whole structure. It was also a clue to the nature of the highest order of the manifestation of being: "God's is an infinite excellency, infinite glory, and beauty itself."[90] Edwards gave beauty ontological priority over all the other categories or orders of being which he found in reality such as unity, goodness, and truth.[91] He also saw beauty as the key to measuring the moral perfection or fullness of being, reaching ultimately to the unity of being and good in God, which Edwards objectively articulated in terms of excellency, goodness, and value. Consequently, he understood both virtue and holiness as forms of beauty, thus conceptualizing the whole process of sanctification from its initial stages to its consummation using aesthetic terms. For him, holiness, moral excellency, and beauty were not merely the same kind of thing; they were essentially and fundamentally the same thing.

As Edwards's formulation of beauty was more structural than evaluative, this enabled him to measure how far being was perfect. "For," as Delattre contended, "only if beauty is the formative inner principle of being-itself, only if the principle of beauty is identical with the principle of being, can even the divine vision of beauty offer a reliable guide to the order of the universal system of being."[92]

Thus Edwards attempted to understand all forms of order and disorder, consent and dissent, in the whole system of being under God. As beauty was the first principle of being, it was ultimately to be resolved into being, rather than the other way round. It was the objective order of beauty rather than the subjective order of sensibility that provided him with the surest guide to the whole system of being, the subjective order of sensibility being ontologically, morally, and conceptually dependent upon, and thus secondary to, the objective order of beauty.

88. Delattre, *Beauty and Sensibility*, 103.

89. Ibid., 45.

90. *WJE* 10:421.

91. Cf. the classic transcendentals of medieval scholasticism (*ens, res, unum, aliquid, verum, bonum*). Maritain contends: "Beauty is the radiance of all transcendentals united." *Creative Intuition in Art and Poetry*, 162. Pseudo-Dionysius gave the beautiful and the good a more equal weighting. *Divine Names* IV.7.704B.

92. Delattre, *Beauty and Sensibility*, 188.

Edwards measured beauty in terms of primary (spiritual, original) beauty, which he defined as "being's consent to being,"[93] and secondary (physical, natural) beauty, which he defined as "a mutual consent and agreement of different things in form, manner, quantity, and visible end or design; called by the various names of regularity, order, uniformity, symmetry, proportion, harmony, etc," and, following Hutcheson, "uniformity in the midst of variety: which is no other than the consent or agreement of different things, in form, quantity, etc."[94] Secondary beauty was analogous to primary beauty, the former being a shadow or image of the latter. Everything which had primary beauty also had secondary beauty, but secondary beauty could not necessarily be described in terms of primary beauty, lacking as it did cordial consent to being. Secondary beauty could not produce primary beauty, the continuity between nature and grace being from the side of grace alone. It was impossible for anyone with no experience or understanding of primary beauty to reason by analogy from the lower secondary beauty to the higher primary beauty, but it was nonetheless true that those who experienced and participated in primary beauty could trace analogously from higher to lower forms of beauty.[95]

At the same time, both forms of beauty consisted in similarness or identity of relation.[96] This view was quite in keeping with the traditional conception of beauty as harmony, uniformity, or symmetry. The distinctive aspect of Edwards's conception of beauty was that there could be different kinds of similarity (in respect of primary and secondary beauty), and that the true quality of a relation of similarity was to be evaluated against the kind of similarity or beauty that made up the beauty of the whole, thus relating beauty to "being in general" which he defined as "comprehending the sum total of universal existence, both Creator and creature,"[97] but in more particular terms: "When we speak of being in general, we may be understood [sic. to speak] of the divine Being, for he is an infinite being."[98] Identifying being in general with the divine presence ensured he did not fall into pantheism, yet at the same time he wanted to show that all things are

---

93. *WJE* 8:624.

94. *WJE* 8:561–62; cf. Hutcheson, *Inquiry* I.II, §III. Coleridge defined beauty as "Multëity in Unity." *SWF* I 372.

95. To put this in Calvin's language, true knowledge of the created order ("secondary beauty") needed knowledge of God ("primary beauty") or it would be restricted.

96. *WJE* 6:332–38.

97. *WJE* 8:423.

98. *WJE* 6:363.

comprehended in God.[99] For Edwards, God was the ultimate criterion and benchmark of beauty.

One key difference between primary and secondary beauty for Edwards was that the former was salvific, whereas the latter was not.[100] Thus Edwards ruled out any form of pantheism or idolization of the created order, keeping the Creator-created distinction, nature being seen by him as the effect not the cause of beauty. Consequently, he rejected Hutcheson's moral theory in which Hutcheson took proportion and harmony to be the primary form of beauty, which for Edwards was to take effect for cause, rather than the other way round. Hutcheson's primary form of beauty was secondary for Edwards. Secondary beauty only held interest for Edwards because it imaged forth or mirrored the primary beauty of spiritual relations based on cordial consent. As Fiering put it: "[F]or Edwards all that is ordinarily meant by 'beauty' was to be understood only as a *symbolic* counterpart to a higher kind of correspondence, that of wills."[101]

Just as Edwards distinguished between two forms of beauty (primary and secondary), so also he described two forms of consent or agreement in conjunction with them (spiritual and natural):

> there are two sorts of agreement or consent of one thing to another. (1) There is a *cordial* agreement that consists in concord and union of heart and mind: which, if not attended (viewing things in general) with more discord than concord, is true virtue, and the original or primary beauty which is the only true *moral* beauty. (2) There is a *natural* union or agreement: which, though some image of the other, is entirely a distinct thing; the will, disposition, or affection of the heart having no concern in it, but consisting only in uniformity and consent of nature, form, quantity, etc. (. . .) wherein lies an inferior secondary sort of beauty which may, in distinction from the other, be called *natural* beauty.[102]

In primary beauty, Edwards understood consent to be an intensive cordial assent or agreement of being to being, involving the cognitive, the volitional, and, essentially, the affectional categories of being, or as Delattre

---

99. Edwards was not a subjective idealist but more an empiricist; cf. Rupp, "The "Idealism" of Jonathan Edwards," 209–26.

100. Arguably, it was Edwards's Calvinism which led him to make such a sharp distinction between primary and secondary beauty, based on the hiatus understood between grace and nature.

101. Fiering, *Jonathan Edwards's Moral Thought*, 82; italics his.

102. *WJE* 8:565; italics his; cf. *De la Recherche* 1.2.9; Ramsey, "The Ineluctable Impulse," 302–22.

put it, "a constitutive principle of intelligent perceiving being."[103] This cordial consent constituted being's inclination toward something loved and desired in order "to be united to, and possessed of" it.[104] Using interchangeably his concept of excellency and that of beauty, Edwards defined excellency as: "The consent of being to being, or being's consent to entity. The more the consent is, and the more extensive, the greater is the excellency."[105] It is what being consented to that determined being in an aesthetic sense, and located being in the universal order of things. "That which is beautiful considered by itself separately (. . .) or beautiful with respect to itself and a few other things (. . .) is false beauty and a confined beauty"; conversely, "[t]hat which is beautiful with respect to the university of things has a generally extended excellence and a true beauty."[106] Thus for Edwards comments Sang Lee, "[a]ll beauty is a relation of consent."[107]

Like Calvin, Edwards is working within a dialectical epistemological framework, positing being in relation to "Being itself"; to do otherwise would collapse knowledge of either pole into falsity or confinement. It was Edwards's structural understanding of "consent" that acted as the relational bond between the two. He defines what he means by consent more tightly as follows (in an ascending ontological order): "Happiness, strictly, consists in the perception of these three things: of the consent of being to its own being; of its own consent to being; and of being's consent to being."[108] The important thing in terms of participation in beauty was that consent was to being rather than to beauty, consent being the first thing in beauty and beauty being the first principle of being. Lack of consent (dissent) meant that there could be no primary beauty or excellence in being. Edwards borrowed the terms consent and dissent from spiritual relations, thus restricting himself to their analogical use in natural relations. Only in spiritual relations, where the will was active and free, could being cordially consent to being and thus participate in primary beauty, for "[t]here [was] no other proper consent but that of minds, even of (. . .) will."[109]

The form of consent in secondary beauty was inferior to that found in primary beauty, secondary beauty being at the very most a shadow or image of primary beauty. In other words, the simple agreements found in material

103. Delattre, *Beauty and Sensibility*, 208.
104. *WJE* 2:394.
105. *WJE* 6:336.
106. *WJE* 6:344.
107. Lee, *Philosophical Theology of Jonathan Edwards*, 180.
108. *WJE* 6:338.
109. *WJE* 6:362.

objects were beautiful only because they resembled to some degree the higher form of consent—the knowing and loving relation of consent. But that did not mean that the lower form of consent did not involve the aesthetic-affectional self to any lesser extent or measure. It was just that primary beauty was to be found particularly in moral agents and relations, whereas secondary beauty (harmony, proportion) was to be found in all kinds of things such as nature, virtue, architecture, and bodies. So, for example, the beauty of earthly music, in terms of harmony and proportion, dimly anticipates that of heaven this wise: "Then perhaps we shall be able fully and easily to apprehend the beauty, where respect is to be had to thousands of different ratios at once to make up the harmony. Such kind of beauties, when fully perceived, are far the sweetest."[110] Like Calvin, Edwards saw nature as a theater of God's glory in the light of what had been revealed in Jesus Christ:

> when we are delighted with flowery meadows and gentle breezes of wind, we may consider that we only see the emanations of the sweet benevolence of Jesus Christ; when we behold the fragrant rose and lily, we see his love and purity. So the green trees and fields, and singing of birds, are the emanations of his infinite joy and benignity; the easiness and naturalness of trees and vines [are] shadows of his infinite beauty and loveliness; the crystal rivers and murmuring streams have the footsteps of his sweet grace and bounty. When we behold the light and brightness of the sun, the golden edges of an evening cloud, or the beauteous bow, we behold the adumbrations of his glory and goodness; and the blue skies, of his mildness and gentleness.[111]

It was crucially the will as moved by the affections which held the key to Edwards's understanding of cordial consent.[112] Edwards used an "is as" formula to articulate his understanding of the determination of the will in the consenting agent, for example: "[T]he will always is as the greatest apparent good is."[113] Beauty was determinative for both sides of this "is as" equation. In primary beauty, both the object of consent and the consenting being were essential to the definition and the process. If the object of consent was other minds, then the form of consent was "love"; if the object of consent was other things, then the form of consent was "choice."[114] Being's

---

110. WJE 13:329.
111. WJE 13:279.
112. Cf. Rom 6:17.
113. WJE 1:142.
114. WJE 6:362.

consent to or "delight in beauty" was called "love of *complacence*,"[115] while being's consent to being in general (which had the higher priority) was called "love of *benevolence*."[116] Thomas Schafer argues that in Edwards's scheme complacence corresponded to self-sufficiency—*ad intra*—and benevolence corresponded to effulgence—*ad extra*—in the divine being, effulgence having priority over self-sufficiency.[117] Delattre argues that "self-sufficiency" is better articulated by the Edwardsean term "sufficiency,"[118] as this reflects more clearly the relation of God's internal being to his creative work.[119] This "sufficiency" communicated *ad extra* was essentially integrated (of-a-piece) with the transcendent being of God *ad intra*, for it was according to God's fullness or "infinite sufficiency"[120] that God created, governed, and redeemed the created order.[121]

Edwards's sliding-scale model of being measured distance, location, and ontological weight in the universal system of being in terms of relations between consent and dissent, proportion and disproportion, goodness and evil, beauty and deformity, and being and nothing. The key elements essential to true, general, primary, spiritual beauty could be summarized in an ascending order: firstly, "consent," defined either by the "cordial consent of being to being" (primary beauty) or by proportion and harmony (secondary beauty); secondly, "consent to being," where primary beauty is defined objectively; thirdly, "consent of being to being," where consent must be given by spiritual being in order to participate in primary beauty; fourthly, "cordial consent of being to being," where consent involved the aesthetic-affectional self and not merely the rational self; and fifthly, "cordial consent or union of being to Being in general," who alone has perfect beauty and is a suitable object for consenting spiritual beings.[122]

The scales of good and evil, being and nothing, consent and dissent, beauty and deformity, all corresponded to each other ontologically as well

---

115. *WJE* 8:543.

116. *WJE* 8:540.

117. Schafer, "Concept of Being in the Thought of Jonathan Edwards," chap. 10.

118. "Goodness or an Inclination to Communicate happiness argues a sufficiency and not a Deficiency[,] for a deficiency Rather Incline[s] to Receive than Communicate." #52. Sermon on Luke 2:14(b), *WJEO* 42 (Edwards's deletions removed).

119. Delattre, *Beauty and Sensibility*, 170.

120. Elwood, *Philosophical Theology of Jonathan Edwards*, 97.

121. Cf. The Augustinian axiom: *opera trinitatis ad extra sunt indivisa* ["the external operations of the Trinity are indivisible"]. *De Trinitate* I.7 [*WSA* 1/5:69–70]; "Letter XI, To Nebridius," *NPNF*² 1:228–30. Nonetheless each of the three Persons of the Trinity *ad intra* has a particular role to play with regard to the economy of communication.

122. *WJE* 8:620.

as morally in Edwards's grand system of being, which ran from the "fullness of being" and beauty in God toward "absolute nothing," his boundary concept for which was "the essence of all contradictions."[123] In the order of beauty, Edwards's scale was from beauty to deformity (a more objective response) rather than from beauty to ugliness (a more subjective response),[124] depending on the level of consent or dissent of being to being. As Delattre put it: "Any partiality of consent (to state it subjectively) or consent to partial being (to state it objectively) constitutes a loss of beauty and a corresponding impoverishment or deprivation of being in any particular consenting-dissenting being."[125] The more cordial or benevolent the consent was, and the larger the system of being to which this consent was extended, the greater the beauty of the subject became.

According to Delattre, beauty was therefore an objective concept for Edwards, being constituted by the objective relations of consent and dissent between beings, which the aesthetic-affectional self could enter into by subjective experience (participation), but the concept remained objective in the sense that beauty was ultimately defined by consent to being. This objectivist understanding of beauty protected Edwards from any charge of aestheticism with regards to taste or of subjectivism (private system of being) as to what constituted goodness or excellence or beauty.[126] Edwards's objective understanding of beauty did not mean there could be any lack of subjective interest or desire on the part of the consenting being or agent in order to participate in that beauty. Rather, a passionate engagement involving the subjective order of pleasure or desire by the spiritual/moral agent with the objective order of primary beauty was absolutely necessary in order for the consenting being to be beautified. A natural corollary of this was that primary beauty was more fully exemplified by the notion of the beautifying

---

123. WJE 13:213; cf. Delattre, Beauty and Sensibility, 78.

124. Edmund Burke held a subjectivist concept of beauty, claiming: "The true opposite to beauty is not disproportion or deformity, but ugliness." Philosophical Enquiry III, §V; italics his. Edwards's objectivist concept of beauty led him to understand deformity as the opposite of beauty.

125. Delattre, Beauty and Sensibility, 105; cf. Edwards: "If being, in itself considered, were not pleasing, being's consent to being would not be pleasing, nor would being's disagreeing with being be displeasing. Therefore, not only may greatness be considered as a capacity of excellency, but a being, by reason of his greatness, considered alone, is the more excellent because he partakes more of being; though if he be great, if he dissents from more general and extensive being, or from universal being, he is the more odious for his greatness, because the dissent or contradiction to being in general is so much the greater." WJE 6:381.

126. Edwards correlated beauty with excellency rather than with subjective pleasantness as in the philosophical aesthetic tradition.

(the object), than by the secondary beauty of the beautified (the subject), the idea of the beautifying being more dynamic and creative in contrast to the idea of the beautified being more static and passive.[127] This was in full accordance with Edwards's understanding that primary beauty had greater ontological and moral weight than secondary beauty, primary beauty being the fundamental structure of being (objective) rather than, as in the case of secondary beauty, simply a description of how well-formed being was (subjective), and so consent was better defined as primary beauty rather than proportion. Accordingly, God was "the foundation and fountain of all being and all beauty,"[128] and the beautified was anything which was related to God. Consent to God therefore constituted participation in primary beauty.

Edwards saw beauty as the central clue not only to the appropriate human response to being in general (as evidenced by a right inclination of the will, by true religious affections, and by true virtue), but also to the nature of the subject of that response, the nature of "Being itself." He developed both his understanding of the divine Being (*ad intra*) and God's relation with the created world (*ad extra*) around his concepts of beauty and sensibility. Divine beauty was "that (...) wherein the truest idea of divinity does consist."[129] And further: "God is God, and distinguished from all other beings, and exalted above 'em, chiefly by his divine beauty, which is infinitely diverse from all other beauty."[130] "Unless this be understood, nothing is understood, that is worthy of the exercise of the noble faculty of understanding. This is the beauty of the Godhead, and the divinity of Divinity (if I may so speak), the good of the infinite Fountain of Good."[131] Ultimately for Edwards:

> Because God is not only infinitely greater and more excellent than all other being, but he is the head of the universal system of existence; the foundation and fountain of all being and all beauty; from whom all is perfectly derived, and on whom all is most absolutely and perfectly dependent; *of whom*, and *through whom*, and *to whom* is all being and all perfection; and whose being and beauty is as it were the sum and comprehension of all existence and excellence: much more than the sun is

---

127. Cf. Shaftesbury: "So that the Beautifying, not the Beautify'd, is the really *Beautiful.*" *Characteristicks*, 2:404; italics his.

128. *WJE* 8:551.

129. *WJE* 2:298.

130. Ibid.

131. *WJE* 2:274.

the fountain and summary comprehension of all the light and brightness of the day.[132]

The distinctive feature of Edwards's understanding of God was his radical elevation of beauty to pre-eminence among the divine perfections (such as righteousness, truthfulness, faithfulness, goodness, omnipotence, omniscience, and omnipresence), making beauty to be the substantive perfection of God.[133] Knowledge of God was thus not to be seen solely in terms of power but in terms of beauty, in which power and goodness were viewed as one. Essentially it was knowledge of God's beauty more than anything else which was salvific.[134]

Edwards was very much concerned with recovering a sense of the "lovely majesty" of God, as opposed to the "awful majesty" of God, the latter an example of the aesthetic category of the "sublime."[135] He prioritized beauty, light, and joy, rather than terror and darkness, as descriptive of "Being itself." This was not to say that he did not find pleasure or delight in the "sublime," as he recorded in his 'Personal Narrative':

> I used to be a person uncommonly terrified with thunder: and it used to strike me with terror, when I saw a thunderstorm rising. But now, on the contrary, it rejoiced me. I felt God at the first appearance of a thunderstorm. And used to take the opportunity at such times, to fix myself to view the clouds, and see the lightnings play, and hear the majestic and awful voice of God's thunder: which often times was exceeding entertaining, leading me to sweet contemplations of my great and glorious God.[136]

It was on the basis of the relational nature of cordial consent that Edwards constructed his ontological understanding of the Trinity. Human consent to being was no less real but comparatively was a mere shadow of

132. *WJE* 8:551.

133. Compare this to the likes of Aquinas, Calvin, Schleiermacher, and Barth, by whom beauty is given at most a peripheral place in their theological schemes. According to Barth: "Reformation and Protestant orthodoxy, so far as I can see, completely ignored it. (. . .) Even Schleiermacher, in whom we might have expected something of this kind, did not achieve anything very striking in this direction." *CD* 2/1:651 [*KD* 2/1:651]. The concept of beauty is more important to the Christian Platonic tradition (from Augustine through Pseudo-Dionysius to the Cambridge Platonists).

134. Cf. *WJE* 2:264–65.

135. Cf. Burke: "Whatever is fitted in any sort to excite the ideas of pain, and danger (. . .) whatever is in any sort terrible, or is conversant about terrible objects, or operates in a manner analogous to terror, is a source of the *sublime.*" *Philosophical Enquiry* I, §VII; italics his.

136. *WJE* 16:794.

God's infinite consent to himself. Unity was essential to being, but that unity was understood by primary beauty (ontologically *a priori*), which in turn was defined by consent, indicating there was plurality and diversity in Being itself. As Edwards put it: "Again, we have shown that one alone cannot be excellent, inasmuch as, in such case, there can be no consent. Therefore, if God is excellent, there must be a plurality in God; otherwise, there can be no consent in him."[137] Beauty thus constituted genuine community, reflecting the relations within the Trinity. So Farley writes: "It is just God's moral disposition, God's consent to being as such, that makes God's power lovely."[138]

Edwards interpreted God's consent to Godself in Augustinian fashion[139] by taking the Holy Spirit to be the subsistent bond of love between the Father and the Son: "The infinite essential love of God is, as it were, an infinite and eternal mutual holy energy between the Father and the Son (. . .) which proceeds from the Father and the Son."[140] Edwards understood the Holy Spirit to be not merely the idea of the consent between the Father and the Son but the consent itself ("'tis God's sweet consent to himself (. . .) which we have shown to be the Holy Spirit"),[141] and consequently "beauty itself" ("the Holy Ghost, being the love and joy of God, is his beauty and happiness").[142] Creaturely consent to being was simply a shadow or image of this cordial consent within the Trinity, the paradigmatic instance and perfect archetype of harmonious diversity. In a more extended entry Edwards writes:

> As to God's excellence, it is evident it consists in the love of himself. For he was as excellent before he created the universe as he is now. But if the excellence of spirits consists in their disposition and action, God could be excellent no other way at that time, for all the exertions of himself were towards himself. But he exerts himself towards himself no other way than in infinitely loving and delighting in himself, in the mutual love of the Father and the Son. This makes the third, the personal Holy Spirit or the holiness of God, which is his infinite beauty, and this is

137. *WJE* 13:284.

138. Farley, *Faith and Beauty*, 46.

139. Augustine, *De Trinitate* XV.29, 30, 37.

140. *WJE* 8:373. "Love is that wherein the very nature of the Holy Spirit consists." *WJE* 4:255–56. "[T]he Spirit of God is spoken of as the love of God, and may with equal foundation and propriety be called the personal love of God." *WJE* 21:183. "The Holy Spirit is the act of God between the Father and the Son infinitely loving and delighting in each other." *WJE* 13:260.

141. *WJE* 13:263.

142. *WJE* 21:130; cf. *WJE* 13:260–63.

God's infinite consent to being in general. And his love to the creature is his excellence, or the communication of himself, his complacency in them, according as they partake of more or less of excellence and beauty; that is, of holiness, which consists in love; that is, according as he communicates more or less of his Holy Spirit. (. . .) 'Tis peculiar to God that he has beauty within himself, consisting in being's consenting with his own being, or the love of himself in his own Holy Spirit (. . .).[143]

It was God's consent to himself that formed the basis for the divine act of creation, God necessarily having highest regard for that which was most worthy. "For 'tis fit that the regard of the Creator should be proportioned to the worthiness of objects, as well as the regard of creatures."[144] The Trinity and creation were therefore the two great divine communications flowing from the two great exercises of consent by God, the one *ad intra* and the other *ad extra*. As Edwards put it:

that which proceeds from God *ad extra* is agreeable to the two-fold subsistences which proceed from Him *ad intra*, which is the Son and the Holy Spirit, the Son being the idea of God, or the knowledge of God [objective], and the Holy Ghost which is the love of God and joy in God [subjective].[145]

Edwards's concept of beauty was highly instrumental in how he understood not only the nature of the transcendence of God but also the providential activity of God described in terms of creation, redemption, and consummation, in all of which "consistence, order, and beauty" could be discerned.[146] As Lee put it regarding Edwards's understanding of the rela-tional order between God and creation: "[B]eauty or excellency is the con-tent of the law according to which God creates and upholds the world, and thus the relational structure entailed in Edwards's doctrine of the laws and habits can only coincide with the relational logic of the concept of beauty."[147]

It was particularly the Holy Spirit's work to bring beauty and perfec-tion to the created order, such as when the Spirit moved upon the face of the waters at the dawn of creation, the Spirit being "the harmony and excellency

---

143. *WJE* 6:364–65; cf. *WJE* 6:337.

144. *WJE* 8:424.

145. *WJE* 23:153. Further: "[T]here are no more than these three really distinct in God: God, and his idea, and his love and delight. We can't conceive of any further real distinctions." *WJE* 13:367.

146. *WJE* 9:519.

147. Lee, *Philosophical Theology of Jonathan Edwards*, 82.

and beauty of the Deity."[148] This was also the case in the redemption of being by "Being itself." The good of the creature was included in and not separable from the glory or beauty of God and in fact consisted in a participation in that very beauty in such a way as to bear the mark or image of the divine beauty in the form of the spiritual beauty of God in humanity.[149] In other words, God's glory and humanity's highest good [summum bonum] were one and the same thing.

The created order as a whole was the external repetition of God's internal being, God being the true beauty or the ultimate form of similarity. Creation proceeded or emanated from the divine being, revealing in a vital and particular way God's fullness, excellency, glory, and beauty. God was a "communicating being"[150] rather than a self-contained or self-sufficient being, giving to the creature from out of his infinite riches ("a 'richness' with maximal reach" as Dan Hardy would put it),[151] it being his nature, as beautiful, to be effulgent. On this basis Delattre argues:

> It is by virtue of God's beauty that effulgence has priority over self-sufficiency in Edwards' conception of God (. . .) Beauty is neither grounded in itself nor does it terminate in itself, but it is grounded in being and terminates in communicating itself to being.[152]

Beauty in creation and in the creature was grounded in the goodness of the Creator, it being "God's goodness which moved him to give them both beauty and being."[153] Holiness or excellency in the creature was therefore an image or reflection of God's beauty. Edwards's theology did not ascend from the "secondary beauty" of the created order to the "primary beauty" of God but rather descended from the latter to the former: "The emanation or communication is of the internal glory or fullness of God, as it is."[154] Thus, the natural beauties were "so immediately derived from God that they are but emanations of his beauty."[155] Edwards recorded how the secondary beauty of creation impacted him in his 'Personal Narrative':

> God's excellency, his wisdom, his purity and love, seemed to appear in everything; in the sun, moon and stars; in the clouds, and

148. WJE 13:384.
149. WJE 8:533.
150. WJE 13:410.
151. Hardy, Finding the Church, 14.
152. Delattre, Beauty and Sensibility, 169.
153. WJE 8:542.
154. WJE 8:528.
155. WJE 13:331.

blue sky; in the grass, flowers, trees; in the water, and all nature; which used greatly to fix my mind. I often used to sit and view the moon, for a long time; and so in the daytime, spent much time in viewing the clouds and sky, to behold the sweet glory of God in these things; in the meantime, singing forth with a low voice, my contemplations of the Creator and Redeemer.[156]

Edwards understood creation as continuous, believing that it involved a movement through time to some teleological end or purpose: "'Tis certain with me that the world exists anew every moment, that the existence of things every moment ceases and is every moment renewed."[157] Further: "It was most agreeable to the Scripture, to suppose creation to be performed new every moment. The Scripture speaks of it not only as past but as a present, remaining, continual act."[158] In bringing things into being, God sought their perfection of being in relation to himself. Creation was therefore governed by divine sovereignty toward an ultimate goal in which the work of creation would reach its eschaton fulfillment. Since the Fall and the introduction of original sin into the created order, that fulfillment necessarily involved redemption. Just as creation was understood as a communication of beauty, so also the "new creation" by God's redemptive act was to be understood as a communication of beauty, for "the beauty of the corporeal world consists chiefly in its imaging forth spiritual beauties."[159] There was thus "both an *emanation* [exit] and *remanation* [return]"[160] of the divine fullness or glory; indeed, all the events of divine providence come "from God" and "its [the providential 'wheel'] return has been to God again."[161] Beauty (harmony, proportion, "some image of the consent of mind")[162] in the natural order was simply an analogy or image of consent in spiritual relations.

The Holy Spirit was both an objective reality (beauty) and a subjective principle (sensibility) to and in the consenting agent, helping to reconstitute the *imago Dei* in created being which had been damaged by the Fall. The Holy Spirit made the consenting being "a partaker of God's beauty and Christ's joy, so that the saint has truly fellowship with the Father and with

156. WJE 16:794.

157. WJE 13:288.

158. WJE 13:418.

159. WJE 13:330.

160. WJE 8:531; italics his.

161. WJE 9:518; cf. Marie-Dominique Chenu, who describes the plan of Aquinas's *Summa Theologiæ* in terms of a Neoplatonic movement of *exitus et reditus*: "*Ia Pars*— emanation from God-the-principle; *IIa Pars*—return to God-the-end.*" Chenu, *Toward Understanding Saint Thomas*, 304.

162. WJE 8:565.

his Son Jesus Christ, in thus having the communion or participation of the Holy Ghost."[163] Edwards's aesthetic concepts are seen here to work in coordination. If the Holy Spirit was the indwelling subjective principle of beauty (internal good) in the soul, then Christ was the objective drawing power of beauty (revealed good) to that self-same soul. As Edwards put it: "And 'tis this sight of the divine beauty of Christ, that bows the wills, and draws the hearts of men."[164] There was again an "is as" correspondence between the divine beauty in Christ and the divine beauty and sensibility of the Holy Spirit, the one beauty being communicated to the "intelligent perceiving being" or consenting agent. Not only did Edwards identify and locate the Holy Spirit with "beauty itself," he also identified the Spirit with the corresponding spiritual sensibility, "the perfectly active flowing affection, holy love and pleasure of God."[165] Further:

> the Holy Ghost is Himself the delight and joyfulness of the Father in that idea, and of the idea in the Father: 'tis still the idea of the Father. So that, if we turn it all the ways in the world, we shall never be able to make more than these three: God, the idea of God, and delight in God.[166]

Like the English aestheticians in vogue in his time, Edwards participated in the subjective turn of locating beauty in "Being itself" in the form of harmony or proportion, but at the same time he held this in tension with a traditional understanding of beauty according to "the Great Theory of beauty"[167] in which the creative order was objectively viewed also in terms of harmony or proportion. Edwards was therefore able to correlate the subjective turn with the traditional objectivist perspective. But where he differed from the traditional understanding was that, instead of viewing the objective relations of harmony and proportion as a primary form of beauty, he took this to be a form of secondary beauty. Although he saw primary beauty as harmonious and proportionate in itself, this did not give him the primary meaning of beauty. Instead, he located primary beauty in what Farley calls a "disposition of benevolence"[168] to being in general, which he named "true virtue." This was beauty in its most pristine and original state. Primary beauty was to be found both subjectively in spiritual beings and objectively in God and in every-

163. *WJE* 2:201.

164. *WJE* 25:635.

165. *WJE* 13:412.

166. *WJE* 13:262; cf. "These three—God, the idea of God, and the inclination, affection or love of God—must be conceived as really distinct." *WJE* 21:131–32.

167. Cf. Tatarkiewicz, "Great Theory of Beauty and Its Decline," 165–80.

168. Farley, *Faith and Beauty*, 45.

thing which mirrored the *imago Dei*. But the subjective order of beauty was not reduced to a "mere subjectivism" but understood in relational terms as constituted in cordial consent or agreement. Edwards's whole ontological order of beauty was therefore inter-connected, linking God to the creative order. All being was part of that order, albeit located at different points of the scale from perfect beauty at the top to total deformity at the bottom (from being to nothingness) depending on the level of consent or dissent of the participating being (with no being exempt from this) to "Being itself." This was crucial in relation to Edwards's understanding of moral and spiritual development, where he took primary beauty as benevolence or cordial consent to being in general to coincide with true, moral virtue.

Edwards's theocentric understanding of beauty set him apart from the other aesthetic theories current during his lifetime. He grounded his aesthetic in God, the ultimate objective referent in which primary beauty was located. All created order revolved around this. However, by dialoguing with Hutcheson's aesthetic theory, for example, Edwards was able to contribute in a unique sense to both the traditional and the relatively new understandings of beauty and being. His understanding of consent helped him to bring about some sort of relational synthesis between the subjective (sensibility) and objective (being) understandings of beauty as found in these two traditions. Edwards's aesthetic theory thus helped him to prevent the idea of beauty from collapsing into a "mere subjectivism" or an "abstract objectivism," neither of which for him bore any relationship to reality. So Farley writes:

> Edwards' analysis (metaphysics) has thus undermined and transcended the conventional duality of the subject and the object. In primary beauty the deepest objective constitution of God and human beings coincides with a self-transcending disposition. Beauty is at the same time subjective and objective, both being and sensibility.[169]

At the same time, Edwards's objective definition of beauty took priority over his subjective definition, thus providing him with what he believed to be the best guide and measurement of beauty both in its primary and secondary aspects.

IMPLICATIONS FOR A THEOLOGY OF CHILDREN

Having explored Edwards's aesthetic theory, there are a number of questions which I would like to raise, the answers to which, whilst drawn from

---

169. Ibid., 47.

the Edwardsean corpus itself, are also pertinent to my book. The first question is: Where could children be located on Edwards's ontological sliding-scale of being and beauty? As we have seen, according to his theological anthropology, children are contaminated by original sin and in a state of total depravity. His language of children merely reflects this theological construal of the child. According to his aesthetic theory, this would mean that children are in a state of dissent to being in general, so would be located low down his sliding-scale of being and beauty. However, as children, in and of themselves, are in a state of existence, they could not be in a state of nothingness or non-being at the same time, for this would be "a state of absolute contradiction."[170] To be a child (in a state of being) but not be (in a state of nothingness) would be an example of what Edwards would call "contrarieties and jars in being."[171] As Edwards further put it, not until we can "think of the same that the sleeping rocks dream of (. . .) shall we get a complete idea of nothing."[172] So to be a child, to exist even at the moment of conception, is *ipso facto* to be in a state of consent to "Being itself," for "God does, by his immediate power, *uphold* every created substance in being."[173] As Delattre comments: "To be anything at all is to be somehow related to God, for to be is to consent to being and therefore involves some measure of participation in the Divine Being and beauty."[174]

If one was to correlate being totally depraved (a state of sinfulness to its maximum effect and intent) with a state of non-being, and if such a state is a contradiction in terms (according to Edwards's sliding-scale), then such a state or condition does not exist. Thus the construal of children as having "black" hearts is a non-entity. Clearly Edwards's claim that children are "totally corrupt and utterly ruined, as they are in themselves," being born into a "natural, blind, wicked, miserable condition" should be strictly interpreted according to the Calvinian construal of the doctrine of total depravity and not in any other way.[175] I would argue that Edwards's

170. *WJE* 6:206.

171. *WJE* 6:363.

172. *WJE* 6:206.

173. *WJE* 3:400; italics his.

174. Delattre, *Beauty and Sensibility*, 167. On the contrariety of being and nothingness, Barth comments: "There is a whole monstrous kingdom, a deep chaos of nothingness, i.e., of what the Creator has excluded and separated from the sphere of being, of what He did not will and therefore did not create, to which He gave no being, which can exist only as non-being, and which thus forms the menacing frontier of what is according to the will of God." *CD* 3/2:143 [*KD* 3/2:171].

175. *WJE* 18:526. Lyman Beecher, a contemporary of Edwards's grandson Timothy Dwight at Yale, used Edwards to redefine the meaning of "depraved nature" as it applied to infants thus: "That nature in infants which is the ground of the certainty that they will

language of children merely reflects this dogmatic understanding and thus should not be interpreted in a literalist fashion. However, according to his aesthetic theory, children, even though contaminated by original sin, must be in a state of consent as they exist in being, and consequently relate in some wise to being in general. At least Edwards would probably have agreed that children participate in secondary beauty in terms of natural, physical beauty (harmony, proportion, etc).

The second question I would raise is: As children are in a state of being and not of nothingness, and thus in some condition of consent to being in general, "for to be is to consent to being," how could this consent be construed from a child's perspective? To put this another way, if cordial consent is "a constitutive principle of intelligent perceiving being" to "Being itself," where does this locate children in Edwards's ontological scale of being and beauty? As Edwards notes: "There is no other proper consent but that of minds, even of their will."[176] Taking this for granted, does this exclude children from having any sort of relationship to being in general and thus condemn them to the lower end of the sliding-scale because they cannot, from a developmental point of view, consciously consent to being in general? Contrariwise, what does this say of children's participation in deformity/original sin when they cannot consciously dissent to being in general?

For me, the answers to these questions lie in the fact that, because children can be located on Edwards's scale of being and beauty, their very being or existence indicates some form of consent even though their cognitive and volitional faculties are hardly developed, for to exist, according to Edwards's scheme, is to be in a state of consent. This is one way he construed what the nature of consent is. On this basis, as children come from being in general in the first place, they must be in a state of consent, even though contaminated by original sin. And to consent is to participate in beauty. This implies that beauty is ontologically prior to any other category of being in this instance. If children are consenting beings in their origins, then at that moment at least they can be described using Edwards's aesthetic terms as being in a state of relationship to "Being itself."[177]

---

be totally, actually depraved as soon as they are capable of accountable action—which renders actual sin certain, I call a depraved nature; and yet I do not mean by 'depraved nature' the same exactly which I mean by the term as applied to the accountable sinful exercises of the hearts of adult men. Nor does Edwards (. . .) Edwards calls it 'a prevailing effectual tendency in their nature' [WJE 3:120] to that sin which brings wrath and eternal undoing; but he does not consider it as being sin in itself considered, in such a sense as to deserve punishment." *Autobiography of Lyman Beecher*, 2:26.

176. *WJE* 6:362.

177. Cf. Plotinus: "[F]rom Him [God] come beauty and all else which falls to the lot of real beings. Or rather, beautifulness is reality, and the other kind of thing is the ugly,

I would therefore argue that Edwards's aesthetic theory, using his structural terms of beauty and consent, offers an alternative way of construing children in relation to God which neither resorts to the dogmatic language of children he did use, nor needs to undermine a properly construed theological *locus* of sin and redemption in the overall scheme of things. Moreover, the biblical pericope I looked at in chapter 1 where the newly-born Moses is described as "beautiful before God" can be linked with this theologically nuanced use of language in relation to children. Earlier I argued that this biblical narrative did not infer a merely physical beauty ("secondary beauty" to use Edwards's terms). I would argue now that the child construed as "beautiful before God" reflects Edwards's objectivist "primary" understanding of being and beauty, using the structural term of "consent" (rather than "cordial consent" which would not be fitting), with due attention given to the fact that this is a new-born child (Moses) which is posited in relation to God.

The question could also be asked: What does baptism do for children? Like Calvin I would argue that children need to be affirmed in who they are in relation to God: "God declares that he adopts our babies as his own before they are born, when he promises that he will be our God and the God of our descendents after us [Gen. 17:7]. Their salvation is embraced in this word."[178] However, in some parts of the Western Church, following Augustine of Hippo, baptism has been seen solely in terms of the washing away of *peccatum originale* although concupiscence remains.[179] By relating Edwards's aesthetic theory to the ecclesial practice of baptism, in particular to the baptismal vows made on behalf of children, the human act of consent could be seen to act as a way of publicly affirming how God sees children, that they are "beautiful" before him. If children, on the sliding-scale of being and beauty, at the very least can be construed in terms of "secondary beauty" by virtue of God's common grace, and at the very most be construed in terms of "primary beauty" by virtue of God's revealed grace, the church rite of baptism should include aesthetic language as theologically intended in the act of affirming how God sees children and before the gathered people of God.[180]

---

and this same is the primary evil (...)." *Enneads* I.6.6.

178. *Institutes* IV.15.20 [*OS* 5:301.12–15].

179. Augustine, *De peccatorum meritis et remissione, et de baptismo parvulorum* I.70.39. For Calvin, infant baptism was a "sign" or "symbol" of God's "preferred grace" to children. *Institutes* IV.16.9 [*OS* 4:312.24, 313.8, 313.18].

180. If baptism affirms what children already are, then this could help to resolve the question of what happens to unbaptized children who die in their infancy, for being beautified depends not on the child but on the one who beautifies, i.e., it is a pure,

This way of understanding baptism also opens up Edwards's construal of consent, whereby other agents who are spiritually active "cordially consent" (deliberate and conscious in terms of decision-making) on the child's behalf. By this cordial consent to being in general, even as it involves other human agents to begin with, the child is kept in being and hence beauty. But biblically speaking, dissent to being in general is also part of creaturely reality (the corruption of the *imago Dei*), and so original sin must be accounted for in this overall scheme of things. According to Edwards's framework, cordial consent (by way of repentance and faith) to Christ and his work of redemption brings about a buying back (re-integration) in terms of subjective sensibility to and objective relations with being in general.[181] Thus Edwards describes himself longing to be like "a little child" whom he pictures as "a little white flower" opening its petals to receive the light from the sun's rays:

> The soul of a true Christian, as I then wrote my meditations, appeared like such a little white flower, as we see in the spring of the year; low and humble on the ground, opening its bosom, to receive the pleasant beams of the sun's glory; rejoicing as it were, in a calm rapture; diffusing around a sweet fragrancy; standing peacefully and lovingly, in the midst of other flowers round about; all in like manner opening their bosoms, to drink in the light of the sun (. . .) It has often appeared sweet to me, to be united to Christ; to have him for my head, and to be a member of his body: and also to have Christ for my teacher and prophet. I very often think with sweetness and longings and pantings of soul, *of being a little child*, taking hold of Christ, to be led by him through the wilderness of this world. That text, Matt. 18 at the

---

unconditional act of prevenient grace without any antecedent merit. Without denying the appropriateness of infant baptism, Wesley argued that prevenient grace cancelled any inherited guilt of original sin from birth, as he comments on Rom 5:12: "That, 'by the offence of one, judgment came upon all men' (all born into the world) 'unto condemnation,' is an undoubted truth, and affects every infant as well as every adult person. But it is equally true that, 'by the righteousness of one, the free gift came upon all men' (all born into the world, infant or adult) 'unto justification.' Therefore no infant ever was or ever will be 'sent to hell for the guilt of Adam's sin,' seeing it is cancelled by the righteousness of Christ as soon as they are sent into the world." *LJW* 6:239–40. The *exitus et reditus* system would also suggest that unbaptized infants are safe in the arms of God.

181. Cf. Kant's correspondence between "the *form of purposiveness* of an object" (the transcendental *a priori* structure or principle of the subjective self) and "the purposiveness of the form" (a property of the spatiotemporal form of the object narrowly understood). *Critique of the Power of Judgment*, §§11, 13 [*KgS* 5:221, 223], leading him to the definition of the beautiful: "Beauty is the form of the purposiveness of an object, insofar as it is perceived in it without representation of an end." Ibid., §17 [*KgS* 5:236]; emphasis his.

beginning, has often been sweet to me, "Except ye be converted, and become as little children" etc.[182]

CONCLUDING REMARKS

This theological construal of children would fit with the following statement by Loder: "Spiritual development consists in increased access between the ego and the Divine center, not in ego development per se."[183] It is that "access" or openness (using Edwards's "little white flower" analogy) between children and God which needs to be carefully protected as children move through the early stages of their development, a role that the home and the church needs to perform, providing an environment which is conducive for "growing temporal wholeness"[184] through the stages of early childhood.[185] In all of this, it is important to hold to a clear distinction between the contingency (and hence the dignity) of the child, a form of natural theology for which Edwards's theological aesthetics provides space, and the flattening or annihilation of the child (at least in its own eyes) which is the logical corollary when children are construed in terms of having "black" hearts.

182. *WJE* 16:796, 799–800; italics mine; cf. "That you may pass a good judgment of the frames you are in, always look upon those the best discourses and the best comforts that have most of these two effects, viz. those that make you least, lowest, and most like a little child; and secondly, those that do most engage and fix your heart in a full and firm disposition to deny yourself for God, and to spend and be spent for him (. . .) In all your course, walk with God and follow Christ as a little, poor, helpless child, taking hold of Christ's hand, keeping your eye on the mark of the wounds on his hands and side, whence came the blood that cleanses you from sin and hiding your nakedness under the skirt of the white shining robe of his righteousness." *WJE* 16:92, 95.

183. Loder and Neidhardt, *Knight's Move*, 284.

184. Wall, *Ethics in Light of Childhood*, 68.

185. "Every Christian family ought to be as it were a little church, consecrated to Christ, and wholly influenced and governed by his rules. And family education and order are some of the chief of the means of grace. If these fail, all other means are like to prove ineffectual. If these are duly maintained, all the means of grace will be like to prosper and be successful." *WJE* 25:484.

Chapter 5

Toward a Theology
of Children

Ring them bells, for the time that flies
For the child who cries
When innocence dies.[1]

THE HIATUS BETWEEN THEOLOGY AND THE
NATURAL SCIENCES

Calvin's theological enterprise of engaging with the world of nature and
with Scripture[2] seems to have lost considerable ground with the birth
of modern times.[3] Even dogmatic Calvinian systems as they appeared in the
late seventeenth-century could be described as "barren rationalisms"[4] in

---

1. Dylan, "Ring Them Bells," Lyrics, 529.

2. Sir Thomas Browne summarizes Calvin's legacy on this: "Thus there are two
bookes from whence I collect my Divinity; besides that written one of God, another
of his servant Nature." Religio Medici, 26; cf. Edwards: "The Book of Scripture is the
interpreter of the book of nature two ways: viz. by declaring to us those spiritual mysteries that are indeed signified or typified in the constitution of the natural world; and
secondly, in actually making application of the signs and types in the book of nature as
representations of those spiritual mysteries in many instances." WJE 11:106.

3. Hardy notes that theology's disengagement from the world has become "the
premise of the 'natural religion' which has been widespread in the West since the eigh-
teenth century." God's Ways with the World, 183.

4. Ibid., 241; cf. Coleridge: "[Modern Calvinism is] Spinosism with all it's Skeleton
unfleshed, bare Bones and Eye-holes, (. . .) [an] iron Chain of Logic, which neither
man or angel could break, (. . .) a rock of adamant." CL IV 548; italics his. The same
critique could be applied to Doherty (see Introduction).

that they attempted to exclude anything perceived as impure in the pursuit of pure knowledge such as that "arising from the senses and materiality,[5] from the less-than-rational self or from a rich transcendence."[6] Hardy elaborates on how this dire state of affairs came to be:

> At that point, the right attempt to assimilate the agency of rational consciousness to Christ's agency (of the agency of God's) wisdom was deflected into an abstractive [rather than concrete] view of logic which was quite at odds with it, evidently drawn from an abstractive view of the Logos as found in Greek philosophy. As a result, the freely rational response to the pattern of God's agency in wisdom was overwhelmed by rationalism. That was a radical distortion, a caricature, but it was readily enough mistaken for Christianity. And subsequent attempts to provide for free scientific inquiry were set up in conscious opposition to this caricature of Christianity (. . .) In effect, consciousness and the world which it studied lost contact with the presence of wisdom in consciousness and materiality. Reference to the wisdom of God present in materiality was forgotten. It was replaced by reference to man's own consciousness of the world, rationalized either through particular pursuits (in the separate sciences) or by a general theory of rational consciousness (as in Descartes, Locke, Kant and Hegel). (. . .) [T]here was a loss "at both ends"—in the richness of materiality and in the richness of wisdom. Thereafter, one could only reconstruct the relations of such abstractions by means of artificial [rather than critically fundamental] connections.[7]

Arguably, all of this is highlighted by the mythic[8] images of children and childhood which arose from the Enlightenment onwards which came from either theological or natural-scientific sources but resulted in, to use an Edwards expression, "contrarieties and jars in being as must necessarily produce jarring and horror in perceiving being."[9] The great swirl of ideas gave rise to various images which either idealized children or demonized them. So, for example, Locke considered children "only as white Paper, or Wax, to be moulded and fashioned as one pleases," and as having "Original Tempers" or

---

5. Cf. René Descartes's classic proposition *"cogito ergo sum"* set up a dichotomy between the thinking subject (mind) and the objective world (body) of scientific observation.

6. Hardy, *God's Ways with the World*, 241.

7. Ibid., 250–51, 256–57.

8. I suggest "mythic" as they appear quite extreme views of children.

9. *WJE* 6:363.

"Characters" which "may perhaps be a little mended; but can hardly be totally alter'd, and transform'd into the contrary."[10] Jean-Jacques Rousseau argued, contra Augustine of Hippo: "God makes all things good; man meddles with them and they become evil."[11] Romantic poets such as William Wordsworth popularized the image of "the innocent child,"[12] musing:

> But trailing clouds of glory do we come,
>
> From God, who is our home:
>
> Heaven lies about us in our infancy![13]

On the other hand, the evangelical and member of the Clapham Sect Hannah More, who was diametrically opposed to Rousseau's understanding of childhood and the educational process, stated:

> Is it not a fundamental error to consider children as innocent beings, whose little weaknesses may perhaps want some correction, rather than as beings who bring into the world a corrupt nature and evil dispositions, which it should be the great end of education to rectify?[14]

Thus James Francis claims: "In the evangelical tradition the purpose of the Sunday School has often been directed to conversion as much as nurture, that the gospel might drive out the wickedness thought to be in the human heart from the beginning."[15] Harsh views of children can be found in the belief-systems of such literary characters as Brocklehurst in Charlotte Brontë's *Jane Eyre* (1847) and the Murdstones in Charles Dickens's *David Copperfield* (1850). George MacDonald also depicts a schoolmaster Mr Malison who, with his harsh blows, reflected his ideas of both God and children:

> theology had come in and taught him that they [his pupils] were in their own nature bad—with a badness for which the

10. Locke, *Some Thoughts concerning Education*, §217, §66. Locke supposed the mind to be as "white Paper, void of all Characters, without any *Ideas*," *Essay* II.i.2:104; italics his; cf. Ezell, "John Locke's Images of Childhood," 139–55.

11. Rousseau, *Émile*, 5 [*OC* IV:245].

12. Brown, *Captured World*, 5.

13. Wordsworth, "Ode: Intimations of Immortality from Recollections of Early Childhood," lines 65–67, in *Poetical Works of William Wordsworth*, 460. Reflecting this Romantic notion in theology, Horace Bushnell went so far as to say: "*That the child is to grow up a Christian, and never know himself as being otherwise.*" Bushnell, *Christian Nurture*, 4; italics his. Arguably this claim removes Bushnell's contribution to a properly construed Calvinian theology of children.

14. More, *Strictures on the Modern System of Female Education*, 1:64.

15. Francis, *Adults as Children*, 13n1.

only set-off he knew or could introduce was blows (. . .) these blows were an embodiment of justice; for "every sin," as the cat-echism teaches, "deserveth God's wrath and curse both in this life and that which is to come." The master therefore was only a co-worker with God in every pandy he inflicted on his pupils.[16]

The complicated cultural status of children and childhood in nine-teenth-century England Peter Coveney characterizes as a "revolution in sensibility,"[17] resulting in "no coherent and stable idea of childhood."[18] Caught up in this maelstrom of ideas with respect to children, MacDonald responded in a particular theological fashion especially through his popular *Princess* novels[19] and *At the Back of the North Wind* (1871), but arguably his ideas and images of children left too much room for the imagination and were not theologically robust enough to survive the century.[20] So when, among others, Lev Vygotsky and Jean Piaget began to publish their findings in child development,[21] the theological world was not necessarily prepared to respond appropriately. Even today the relations between anthropological findings in the natural sciences with regards to child development (a flour-ishing field of research) and how theology may approach and contribute to this area of research remain fragmentary at best. Angela Shier-Jones is not far off the mark when she claims that there is a "paucity in all of the

16. MacDonald, *Alec Forbes of Howglen*, 1:132–33.

17. Coveney, *Image of Childhood*, 29.

18. Andrews, *Dickens and the Grown-Up Child*, 146.

19. MacDonald, *Princess and the Goblin* (1872); *Princess and Curdie* (1883).

20. Henry Drummond sought to readdress the impasse between theology and the natural sciences in his *Natural Law in the Spiritual World* (1883) and *Ascent of Man* (1894). In an essay he concludes: "Nature in Genesis has no link with geology, seeks none and needs none: man has no link with biology, and misses none. What he really needs and really misses—for he can get it nowhere else—Genesis gives him; it links nature and man with their Maker (. . .) The scientific man must go there to complete his science, or remains for ever incomplete (. . .) What is really there he cannot attack, for he cannot do without it. Nor let religion plant positions there which can only keep science out. Then only can the interpreters of Nature and the interpreters of Genesis understand each other." Drummond, "Mr. Gladstone and Genesis," 214.

21. Vygotsky's definition: "We believe that child development is a complex dialecti-cal process characterized by periodicity, unevenness in the development of different functions, metamorphosis or qualitative transformation of one form into another, intertwining of external and internal factors, and adaptive processes which overcome impediments that the child encounters." Vygotsky, *Mind in Society*, 73. For Piaget, by a cumulative process involving assimilation, accommodation, and adaptation, a state of "organized totality" in the relation between the developing child and its context is constantly renewed and reached (in its idealized sense), from a first "generalizing assimilation" through to final motor recognition. Piaget, *Origin of Intelligence in the Child*, 34–42.

major [Christian] traditions of fully coherent or systematic theologies of childhood."[22] It is to this situation that I seek to respond.

CONVERTING CALVIN'S DIALECTICAL PRINCIPLE INTO A BIBLICAL "HERMENEUTIC OF WISDOM"[23]

What I seek to articulate at this point is a structural way of understanding the developing child in which relational, dynamic notions of human personhood can be sustained, rather than essentialist, static notions,[24] and which allows space for knowledge of children to be endlessly qualified by their relationship to God.[25] Arguably, each propensity, if taken exclusively on its own, potentially distorts any knowledge claims of the dialectical partnership, resulting in flat, one-dimensional, reductionist caricatures which do not fully reflect the reality of either. Only in relationship can one begin to articulate a right ordering and construal of the developing child vis-à-vis God. It is vital to hold the dialectical tension, where each is granted full personhood without collapsing one into the other—as can be found in various forms of kenotic self-emptying theological anthropologies, such as, for example, in "oneness" absorption mystical ideas governed by esoteric principles[26]—for only a "complete unto itself, full, flowing" self in dialectical

22. Shier-Jones, *Children of God*, 186. For historical theological overviews of children see, for example, Bunge, *Child in Christian Thought*; Wood, *Church and Childhood*; Reynolds, "The Infants of Eden," 89–102.

23. Cf. Kant: "[A] principle that would otherwise be dialectical will be transformed into a doctrinal principle." *Critique of Pure Reason*, A516/B544 [*KgS* 3:353.27–28]; emphasis his.

24. See above Introduction.

25. Cf. 1 Cor 2:10–11; Rom 8:16.

26. In my reading of Paul, although he had identified himself with the death of Christ (Gal 2:20), this did not mean that the "I" had been totally abolished or violated, rather that he had become a new creature in Christ (2 Cor 5:17) such that the life he now lived in the flesh (the new Paul) he lived "by faith in the son of God" (Gal 2:21), thus maintaining certain ego boundaries without loss of the self's identity in the "I-Thou" relationship, albeit divinely construed (the self recentered) and sustained as "spirit"; cf. John 4:24. Transparency within this relationship was, for Loder, "a direct relationship of love with God." *Knight's Move*, 292. Some theologians such as Pannenberg (under the influence of Hegel) have tended to dissolve the human spirit into the divine Spirit, thus reducing human freedom to an expression of the divine life. Hence Loder writes: "In the idealistic tradition [from Plato to Hegel], dialectics are only a via media to a higher all-encompassing universality in which all relationality is finally consumed (. . .) [i.e.] where the integrity of the knower as well as the empirical evidence itself is swallowed up by the system." Ibid., 53, 77. Kierkegaard also believed that a higher order synthesis was a violation of the ontology of human nature and was thus fundamentally contrary

relationship can yield to another "complete unto itself, full, flowing" self.[27] Just as in Patristic perichoretic trinitarian thinking, individuality and mutuality are simultaneously affirmed, so for Brümmer, "a personal relationship with God assumes that the human partner also remains a person in the relationship and that his or her free choice is equally a necessary condition for the relationship to be brought about."[28] Contra the Idealistic tradition, then, with its tendency to collapse the "I" into the "Thou" (a form of universality), the theological realism for which I would contend is the relationality expressed in dialectics. It is here that the final outcome of the epistemological search can be placed, grounded in the empirically contingent.

Brunner suggests that the divine-human dialectical relationship is not an equal partnership, as it is *a priori* "God who approaches man," and not the other way round. On the other hand, it is "man who comes from God."[29] Nonetheless, epistemological disclosure of either only comes when they are placed in relationship to each other. Splendid isolation does not impart any genuine knowledge of either. Brunner also argues that this relationship can

---

to Christianity; cf. the ultimate dichotomy between "Religiousness *A*" and "Religiousness *B*." *KW* 12.1:555–61. Only in the case of the human person who freely chooses (an act of responsibility thus owning the decision for oneself) from within (Kierkegaard's passionate "leap of faith" across Lessing's "ugly ditch") can the kinetic nature of existence (including the nature of human personhood) be said to be properly constituted or established and not distorted. The ultimate form of this dialectical movement is to be found in Jesus who freely chose to lay down his life for others (cf. Phil 2:5–11). "To see it like it *is*, is to let God be God and find that, lo and behold, a "transparent" relationship to God's Spirit *does* put things together in an astonishing way (. . .) The self at its very center has been sealed into a covenant with God by the very life of God [*divine* causality], the Creator Spirit." Loder and Neidhart, *Knight's Move*, 207, 236; italics his. The reductive terms such as those used by Doherty do not allow for such a transparent dialectical relationship to happen; indeed the dialectic collapses.

27. As Loder put it: "[H]uman nature requires both completeness and equal necessity (. . .) the freedom to be totally human is simultaneously a freedom to let God be God (. . .) letting God be God for oneself thrusts one most profoundly into the created order of human existence." *Knight's Move*, 112–13. For Brueggemann, "self-denial is fraudulent and pathological unless one has arrived at a self that can be willingly ceded and surrendered. Without such a self to give, self-denial is simply a refusal to live one's life [i.e., to take responsibility]." *Theology of the Old Testament*, 479n58. Loder states: "The Holy Spirit in Christian theology (. . .) puts us more decisively into the body." *Knight's Move*, 11.

28. Brümmer, *Speaking of a Personal God*, 75.

29. "The Biblical revelation in the Old and New Testaments deals with the relation of God to men and of men to God. It contains no doctrine of God as He is in Himself [*Gott-an-sich*], none of man as he is in himself [*Menschen-an-sich*]. It always speaks of God as the God who approaches man [*Gott-zum Menschen-hin*] and of man as the man who comes from God [*Menschen-von-Gott-her*]." Brunner, *Divine-Human Encounter*, 31.

only be described in "verbal, historical, and personal" terms rather than in "substantival, neuter and abstract" terms, as he believed that the relationship was both dynamic and event-based, rooted in spatio-temporal reality, and thus could only be described in narrative form.[30] This for me is an important hermeneutical key for explicating the relationship between children and God in the biblical narratives I explored in chapter 1.

However, James Barr has argued that Brunner's epistemological approach is problematic in that it includes a certain "existentialist personalism"[31] which Barr believed tended toward epistemological closure rather than open-ended disclosure. In order to make epistemological progress, Barr suggested that a certain kind of objectivity was essential whereby analytical questions could be raised and explored, something for which, he contentiously states, Brunner and Barth did not provide space. Instead, Barr claims that they only made "synthetic claims about wholes" in their respective systematic theologies, and that they were not analytical enough in their approach, concluding on their behalf: "One is not concerned with being and becoming, with causes and results; one is interested in confrontations, in events, in demands."[32]

Although this is a rather bold and misleading claim,[33] I would still suggest that there is a problematic toward which Barr points in terms of finding a way to make it possible to discern and articulate analytically how the dynamic relationality between knowledge of God and knowledge of children may operate from an empirical point of view. Barr's claim that the "I-Thou relationship" was paramount to Barth does seem by-and-large justifiable,

---

30. "It is not a timeless or static relation, arising from the world of ideas—and only for such is doctrine an adequate form: rather the relation is an event, and hence narration is the proper form to describe it. The decisive word-form in the language of the Bible is not the substantive, as in Greek, but the verb, the word of action. The thought of the Bible is not substantival, neuter and abstract, but verbal, historical and personal." Brunner, *Divine-Human Encounter*, 32.

31. Barr: "[I]t was the dialectical theologians who exploited the contours of biblical thought, which, as it turned out, was remarkably similar to the existentialism we have already seen them to support. In essence, most of the time it has been a sort of existentialist personalism. The I-Thou relationship is paramount, the I-It relationship is suspect. Self-involvement is central and the idea of objectivity is to be deplored. Analytic questions, dividing up a problem between distinguishable meanings and elements, are to be ignored; synthetic claims about wholes are to be made." *Concept of Biblical Theology*, 159.

32. Ibid.

33. I would argue that the charge of non-objectivity, existentialism, and non-analytical thinking can hardly be sustained in relation to either Brunner or Barth's theological enterprises. Barr's comment seems on the whole to be rather bizarre and lacking in critical awareness and analysis. So, for example, Barr seems badly to misunderstand Barth, as if Barth attempted to collapse the divine-human dialectical relationship into some sort of subjective personalism which surely Barth would have rejected.

and it is also a fact that Barth had very little time for any form of natural the-ology.[34] If indeed Barth posited a divine transcendence in direct opposition to the earthly sphere, this would only have served to remove the possibility of how one could discern divine causality in the created order, the "being and becoming (. . .) causes and results" to which Barr refers.[35] This is not to suggest that Barth did not provide some very important correctives to the state of theology and the condition of the church in which he found himself, but critically he did not offer a way forward in which theology and the natural sciences could engage with each other.[36]

Similar to Barr, Brueggemann believed that the net result of this kind of Barthian dialectical theology which resisted any reduction of the divine to the natural was a theology which was "removed from human birth, suffering,

34. Arguably Barth's "Nein!" was directed toward a natural theology that was independent of God's self-revelation in Jesus Christ. It was his respect for the utter difference between God and humanity (no *analogia entis* in Barth) that ruled out of court what he described as "the sorry hypothesis of a so-called 'natural theology' (i.e., a knowledge of God given in and with the natural force of reason or to be attained in its exercise)." *CD* 4:117 [*KD* 4/3:131]. But it could be argued that Barth swung the theo-logical pendulum too far the other way and closed down the possibility of how God's ways with the world (including providential activity in child development) could be discerned. However, according to Torrance, Barth in his later years was open to the idea that a theology of nature did begin with faith seeking understanding [*fides quaerens intellectum*] that was dependent upon God's redemptive self-revelation in Jesus Christ. Further, Torrance argues that the dualism often attributed to Barth ought to be replaced by "[Barth's] restoration of an interactionist understanding of the relation between God and the world in which he operated with an ontological and cognitive bridge between the world and God, which God himself has already established. Thus Barth's objections to traditional natural theology are on grounds precisely the opposite of those attributed to him!" Torrance, *Ground and Grammar of Theology*, 87; cf. Torrance, *Space, Time and Resurrection*, ix–xi; Torrance, *Karl Barth, Biblical and Evangelical Theologian*, chap. 5; Willis, *Calvin's Catholic Christology*, 101–5; Barr, *Biblical Faith and Natural Theol-ogy*, 111–17; Dowey, *Knowledge of God in Calvin's Theology*, Appendix 3; O'Donovan, "Man in the Image of God," 433–59; Thiselton, "Barr on Barth and Natural Theology," 519–28; Molnar, "Natural Theology Revisited," 53–83.

35. Arguably the natural theology that emerged through Aquinas's use of Aristo-telian atomistic logic led to a hardening of the dualism between nature and God; cf. Aquinas's subordination of God's interaction with nature to an Aristotelian container (like a definitive border) notion of space worked out apart from God as the context within which the life and work of God was to be conceived. In other words, the dy-namic dialectical relationship between God and the created order for which I want to argue is reduced or collapsed in the Thomist medieval scholastic synthesis.

36. At the same time, I would suggest that Barth was right to contend with those who had collapsed the transcendence of God into a mere immanence, ending up with a subjectivism which put humanity at the center, and not God, in the theological enter-prise. This is not to negate the mundane (the created order, material reality) but to see it in relationship to the transcendent, thus mutually correcting, enriching, and informing knowledge of either.

and dying—bodily and communal processes in which the mystery of life is lodged."[37] He goes on to suggest that such a Barthian perspective did not give sufficient weight to "the feminine-maternal hosting of the mystery of God-given life as an important theological dictum."[38] Like Brueggemann, Walter Harrelson also argues that the generative powers of God are embedded in the natural processes of the created order and writes, for example: "The theologians of ancient Israel came to understand Yahweh to be the creator of all fertility, providing within the natural order for a continuing appearance of life."[39] Herein both Brueggemann and Harrelson provide a vital clue as to how a child may be construed in relation to God: by seeking the patterns and signatures of providential activity in child development, or what Jonathan Edwards calls "the proportion of God's acting."[40]

Moberly has detected a particular dialectical circle in the biblical Johannine literature which he construes as "an ascending spiral"[41] wherein a deepening understanding of knowledge of God in relation to humanity (and vice versa)[42] is opened up, rather than "a closed, or vicious" one.[43] As I have argued in chapter 3, the shape of the dialectical epistemological framework in which Calvin worked, as dictated by his construal of the theological categories of sin and grace, could be described as narrow or vertical. On the other hand, the dialectical shape found in the writings of various proponents of children's "innate spirituality," which have no biblical narrative of sin embedded in them, could be described as flattened or horizontal. I would argue that both these dialectical formulations provide good illustrations of Moberly's "closed, or vicious" dialectical circle.

---

37. Brueggemann, *Book That Breathes New Life*, 85. The cornerstone of Vygotsky's "dialectical method" is the idea that everything in time must be understood in its development. Accordingly, he argues that to understand the mature mind we must comprehend the process from which it emerges. "To encompass in research the process of a given thing's development in all its phases and changes—from birth to death—fundamentally means to discover its nature, its essence, for 'it is only in movement that a body shows what it is.'" *Mind in Society*, 65.

38. Ibid.

39. Harrelson, *From Fertility Cult to Worship*, 68. Consequently, communities and families who have children born into them have "the awesome responsibility to identify the child as God's child" regardless of how costly or dangerous this may be. Ibid., 40, 136.

40. *WJE* 6:353.

41. Cf. "So the circle is not something fixed but involves the dynamics of responsiveness and growth, and is more akin to a spiral." Moberly, *Prophecy and Discernment*, 159.

42. "To understand humanity and to know God are different facets of a single, complex reality." Moberly, *Prophecy and Discernment*, 245.

43. Moberly, "How Can We Know the Truth?," in Davis and Hays, eds., *Art of Reading Scripture*, 252–53.

Moberly notes how these different shapes of dialectical movement are crucially formational when understood in relation to human growth and development. If so, a "closed-circle" narrow dialectical shape such as found in Calvin's thinking could arguably do pathological damage to the developing child's self-awareness and self-confidence. On the other hand, a "closed-circle" flattened dialectical shape could arguably lead to self-centered, self-aggrandizing behavioral patterns in the developing child. Both these dialectical movements could also lead to warped understandings of the nature and character of God. However, construing the child in relation to God in an "open-circle" dialectical shape in which "heart speaks to heart" and "deep calls to deep"[44] could lead to a more theologically robust and realist understanding of the child.

It is the dialectical tension which pushes the probing of reality deeper and deeper in endless motion without evading or running away from any problematic issues that arise. Indeed, MacDonald's "gently ascending stair"[45] could be described as an endlessly open-circle dialectical shape/formulation in which, to take one particular example in MacDonald's *Princess* novels, growing awareness and mutual understanding between the great-great-grandmother and the Princess Irene could potentially occur (connected by a literal staircase), leading to healthy child development and maturation. According to Loder, the theological logic that lies behind such thinking is one of coherent "bipolar-relational *differentiated* unity" (which is asymmetrical in shape) such as is revealed in Jesus Christ (the God-human).[46]

Shedding further light on this open dialectic, hermeneutical theory has repeatedly shown how the necessarily "circular" relationship between preunderstanding and text need not be closed and predictable (though sadly it can become such) but rather can be open and unpredictable, thus entailing dialectical processes that potentially could lead to correction and true growth in knowledge and understanding. The same holds true, I would suggest, in terms of the developing child in relation to God.

Moberly goes on to suggest that the Johannine formulations of "love" and "faith" (appealing to the whole human person and not just to the cognitive faculty)[47] are crucial in this open circle dialectical shape in order to

44. Ps 42:7.

45. "The Truth," *Unspoken Sermons Third Series*, 57; cf. Kierkegaard's "eternal essential qualitative difference" [*KW* 24:181] and Niels Bohr's "complementarity" in quantum theory, which were also construed as relational epistemological frames in which they could do their respective research.

46. Loder and Neidhardt, *Knight's Move*, 2n3, 32–33; italics his.

47. Stanley Greenspan: "The abstract concept represented by a word like *love*, for example, begins to be formed not from any dictionary definition but, quite literally, in

promote healthy formation of the human person, both categories being construed in a dynamic, relational fashion rather than statically.[48] The spiral dialectical movement which Moberly detects in the Johannine narratives could also be described in terms of an epistemological sliding-scale in which the basic polarity of human "responsiveness," or lack of it, is determinative of where the human person can be placed on the scale in relationship to the divine.[49] As Moberly observes:

> there are the narrative portrayals of Jesus' encounters with particular people in which the dynamics are rarely straightforward and a sense of movement, for good and for bad, characterizes the response to Jesus. The movement may be hesitant and partial, and it cannot be predicted at the outset of the encounter. The steady journey into light of the man born blind is paralleled by the authorities' progress in embracing darkness (John 9, the story that most clearly portrays the dynamics of right and wrong response, dynamics that are worked out even when Jesus is most of the time off-scene); Pilate moves first a little forward but then right back when his incipient intuitions that Jesus is innocent are snuffed out by his concern for self-preservation ([John] 18:33—19:16; esp. 19:12).[50]

Moberly describes three categories, the "moral," "spiritual," and "contemplative," which have traditionally been used to probe knowledge of God in relation to humanity. Although Moberly deems these to be useful, they do not, for him, go far enough in probing the true depths of human reality,

---

the heart." *Growth of the Mind*, 26–27; italics his.

48. "There is a world of difference between a closed, or vicious, circle (with no apparent points of entry or exit, where all is predictable in terms of certain premises) and an open circle (where the necessary and mutual relationship between certain factors can be engaged or evaded according to a person's degree of openness and where the outworking may be endlessly variable)—a circle that is really an ascending spiral. (. . .) Human awareness is complex and variegated, formed by many factors and responding variously in varied contexts; yet it is possible, at least sometimes, to recognize certain factors that form a person more fundamentally than do others and that may, from sometimes ambiguous beginnings, come over time to be determinative. Love is one such factor, and the close relationship between 'love' and 'faith' in a Johannine context (as, in varied ways, in other New Testament contexts as well) helps the interpreter see what is at stake in John's characteristic formulations." Moberly, "How Can We Know the Truth?" in Davis and Hays, eds., *Art of Reading Scripture*, 252–53.

49. "[R]*esponsiveness*, envisaged in terms of *movement*, gives content to the hermeneutical spiral of revelation and reception depicted by John." Moberly, "How Can We Know the Truth?" in ibid., 253; italics his. Cf. Edwards's sliding-scale of being and beauty ("consent" and "dissent").

50. Ibid.

and hence can be potentially misleading.[51] He suggests that something more is needed in order to make progress in the search for true knowledge of humanity in relation to God. The category which Moberly proposes is "the fear of YHWH" [יִרְאַת יְהוָה]][52] for which von Rad provides an important lead.

Interestingly, von Rad also describes a dialectical epistemological framework in terms of knowledge of God and self-knowledge. He suggests that this can only open up in the context of appropriate responsiveness to God, which he argues is described primarily in the Old Testament as "the fear of YHWH [which] is the beginning of knowledge/wisdom,"[53] the analogous term in the New Testament being "faith." On this Old Testament category of "the fear of YHWH," von Rad comments:

> There is no knowledge which does not, before long, throw the one who seeks the knowledge back upon the question of his self-knowledge and his self-understanding. Even Israel did not give herself uncritically to her drive for knowledge, but went on to ask the question about the possibility of and the authority for knowledge. She made intellect itself the object of her knowledge. The thesis that all human knowledge comes back to the question about commitment to God is a statement of penetrating perspicacity. It has, of course, been so worn by centuries of Christian teaching that it has to be seen anew in all its provocative pungency. In the most concise phraseology it encompasses a wide range of intellectual content and can itself be understood only as a result of a long process of thought. It contains in a nutshell the whole Israelite theory of knowledge.[54]

However, von Rad seems to restrict his understanding of Israel's epistemological quest merely to the cognitive faculty, which seems rather peculiar considering the fact that the affective and the experiential are very much to the fore in the very writings in which the category of "the fear of YHWH" appears.[55] Von Rad's limitation here seems to be taken up by Moberly when

51. "One of the difficulties in understanding the Johannine spiral of divine revelation and human response is the poverty of categories for depicting the kind of human reality that is envisaged—and our awkwardness in using such categories as we do possess." Ibid.

52. This term is used significantly five times in the didactic literature of the Old Testament: Prov 1:7; 9:10; 15:33; Ps 111:10; Job 28:28; cf. Moltmann, *Experiences in Theology*, Epilogue.

53. Prov 1:7; 9:10.

54. Von Rad, *Wisdom in Israel*, 67.

55. Nonetheless von Rad, in my estimation, is correct to suggest that the only way to get "the orders of life" right (the path of true wisdom) is to begin with "knowledge of God" (like building on a good foundation), otherwise one's life-path can become

he extends and deepens von Rad's proposal by suggesting that within the category "the fear of YHWH" there must necessarily be a certain letting go or a "self-dispossession" in order for the human subject to make progress in epistemological discernment and wisdom, which is in effect the only way to become spiritually mature. The human person's intellectual capacities will not be solely sufficient for this because the human person is, naturally speaking, in non-relationship to the divine due to the Fall and thus in a state of sin (described in Johannine terms of ἀδικία, "injustice, falsehood"), which directly impedes or blocks the dialectical "ascending-spiral" movement towards true knowledge of the human person in relation to the divine. Only a particular way of being in the world, for which Moberly uses the category of "integrity," as embodied primarily and ultimately by "Jesus's way to the cross," can achieve such a task to the fullest extent, albeit limited by finite reality on the human plane. Christologically speaking, only the God-human, in a crucially fundamental sense, knew the secret to such epistemological discernment,[56] and thus only those who follow in his steps, in true Christian discipleship, can grow likewise in this awareness of self in relation to God.

Arguably then Jesus's dictum "follow me"[57] is not simply a matter of believing certain things about the gospel using the cognitive faculties, but more complexly yet holistically, about a way of being and living in the world which involves the whole of the human person (including the cognitive and affective faculties),[58] a life lived in the power and grace of the gospel which a certain "fullness of life"[59] (not self-generated) both initiates[60] and sustains.[61] Torrance has called this a divine contingency on which the whole order of creation is dependent for its life and being.[62] Holding this to be the case,

---

strewn with mistakes and misjudgments, all "because of one single mistake at the beginning." von Rad, *Wisdom in Israel*, 67–68.

56. Perhaps there is a clue here to the reason why, as evidenced in the Synoptic Gospels, Jesus treasured children and childhood so highly and encouraged his disciples to do likewise; cf. Rahner, "Ideas for a Theology of Childhood," in *TI* 8:33–50 [*SZT* 7:515–29]; von Balthasar, *Unless You Become like This Child*; von Balthasar, "Jesus as Child and His Praise of the Child," 625–34.

57. Mark 1:17.

58. Piaget argues that "affectivity and intelligence are indissociable and constitute the two complimentary aspects of all human behaviour." Piaget, *Six Psychological Studies*, 15. Similarly, Vygotsky postulates "the existence of a dynamic system of meaning in which the affective and the intellectual unite." Vygotsky, *Thought and Language*, 10.

59. John 10:10.

60. Cf. Eph 2:4; Col 2:13.

61. Cf. Col 2:19.

62. Torrance, *Divine and Contingent Order*; cf. Col 1:17. In analyzing the category "Christian," missiologist Paul Hiebert suggests that we make use of the mathematical

Loder states: "The natural order then becomes, remarkably, the creation of God in which every moment is sustained by God's grace alone."[63]

For would-be Christian disciples today, one could say that this is a life anchored in a broadly canonical context which places human life in a historical narrative form as revealed in the Christian Scriptures, stretching from the origins of life in creation to its future eschatological consummation, a narrative which contains within it both the story of human fallenness (described in biblical terms of "death" and "darkness") as epitomized by Genesis 3, and the story of human redemption (described in biblical terms of "life" and "light") centered in the life, death, and resurrection of Jesus Christ. How human life and existence, including the developing child, can be construed theologically within these parameters in both its historical extensity through time and space, and also in its particular intensity in the life of any one human person in its path from birth to death, are some of the broad-ranging issues within which my epistemological enquiry into the dialectical relationship between God and the developing child can be placed.

How a developing child is theologically conceptualized and understood obviously will have a huge bearing on how a child is nurtured and formed. There is a real danger for a human life sequence to be disrupted or be violated because of its fragility and vulnerability, especially in its beginnings. Arguably, a static, essentialist notion of a child's nature and an interventionist understanding of grace can do damage to the delicate fabric of a child's identity. In this regard, Gordon Kaufman points out that before we can think of God acting over time in an orderly fashion, we must first overcome the standard, conventional way of viewing "an act of God" as "a new event that suddenly and without adequate prior conditions rips inexplicably into the fabric of experience."[64] Once we succeed in discarding this common, and in some instances legal, definition of an act of God, and think rather about God's act in analogous relationship with human acts, we can then conceive of "the whole course of history, from its initiation in God's creative activity to its

---

categories of "bounded," "fuzzy," and "centered sets." Bounded sets function on the principle "either/or": an apple is an apple or it is not; it cannot be partly apple and partly pear. Fuzzy sets, on the other hand, have no sharp boundaries; things are fluid with no stable point of reference and with various degrees of inclusion—as when a mountain merges into the plains. A centered set is defined by a center and the relationship of things to that center, by a *movement* toward it or away from it. The category "Christian," Hiebert suggests, should be understood as a centered set. A demarcation line exists, but the focus is not on "maintaining the boundary" but "on reaffirming the center." Hiebert, "Category "Christian" in the Missionary Task," 424.

63. Loder and Neidhardt, *Knight's Move*, 49.

64. Kaufman, *God the Problem*, 137.

consummation when God ultimately achieves his purposes,"[65] as one whole complex providential act or activity of God.[66] What I would like to articulate then is a biblical understanding of the relationship between the eternal act of grace on God's part[67] and how that act is appropriated on the spatio-temporal level, without collapsing the latter into some form of interventionism or confrontationalism[68] which could disturb the developmental history of the child itself. In respect of interpreting salvation as a state caused in humanity by God, using a form of Aristotelian logic, Brümmer argues: "This does not provide an adequate account of the complex reciprocal nature of personal relationships in general, and of the personal relationship which we have with God in particular."[69] In other words, static anthropological and soteriological notions are narrowly conceived and simplistic, and do not reflect human reality or indeed biblical revelation.

At the same time, I would not deny that there may be moments in the developing child when that grace of God may be comprehended, acknowledged and grasped, but ultimately those particular acts of grace are only tastes of a greater fullness, for divine fullness always exceeds human appropriation,[70] God's grace not being limited even when revealed by divine illumination on the human plane.[71] Nor would it be biblically or theologically correct to limit God's grace to the cognitive development of the child, for surely that would make grace conditional rather a gift.[72] I would therefore argue that to limit that grace to the finite moment or moments is to do epistemological damage both to the idea of God and to the idea of the child.[73] Instead, I would suggest that the developing child needs to be understood in the context of divine providence in which grace always come before, and

65. Ibid.

66. This is analogous to Coleridge's definition of the primary imagination: "[A] repetition in the finite mind of the eternal act of creation in the infinite I AM." *BL* I 304.

67. Bishop Maximos Aghiorgoussis argues: "[W]hen Paul distinguished in Rom. 8:8–30 among predestination, calling, justification, and glorification, these are all stages in one process, that of salvation." Aghiorgoussis, "Orthodox Soteriology," in Meyendorff and Tobias, eds., *Salvation in Christ*, 48–49.

68. Barth states: "between the real God and real man judgment *must* become an event." *CD* 1/2:92; italics his [*KD* 1/2:91]; cf. Barth's characterization of Billy Graham's preaching: "It was the gospel at gun-point." *KBL*, 462; *ET*, 446. In response, Billy Graham comments that Barth, in contrast to Brunner, did not like his use of the word *"must."* Graham, *Just As I Am*, 694; italics his.

69. Brümmer, *Speaking of a Personal God*, 86.

70. Cf. Paul's prayer in Eph 3:16–21.

71. Cf. Edwards's sermon, "A Divine and Supernatural Light," *WJE* 17:408–26.

72. Cf. Eph 2:8.

73. I am thinking in terms of Moberly's "ascending spiral" dialectical movement.

that the child needs only to be gently instructed that this is so. The biblical record, as we have seen, does understand a developing child in its dynamic spatio-temporality as a life-history (and thus not in static categories), and it is in the providential that a child's primary nurture and formation as a developing human person biblically seems to lie.

In response to the perceived hiatus between theology and the natural sciences, Hardy argues theologians "must attempt to reappropriate the intrinsic connection of knowledge and rationality, as mediated in materiality and history, to the nature and presence of God," and, further, they "need to face the kinds of distortion which afflict the understanding of God, knowledge and rationality, materiality and history, and which have severed the proper connections between them."[74] Clearly this includes a place for a proper theological account of children in their development if theology is "to begin from God's presence to the world."[75] The methodology involved becomes one of abduction—that is, arguing backwards from what is accessible and may be observed to what may lie behind it,[76] a task which I see as the next step in my ongoing project.[77]

According to Jonathan Edwards's scheme of thinking, it is vital that the church is prepared to engage with the discoveries of the natural sciences, then re-interpret this knowledge *sub specie aeternitatis* and use it to the glory of God. Such a procedure could be placed within Watson's understanding of the task of theology in the ongoing relationship between the church and the world within which it is set if the church is to remain true to its calling of bearing witness to the truth as it understands it to the world round about, as he claims:

> Movements within the world beyond the ecclesial community continually pose a question to the community. They bring before it the question whether particular aspects of its existing self-understanding, beliefs and practices are still to be regarded as authentically Christian, or whether they require critical reappraisal or outright rejection. This process of questioning from outside is one of the ways in which the Spirit leads the

74. Hardy, *God's Ways with the World*, 236.

75. Ibid., 234. Loder has made some attempt toward this end but, arguably, it lacks the biblical robustness required. *Logic of the Spirit*, chap. 5.

76. Cf. Harman, "The Inference to the Best Explanation," 88–95.

77. I see the hermeneutical task as measuring and describing the distance (if such) between biblical accounts of child development and direct observations of infancy/childhood, so that the tension between the two, when clarified, can operate as a corrective to both, without in any way undermining the truth claims of the natural sciences or the authority of Scripture (a spiral hermeneutic); cf. Stern, *Interpersonal World of the Infant*.

community out of distorted and inadequate positions into all the truth (cf. John 16:13); and it is one of the ways in which oppressive law is distinguished from life-giving gospel as holy scripture is read and interpreted.[78]

I would argue for a biblical objectivism or realism which seeks to trace the workings of God in the materiality of child development.[79] Such a form of discernment David Ford would call a "theological motif of wisdom" which does not bury itself in the sand when faced with new scientific discoveries,[80] but rather seeks "to respond appropriately to the new advances in the biological sciences."[81] Moltmann also allows for this kind of theological space in his thinking when he articulates a *"Wisdom theology"* in which "God is perceived from the life and orders of nature, and then recognized again in human wisdom about life."[82]

Richard Hays uses the resurrection narratives in the Gospels in order to provide the human subject with a hermeneutical device to discern God's ways with the world by suggesting:

> [they] expand our imagination and lead us to discern that God is at work within the sphere of physical time-space reality to transform and restore all things, negating death's power over the body (. . .) That is why the gospel's epistemology privileges concreteness and anathematizes all docetism, Neoplatonism, and Kantian epistemological dualism. God the Creator raised Jesus from the dead; therefore, "flesh is precious."[83]

Rainer Albertz also suggests a useful hermeneutical lens with which to approach the Christian Scriptures when he states: "From the start Yahweh religion is more closely focussed on a correspondence between divine and human conduct."[84] Speaking from a less personal and more communal basis, Brueggemann argues: "These two, Yahweh and Israel, are lodged in a common theology on their way together. But it is important that they are on

---

78. Watson, *Text, Church and World*, 240.

79. This could be described in terms of a diagonal dialectic (a theological Panentheism) which neither abstracts God from materiality nor collapses God into materiality, thus sustaining the Creator-creature distinction.

80. As in various forms of Protestant fundamentalist obscurantism.

81. Ford, *Christian Wisdom*, 271.

82. Moltmann, *Science and Wisdom*, 148; italics his.

83. Hays, "Reading Scripture in the Light of the Resurrection," in Davis and Hays, eds., *Art of Reading Scripture*, 236.

84. Albertz, *History of Israelite Religion in the Old Testament Period*, 1:49.

the way together and not in a resting-place together."[85] In other words, one cannot do without the other, for *the inner movement of God is intrinsic to the dynamics of human life.*"[86]

This comment exhibits some sort of affinity or kinship with MacDonald's assertion of God's intent for the created order which he stated in the following way: "The whole history is a divine agony to give divine life to creatures. The outcome of that agony, the victory of that creative and again creative energy, will be radiant life, whereof joy unspeakable is the flower. Every child will look in the eyes of the Father, and the eyes of the Father will receive the child with an infinite embrace."[87] MacDonald here points toward a divine causality which potentially can be seen (a form of discernment) operating in the lives of young children. This may provide a meaningful and rich hermeneutic with which to open up the presently dense and, in many senses, closed subject (in terms of entrenched positions) of how a child is perceived or construed, a subject which I have suggested has a confusing history which arguably has tended toward quite rationalistic, reductionist and simplistic ideas of children.[88] MacDonald's hermeneutic may be viewed as simple, but it may open up the subject rather than close it down, and may provide further insights into the rich complexities of the created order (reflecting the *imago Dei*), of which children are a distinct part. Mary Taylor also points in this direction (dialectical relationship between divine causality and the meaning of childhood) when she writes: "Investigations of the beginnings and development of life return us to the question of *why*, a realm that contemplates the possibility of a constant intentionality and purpose deep within vibrant and variable ways and means."[89]

It should also be said that this hermeneutic not only acknowledges that "[God] gives life to all things,"[90] including children, but that God also uses human means to channel or impart this fullness of life ("rivers of living water")[91] to those who come under its care, especially young children who yet remain in a vulnerable state, dependent on others for their well-being.[92]

85. Brueggemann, *Old Testament Theology*, 23.

86. Hardy, "Reason, Wisdom and the Interpretation of Scripture," in Ford and Stanton, eds., *Reading Texts, Seeking Wisdom*, 73–74; italics his.

87. "Life," *Unspoken Sermons Second Series*, 172–73.

88. Cf. Wall, "Fallen Angels," 160–84.

89. Taylor, *George MacDonald Exposes False Conflicts*, 79; italics hers.

90. 1 Tim 6:13.

91. John 7:38.

92. Such as Paul describes in Col 1:29—"For this [that we may present everyone mature in Christ] I toil and struggle with all the energy that he powerfully inspires within me." Cf. Col 4:12.

As we have seen, in the biblical narrative a divine causality can be discerned in the lives of children, of which Timothy is a prime example.

As suggested earlier, there may be room for such an endeavor which neither follows the fundamentalist route nor the Barthian route, but operates upon the understanding that the God of the Bible is the Creator of human life, such as Wolfhart Pannenberg advances: "[theologians] must expect that a critical appropriation of these findings for theological use is also possible, if the God of the Bible is indeed the creator of all reality."[93] What Pannenberg offers here is a vital critical space in which child-developmental ideas can potentially be brought into dialogue with a dynamic, relational understanding of children as found in the biblical narrative, which could thus provide a critical apparatus to engage with the Calvinian tradition. Arguably, there is a theological and biblical warrant for such a developmental understanding of children, as Paul Janz helpfully suggests:

> God works and reveals himself incarnationally *even today*, and this means *causally* in the real affairs of sensibly embodied human beings today in space and time, with real, life-changing effects (. . .) It is rather a *divine* causality whose origin is not temporal or finite, but infinite; yet whose effects are no less dynamic, no less empirical, no less real for human embodied life today than any natural causality, however infinite these effects may *also* be for the eternal redemption of human beings beyond this life, and for God's reconciliation of the whole world to himself.[94]

On this basis, I would suggest that there is a need to discern *a posteriori* this "*divine* causality" in how children develop, theologically articulating this with both conceptual rigor and empirical attentiveness "in the way that Christianity as a genuinely *incarnational* confession of faith demands."[95] Essentially that is what Torrance's prolegomenal theological-scientific project is all about, the uncovering through scientific inquiry of the rational patterns which God has conferred upon creation, which he describes as "the signature of the Creator in the depths of contingent being."[96] What kind of world should we find when looking at how children develop? To quote Eric Mascall, although speaking more generally:

> it will be both contingent and orderly, since it is the work of a God who is both free and rational. It will embody regularities

93. Pannenberg, *Anthropology in Theological Perspective*, 19.

94. Janz, "Divine Causality and the Nature of Theological Questioning," 324; italics his.

95. Ibid.; italics his.

96. Torrance, *Divine and Contingent Order*, 73.

and patterns, since its Creator is rational, but the particular regularities and patterns which it embodies cannot be predicted *a priori*, since he is free; they can only be discovered by examination. The world of Christian theism will thus be one whose investigation requires the empirical method, that is to say the method of modern natural science, with its twin techniques of observation and experiment.[97]

Vygotsky points to the areas of child development that need to be properly engaged with "true causal-genetic analysis, systematic study of the relations between the growth of the child's thinking ability and his social development."[98] Arguably it is by attending to sequences and connections in children's discovery of the mind[99] and how children grow into social beings[100] that, in the words of Janz:

> we will again and again come up against features or forces which we recognize unmistakeably as being *not* [solely] the *products* of intellection or interpretive consciousness [such as can be found, Janz contends, in much contemporary phenomenological and idealistic studies today], but rather as being forces which confront the reflecting perceiver with their own originary causal authority through sensibility.[101]

97. Mascall, *Christian Theology and Natural Science*, 94.

98. Vygotsky, *Thought and Language*, 9. Vygotsky sought for "a causal-dynamic explanation of concept formation" in the developing child. Ibid., 103.

99. In accord with a general Piagetian perspective. Used to refer to various phenomena: a cognitive structure leading to certain abilities; the development of these abilities; and a theoretical perspective explaining this development; cf. Astington, *Child's Discovery of the Mind*.

100. In accord with a general Vygotskian perspective; cf. Wertsch, *Vygotsky and the Social Formation of Mind*. For Erikson, a good nurturing environment provides resources for growth in motivational drive, self-control, direction, method, devotion, affiliation, production, and renunciation. Erikson, *Childhood and Society*, 247.

101. Janz, "Divine Causality and the Nature of Theological Questioning," 325; italics his; cf. Farrer's notion of the "causal joint (. . .) between God's action and ours." Farrer, *Faith and Speculation*, 66. Edward Henderson summarizes: "According to the idea of double agency, God acts instead by acting in the actions of creatures in a way that preserves their natural modes of operation and their integrity as creatures enjoying a being of their own." Henderson, "Double Agency and the Relations of Persons to God," in Hebblethwaite and Hedley, eds., *Human Person in God's World*, 38. Developmental psychology arguably sidelines these "actions" as it primarily focuses on the outcome of development, namely adulthood.

CONCLUDING REMARKS

MacDonald, like Calvin and Edwards before him, saw the glory of God in the beauty of creation. He also saw "how in all God's works the laws of beauty are wrought out in evanishment, in birth and death. There, there is no hoarding, but an everfresh creating, an eternal flow of life from the heart of the All-beautiful."[102]

The development of children is achieved by maintaining the delicate fabric of human life and should not be disrupted any more than necessary. The divine purpose for children occurs within this life sequence, not simply in a moment when a child 'knows' it, but rather when it lives within it. If life is an extensity or a sequence, then the 'gate' for the intensity of the divine presence is in the sequence not in the instantaneous. Grace is the condition by which the child grows and moves forward, rather than something that kick-starts it instantaneously. The child experiences this grace; indeed to grow is to experience this. The goal is a security in the grace of God that the child will not be knocked off no matter the difficulty. Grace is thus intertwined with the child in who they are in a way that does not inhibit them but is conducive to their development and growth to a mature form of human flourishing.

It is in its living out this high calling that Ford writes of the community at Ephesus which included children: "In Ephesians the theme of energy, strength, power and 'dynamism' is pervasive (. . .) The picture by the end of the letter is of an energetic, resilient gentleness growing in members of a community who can sing to each other and to God as they resist whatever evils come."[103] Here we have a holistic vision where the whole human person within the community is actively engaged in the journey into the inexhaustible "treasures of darkness."[104] If "totalitarian" art tells us what to feel, this biblical landscape feels, and invites children to be part of it.

102. MacDonald, *Seaboard Parish*, 3:26.

103. Ford, *Self and Salvation*, 124.

104. Isa 45:3—"the treasures beyond all beauty"; cf. Pseudo-Dionysius, *Mystical Theology* I.1.

Bibliography

CALVIN PRIMARY SOURCES

"L'abécédaire genevois ou catéchisme élémentaire de Calvin." *Revue d'histoire et de Philosophie Religieuses* 45 (1965) 11–45.

De aeterna Dei praedestinatione / De la prédestination éternelle. In *COR* 3/1, edited by Wilhelm H. Neuser. Geneva: Droz, 1998.

The Bondage and Liberation of the Will: A Defence of the Orthodox Doctrine of Human Choice against Pighius. Edited by Anthony N. S. Lane. Translated by Graham I. Davies. Grand Rapids: Baker, 1996.

Briève instruction pour armer tous bons fidèles contre les erreurs de la secte commune des anabaptistes. Vol. 4/2 of *COR*. Edited by Myriam van Veen. Geneva: Droz, 2007.

Calvin: Commentaries. Edited and translated by Joseph Haroutunian. London: SCM, 1958.

Calvin's Commentary on Seneca's De Clementia,. Edited and translated by Ford L. Battles and André M. Hugo. Leiden: Brill, 1969.

"Calvin's Latin Preface to his Proposed French Edition of Chrysostom's Homilies: Translation and Commentary" [CO 9:831–38]. In *Humanism and Reform: The Church in Europe, England and Scotland, 1400–1643. Essays in Honour of James K. Cameron,* edited by James Kirk, translated by Ian P. Hazlett, 129–50. Studies in Church History: Subsidia 8. Oxford: Blackwell, 1991.

"Calvin's Treatise 'Against the Libertines.'" Translated by Robert G. Wilkie and Allen Verhey. *CTJ* 15 (1980) 190–219.

"Calvin's XXXIX Sermon on First Samuel (1 Samuel 8:11–22)." Translated by Douglas F. Kelly. In *Calvin Studies I,* edited by John H. Leith, 66–77. Davidson, NC: Davidson College, 1982.

Le Catéchisme français de Calvin: publié en 1537, réimprimé pour la première fois d'après un exemplaire nouvellement retrouvé, et suivi de la plus ancienne Confession de foi de l'Église de Genève, avec deux notices. Edited by Albert Rilliet and Théophile Dufour. Geneva: Fick, 1878.

"De catechese in Geneve." In *De catechese van de Reformatie en de Nadere Reformatie,* edited and translated by Willem Verboom, 53–65. Amsterdam: Buijten & Schipperheijn, 1986.

Come Out from among Them: "Anti-Nicodemite" Writings of John Calvin. Translated by Seth Scolnitsky. Dallas: Protestant Heritage, 2001.

Commentarii in Epistolas Canonicas sive Catholicas Commentarius. Vol. 2/20 of *COR.* Edited by Kenneth Hagen. Geneva: Droz, 2009.

Commentarii in Pauli Epistolas ad Galatas, ad Ephesios, ad Philippenses, ad Colossenses. Vol. 2/16 of *COR.* Edited by Helmut Feld. Geneva: Droz, 1992.

Commentarii in secundam Pauli Epistolam ad Corinthios. Edited by Helmut Feld. Geneva: Droz, 1994, in *COR* 2/15.

Commentariorum in Acta Apostolorum liber primus et liber posterior. Vols. 2/12/1–2 of *COR.* Edited by Helmut Feld. Geneva: Droz, 2001.

Commentarius in Epistolam ad Hebraeos. Vol. 2/19 of *COR.* Edited by Thomas H.L. Parker. Geneva: Droz, 1996.

Commentarius in Epistolam Pauli ad Romanos. Vol. 2/13 of *COR.* Edited by Thomas H. L. Parker and David C. Parker. Geneva: Droz, 1999.

Concerning the Eternal Predestination of God. Translated by John K. S. Reid. Cambridge: Clarke, 1961.

Concerning Scandals. Translated by John W. Fraser. Grand Rapids: Eerdmans, 1978.

Confessions et catéchismes de la foi réformée. Edited by Olivier Fatio et al. 2nd ed. Geneva: Labor et Fides, 2005.

Congrégations et Disputations. Vol. 7/1 of *COR.* Edited by Erik A. de Boer. Geneva: Droz, 2014.

Contre la secte phantastique et furieuse des libertins qui se nomment spirituelz (avec une epistre de la mesme matiere, contre un certain cordelier, suppost de la secte: lequel est prisonnier à Roan) en Response à un certain holandois, lequel sous ombre de faire les chrestiens tout spirtuels, leur permet de polluer leurs corps en toutes idolatries. Vol. 4/1 of *COR.* Edited by Mirjam van Veen. Geneva: Droz, 2005.

Correspondance française de Calvin avec Louis du Tillet. Edited by Alexandre C. Crottet. Geneva: Cherruliez, 1850.

Defensio Orthodoxae Fidei de Sacra Trinitate, Contra Prodigiosos Errores Michaelis Serueti Hispani. Vol. 4/5 of *COR.* Edited by Joy Kleinstuber. Geneva: Droz, 2009.

Defensio sanae et orthodoxae doctrinae de servitute et liberatione humani arbitrii. Vol. 4/3 of *COR.* Edited by Graham I. Davies and Anthony N. S. Lane. Geneva: Droz, 2008.

Epistolae, 1530–Sep. 1538. Vol. 6/1 of *COR.* Edited by Cornelis Augustijn and Frans P. van Stam. Geneva: Droz, 2005.

Epistolae duae (1537), Deux discours (Oct. 1536). Vol. 4/4 of *COR.* Edited by Erik A. de Boer and Frans P. van Stam. Geneva: Droz, 2009.

"Épître à tous amateurs de Jésus-Christ (1535)." In *"La vraie piété": divers traités de Jean Calvin et Confession de foi de Guillaume Farel,* edited by Irena Backus and Claire Chimelli, 17–23. Geneva: Labor et Fides, 1986.

In evangelium secundum Johannem commentarius pars prior et pars altera. Vol. 2/11/1–2 of *COR.* Edited by Helmut Feld. Geneva: Droz, 1997, 1998.

La Famine Spirituelle: Sermon inédit sur Esaïe 55, 1–2. Edited by Max Engammare. Translated by Francis M. Higman. Geneva: Droz, 2000.

"The Form of Prayers, 1542" [*CO* 6:185–92]. ET in *Christian Initiation: The Reformation Period,* translated by John D. C. Fisher, 113–17. London: SPCK, 1970.

"The French Gallican Confession (1559)" [*OS* 2:297–324]. Translated by Emily O. Butler. In *The Faith of Christendom: A Source Book of Creeds and Confessions,* edited by Brian A. Gerrish, 126–63. New York: World, 1963.

Instruction et confession de foy dont on use en l'Eglise de Genève. Catechismus seu Christianæ religionis institutio ecclesiæ Genevensis, Confessio Genevensium prædicatorum de Trinitate. Vol. 3/2. Edited by Anette Zillenbiller and Marc Vial. Geneva: Droz, 2002.

John Calvin: Selections from His Writings. Edited by John Dillenberger. Atlanta: Scholars, 1975.

John Calvin: Writings on Pastoral Piety. Edited and translated by Elsie A. McKee. New York: Paulist, 2001.

John Calvin's Ecclesiastical Advice. Translated by Mary Beaty and Benjamin W. Farley. Edinburgh: T. & T. Clark, 1991.

The Lectures or Daily Sermons, of that Reverend Divine, M. John Calvine, upon the Prophet Jonas: Whereunto is annexed an excellent exposition of the two last Epistles of S. John. Translated by Nathaniel Baxter. London: Kingston, 1578.

Men, Women, and Order in the Church: Three Sermons by John Calvin. Translated by Seth Scolnitsky. Dallas: Presbyterian Heritage, 1992.

The Mystery of Godliness and Other Sermons. Morgan, PA: Soli Deo Gloria, 1999.

Notice Bibliographique sur le Catéchisme et la Confession de Foi de Calvin (1537) et sur les autres livres imprimés à Genève et à Neuchâtel dans les premiers temps de la réforme (1533-1540). Edited by Théophile Dufour. Geneva: Fick, 1878.

Peter, Rudolphe. "The Geneva Primer or Calvin's Elementary Catechism (1551)." Translated by Charles Raynal. In *Calvin Studies V*, edited by John H. Leith, 135–61. Davidson, NC: Davidson College, 1990.

Plusieurs Sermons de Jean Calvin. Vol. 5/8 of *COR*. Edited by Wilhelmus H. Th. Moehn. Geneva: Droz, 2011.

Praelectiones in librum Prophetiarum Ieremiae. Vol. 6/1–2 of *COR*. Edited by Nicole Gueunier. Geneva: Droz, 2016.

Predigten über das 2: Buch Samuelis. Vol. 1 of *SC*. Edited by Hanns Rückert. Neukirchen-Vluyn: Neukirchener, 1961.

Psalmenpredigten, Passions-, Oster-und Pfingstpredigten. Vol. 7 of *SC*. Edited by Erwin Mühlhaupt. Neukirchen-Vluyn: Neukirchener, 1981.

Psychopannychia: Tracts and Treatises, with a Short Life of John Calvin. 3 vols. Edited by Thomas F. Torrance. Translated by Henry Beveridge. Grand Rapids: Eerdmans, 1958.

The Register of the Company of Pastors of Geneva in the Time of Calvin. Edited and translated by Philip E. Hughes. Grand Rapids: Eerdmans, 1966.

Registers of the Consistory of Geneva in the Time of Calvin. Vol. 1, *1542-1544.* Edited by Thomas A. Lambert and Isabella M. Watt. Translated by M. Wallace McDonald. Grand Rapids: Eerdmans, 2000.

Des Scandales, edited by Olivier Fatio. Geneva: Droz, 1984.

The Secret Providence of God. Edited by Paul Helm. Translated by Keith Goad. Wheaton, IL: Crossway, 2010.

Sermons on the Acts of the Apostles Chapters 1–7. Translated by Rob R. McGregor. Edinburgh: Banner of Truth Trust, 2008.

Sermons on the Acts of the Apostles, Chapitres 1–7. Vol. 8 of *SC*. Edited by Willem Balke and Wilhelmus H. Th. Moehn. Neukirchen-Vluyn: Neukirchener, 1994.

Sermons on the Beatitudes. Translated by Robert White. Edinburgh: Banner of Truth Trust, 2007.

Sermons on the Book of Micah. Edited and translated by Benjamin W. Farley. Phillipsburg, NJ: P&R, 2003.

Sermons on the Deity of Christ. Translated by Leroy Nixon. 1581. Updated version: Audubon, NJ: Old Paths, 1997.

Sermons on Deuteronomy. Translated by Arthur Golding. 1583. Repr., Edinburgh: Banner of Truth Trust, 1987.

Sermons on Election and Reprobation. Translated by John Fielde. 1579. Updated version: Audubon, NJ: Old Paths, 1996.

Sermons on the Epistle to the Ephesians. Translated by Arthur Golding. 1577. Revised translation by Leslie Rawlinson and Sidney M. Houghton, Edinburgh: Banner of Truth Trust, 1973.

Sermons on the Epistle to the Galatians. Translated by Kathy Childress. Edinburgh: Banner of Truth Trust, 1997.

Sermons on the Epistles to Timothy & Titus. Translated by Laurence Tomson. 1579. Repr., Edinburgh: Banner of Truth Trust, 1983.

Sermons sur la Genèse, Chapitres 1,1—11,4. Vol. 11/1 of SC. Edited by Max Engammare. Neukirchen-Vluyn: Neukirchener, 2000.

Sermons sur la Genèse, Chapitres 11,5—20,7. Vol. 11/2 of SC. Edited by Max Engammare. Neukirchen-Vluyn: Neukirchener, 2000.

Sermons on Genesis Chapters 1:1—11:4. Translated by Rob R. McGregor. Edinburgh: Banner of Truth Trust, 2009.

Sermons on Genesis Chapters 11-20. Translated by Rob R. McGregor. Edinburgh: Banner of Truth Trust, 2012.

Sermons on Isaiah's Prophecy of the Death and Passion of Christ. Edited and translated by Thomas H. L. Parker. Cambridge: Clarke, 1956.

Sermons on Jeremiah. Translated by Blair Reynolds. Lampeter, Wales: Mellor, 1993.

Sermons on Job. Translated by Arthur Golding. 1574. Repr., Edinburgh: Banner of Truth Trust, 1993.

Sermons on Job. Translated by Leroy Nixon. Grand Rapids: Baker, 1952.

Sermons sur le Livre d'Esaïe, Chapitres 13-29. Vol. 2 of SC. Edited by Georges A. Barrois. Neukirchen-Vluyn: Neukirchener, 1961.

Sermons sur le Livre d'Esaïe, Chapitres 30-41. Vol. 3 of SC. Edited by Francis M. Higman et al. Neukirchen-Vluyn: Neukirchener, 1995.

Sermons sur les Livres de Jérémie et des Lamentations. Vol. 6 of SC. Edited by Rudolph Peter. Neukirchen-Vluyn: Neukirchener, 1971.

Sermons sur le Livre de Michée. In Vol. 5 of SC. Edited by Jean-Daniel Benoît. Neukirchen-Vluyn: Neukirchener, 1964.

Sermons sur le Livre des Révélations du prophète Ézéchiel, Chapitres 36 à 48. Vol. 10/3 of SC. Edited by Erik A. de Boer and Barnabas Nagy. Neukirchen-Vluyn: Neukirchener, 2006.

Sermons on Melchizedek and Abraham: Justification, Faith and Obedience. Translated by Thomas Stocker. 1592. Updated version: Willow Street, PA: Old Paths, 2000.

Sermons on Psalm 119. Translated by Thomas Stocker. 1580. Updated version: Audubon, NJ: Old Paths, 1996.

Sermons on 2 Samuel Chapters 1-13. Translated by Douglas F. Kelly. Edinburgh: Banner of Truth Trust, 1992.

Sermons on the Saving Work of Christ. Translated by Leroy Nixon. Grand Rapids: Baker, 1980.

Sermons on the Ten Commandments. Edited and translated by Benjamin W. Farley. Grand Rapids: Baker, 1980.

Sermons on Titus. Translated by Robert White. Edinburgh: Banner of Truth Trust, 2015.

Sex, Marriage, and Family in John Calvin's Geneva. Vol. 1, *Courtship, Engagement, and Marriage.* Edited by John Witte, Jr. and Robert M. Kingdon. Grand Rapids: Eerdmans, 2005.

Six Psalms of John Calvin: Psalms 25, 36, 46, 91, 113, 138. Translated by Ford L. Battles. Grand Rapids: Baker, 1978.

Songs of the Nativity: Selected Sermons on Luke 1 & 2. Translated by Robert White. Edinburgh: Banner of Truth Trust, 2008.

Three French Treatises. Edited by Francis M. Higdon. London: Athlone, 1970.

Treatises against the Anabaptists and against the Libertines. Edited and translated by Benjamin W. Farley. Grand Rapids: Baker, 1982.

Treatises on the Sacraments: Catechism of the Church of Geneva Forms of Prayer, and Confessions of Faith. Translated by Henry Beveridge. Fearn, UK: Christian Focus, 2002.

Trois libellés anonymes. Edited by Francis M. Higman and Olivier Millet. Geneva: Droz, 2006.

"A Warning against Judicial Astrology and Other Prevalent Curiosities (1549)." Translated by Mary Potter. *CTJ* 18 (1983) 157–89.

EDWARDS PRIMARY SOURCES

Apocalyptic Writings. Vol. 5 of *WJE.* Edited by Stephen J. Stein. New Haven: Yale University Press, 1977.

The "Blank Bible." 2 vols. Vol. 24/1–2 of *WJE.* Edited by Stephen J. Stein. New Haven: Yale University Press, 2006.

The Blessing of God: Previously Unpublished Sermons of Jonathan Edwards. Vol. 1. Edited by Michael D. McMullen. Nashville: Broadman & Holman, 2003.

Catalogues of Books. Vol. 26 of *WJE.* Edited by Peter J. Thuesen. New Haven: Yale University Press, 2008.

Doctrine of Original Sin Defended. Vol. 3 of *WJE.* Edited by Clyde A. Holbrook. New Haven: Yale University Press, 1970.

Ecclesiastical Writings. Vol. 12 of *WJE.* Edited by David D. Hall. New Haven: Yale University Press, 1994.

Ethical Writings. Vol. 8 of *WJE.* Edited by Paul Ramsey. New Haven: Yale University Press, 1989.

Freedom of the Will. Vol. 1 of *WJE.* Edited by Paul Ramsey. New Haven: Yale University Press, 1957.

The Glory and Honor of God: Previously Unpublished Sermons of Jonathan Edwards. Vol. 2. Edited by Michael D. McMullen. Nashville: Broadman & Holman, 2004.

The Great Awakening. Vol. 4 of *WJE.* Edited by Clarence C. Goen. New Haven: Yale University Press, 1972.

A History of the Work of Redemption. Vol. 9 of *WJE.* Edited by John Wilson. New Haven: Yale University Press, 1989.

A Just and Righteous God: 18 sermons (13 Previously Unpublished). Edited by Don Kistler. Morgan, MA: SDG, 2006.

Jonathan Edwards: The Unpublished Sermons. Edited by Michael D. Mcmullen. Mountain Home, AR: Borderstone, 2012.

Knowing the Heart: Jonathan Edwards on True and False Conversion. Edited by William C. Nichols. Ames, IA: International Outreach, 2003.

Letters and Personal Writings. Vol. 16 of *WJE.* Edited by George S. Claghorn. New Haven: Yale University Press, 1998.

The Life of David Brainerd. Vol. 7 of *WJE.* Edited by Norman Petit. New Haven: Yale University Press, 1985.

"The Miscellanies," a–500. Vol. 13 of *WJE.* Edited by Thomas A. Schafer. New Haven: Yale University Press, 1994.

"The Miscellanies," 501–832. Vol. 18 of *WJE.* Edited by Ava Chamberlain. New Haven: Yale University Press, 2000.

"The Miscellanies," 833–1152. Vol. 20 of *WJE.* Edited by Amy P. Pauw. New Haven: Yale University Press, 2002.

"The Miscellanies," 1153–1360. Vol. 23 of *WJE.* Edited by Douglas A. Sweeney. New Haven: Yale University Press, 2004.

Notes on Scripture. Vol. 15 of *WJE.* Edited by Stephen J. Stein. New Haven: Yale University Press, 1998.

The Puritan Pulpit: Jonathan Edwards. Edited by Don Kistler. Morgan, MA: SDG, 2004.

Religious Affections. Vol. 2 of *WJE.* Edited by John Smith. New Haven: Yale University Press, 1959.

Resolutions and Advice to Young Converts. Edited by Stephen J. Nichols. Phillipsburg, NJ: P&R, 2001.

To the Rising Generation: Addresses Given to Children and Young Adults. Edited by Don Kistler. Morgan, MA: SDG, 2005.

The Salvation of Souls: Nine Previously Unpublished Sermons on the Call of Ministry and the Gospel by Jonathan Edwards. Edited by Richard A. Bailey and Gregory A. Wills. Wheaton, IL: Crossway, 2002.

Scientific and Philosophical Writings. Vol. 6 of *WJE.* Edited by Wallace E. Anderson. New Haven: Yale University Press, 1980.

Seeking God: Jonathan Edwards' Evangelism Contrasted with Modern Methodologies. Edited by William C. Nichols. Ames, IA: International Outreach, 2001.

Sermons and Discourses, 1720–1723. Vol. 10 of *WJE.* Edited by Wilson H. Kilmnach. New Haven: Yale University Press, 1992.

Sermons and Discourses, 1723–1729. Vol. 14 of *WJE.* Edited by Kenneth P. Minkema. New Haven: Yale University Press, 1977.

Sermons and Discourses, 1730–1733. Vol. 17 of *WJE.* Edited by Mark Valeri. New Haven: Yale University Press, 1999.

Sermons and Discourses, 1734–1738. Vol. 19 of *WJE.* Edited by Max X. Lesser. New Haven: Yale University Press, 2001.

Sermons and Discourses, 1739–1742. Vol. 22 of *WJE.* Edited by Harry S. Stout and Nathan O. Hatch. New Haven: Yale University Press, 2003.

Sermons and Discourses, 1743–1758. Vol. 25 of *WJE.* Edited by Wilson H. Kimnath. New Haven: Yale University Press, 2006.

Sermons by Jonathan Edwards on the Matthean Parables. Vol. 1, *True and False Christians.* Edited by Kenneth P. Minkema et al. Eugene, OR: Cascade, 2012.

Sermons by Jonathan Edwards on the Matthean Parables. Vol. 2, *Divine Husbandman.* Edited by Kenneth P. Minkema and Adriaan C. Neele. Eugene, OR: Cascade, 2012.

Sermons by Jonathan Edwards on the Matthean Parables. Vol. 3, *Fish Out of Their Element*. Edited by Kenneth P. Minkema and Adriaan C. Neele. Eugene, OR: Cascade, 2012.

Sermons on the Lord's Supper. Edited by Don Kistler. Orlando: Northampton, 2007.

The Torments of Hell: Jonathan Edwards on Eternal Damnation. Edited by William C. Nichols. Ames, IA: International Outreach, 2006.

Typological Writings. Vol. 11 of *WJE*. Edited by Wallace E. Anderson and Mason I. Lowance, Jr. New Haven: Yale University Press, 1993.

Unless You Repent: 15 Previously Unpublished Sermons on the Fate Awaiting the Impenitent. Edited by Don Kistler. Morgan, MA: SDG, 2005.

Writings on the Trinity, Grace and Faith. Vol. 21 of *WJE*. Edited by Sang H. Lee. New Haven: Yale University Press, 2003.

OTHER SOURCES

Albertz, Rainer. *A History of Israelite Religion in the Old Testament Period*. 2 vols. London: SCM, 1994.

Albright, William F. "The Archaeological Background of the Hebrew Prophets of the Eighth Century." *JBR* 8 (1940) 131–36.

———. *Archaeology and the Religion of Israel*. Louisville: Westminster John Knox, 2006.

———. *From the Stone Age to Christianity: Monotheism and the Historical Process*. New York: Doubleday, 1957.

———. "Samuel and the Beginnings of the Prophetic Movement." In *Interpreting the Prophetic Tradition*, edited by Harry M. Orlinsky, 149–76. Cincinnati: Hebrew Union College Press, 1969.

Alston, William P. "Two Cheers for Mystery!" In *God and the Ethics of Belief: New Essays in the Philosophy of Religion*, edited by Andrew Dole et al., 99–114. Cambridge: Cambridge University Press, 2005.

Andrews, Malcolm. *Dickens and the Grown-Up Child*. Basingstoke, UK: Macmillan, 1994.

Armstrong, Brian G. *Calvinism and the Amyraut Heresy: Protestant Scholasticism and Humanism in Seventeenth-Century France*. Madison: University of Wisconsin Press, 1969.

Astington, Janet W. *The Child's Discovery of the Mind*. London: Fontana, 1994.

Augustine. *The Confessions*. Vol. 1/1 of *WA*. Edited by John E. Rotelle. Translated by Maria Boulding. New York: New City, 1997.

Ayres, Lewis. "Being (*esse/essentia*)." In *Augustine through the Ages*, edited by Allan D. Fitzgerald, 96–98. Grand Rapids: Eerdmans, 1999.

———. *Unless You Become Like This Child*. Translated by Erasmo Leiva-Merikakis. San Francisco: Ignatius, 1991.

Baltzer, Klaus. "Considerations concerning the Office and Calling of the Prophet." *HTR* 61 (1968) 567–81.

Bannon, Brad. "President Edwards and the Sage of Highgate: Determinism, Depravity, and the Supernatural Will." *JHI* 77 (2016) 27–47.

Barr, James. *Biblical Faith and Natural Theology*. Oxford: Oxford University Press, 1993.

————. *The Concept of Biblical Theology: An Old Testament Perspective.* London: SCM, 1999.

Barrett, C. Kingsley. *A Critical and Exegetical Commentary on the Acts of the Apostles.* ICC. 2 vols. London: T. & T. Clark, 2004.

Barth, Karl. *The Humanity of God.* Translated by John Newton Thomas. London: Collins, 1961.

————. *The Knowledge of God and the Service of God according to the Teaching of the Reformation: Recalling the Scottish Confession of 1560.* Translated by James L. M. Haire and Ian Henderson. London: Hodder & Stoughton, 1938.

————. *Theology and Church: Shorter Writings 1920–1928.* Translated by Louise P. Smith. New York: Harper & Row, 1962.

Bartsch, Karen, and Henry M. Wellman. *Children Talk about the Mind.* Oxford: Oxford University Press, 1995.

Batten, Loring W. "The Sanctuary at Shiloh, and Samuel's Sleeping Therein." *JBL* 19 (1900) 29–33.

Battles, Ford L. *Interpreting John Calvin.* Edited by Robert Benedetto. Grand Rapids: Baker, 1996.

Bauke, Hermann. *Die Probleme der Theologie Calvins.* Leipzig: Hinrichs'schen, 1922.

Baumgarten, Alexander G. *Meditationes Philosophicae de Nonnullis ad Poema Pertinentibus.* ET: *Reflections on Poetry: Alexander Gottlieb Baumgarten's Meditationes Philosophicae de Nonnullis ad Poema Pertinentibus.* Translated by Karl Aschenbrenner and William B. Holther. Los Angeles: University of California Press, 1954.

Beecher, Lyman. *The Autobiography of Lyman Beecher.* 2 vols. New York: Harper, 1865.

Berryman, Jerome W. *The Complete Guide to Godly Play.* 7 vols. Denver: Church Publishing, 2002–2008.

Bèze, Théodore. *Ioannis Calvini Vita.* In *CO* 21:119–72. Geneva, 1575; ET in *CTL* 1:xlviii–xlix.

————. *Théodore de Besze au Lecteur chrestian.* Preface to *Commentaires sur le livre de Iosue* [CO 21:21–50]. Geneva, 1564; ET in *The Life of John Calvin.* Darlington, UK: Evangelical, 1997.

————. "Zum 400. Todestag Calvins." *EvTh* 24 (1964) 225–29.

Billings, J. Todd. "John Calvin: United to God through Christ." In *Partakers of the Divine Nature: The History and Development of Deification in the Christian Traditions,* edited by Michael J. Christensen and Jeffrey A. Wittung, 200–218. Grand Rapids: Baker, 2008.

Blacketer, Raymond A. *The School of God: Pedagogy and Rhetoric in Calvin's Interpretation of Deuteronomy.* Dordrecht: Springer, 2006.

Bohatec, Josef. *Budé und Calvin: Studien zur Gedankenwelt des französischen Frühumanismus.* Graz: Böhlaus Nachfolger, 1950.

Bonhoeffer, Dietrich. *Barcelona, Berlin, New York: 1928–1931.* Translated by Douglas W. Scott. *DBWE* 10. Minneapolis: Fortress, 2008.

————. *Letters and Papers from Prison.* Translated by Isabel Best et al. *DBWE* 8. Minneapolis: Fortress, 2010.

Boston, Thomas. *Human Nature in its Fourfold State.* Edinburgh: Banner of Truth Trust, 1964.

Bourke, Joseph. "Samuel and the Ark: A Study in Contrasts." *DS* 7 (1954) 73–103.

Breed, David R. "The New Era in Evangelism." *PrTR* 1 (1903) 227–38.

Breen, Quirinus. "John Calvin and the Rhetorical Tradition." *CH* 26 (1957) 3–21.

———. *John Calvin: A Study in French Humanism*. 2nd ed. Hamden, CT: Archon, 1968.

Brodie, Louis. "Creative Writing: Missing Link in Biblical Research." *BTB* 8 (1978) 34–39.

Brown, Abner W. *Recollections of the Conversation Parties of the Rev. Charles Simeon*. London: Hamilton, Adams, 1863.

Brown, Penny. *The Captured World: The Child and Childhood in Nineteenth-Century Women's Writing in England*. London: Harvester Wheatsheaf, 1993.

Brown, Robert E. *Jonathan Edwards and the Bible*. Bloomington: Indiana University Press, 2002.

Browne, Thomas. *Religio Medici*. London: Crooke, 1642.

Bruce, Frederick F. *The Acts of the Apostles: The Greek Text with Introduction and Commentary*. 3rd rev. ed. Grand Rapids: Eerdmans, 1990.

Brueggemann, Walter. *The Book That Breathes New Life: Scriptural Authority and Biblical Theology*, edited by Patrick D. Miller. Minneapolis: Fortress, 2005.

———. *Old Testament Theology: Essays on Structure, Themes and Text*. Edited by Patrick D. Miller. Minneapolis: Fortress, 1992.

———. *Theology of the Old Testament: Testimony, Dispute, Advocacy*. Minneapolis: Fortress, 1997.

Brümmer, Vincent. *Speaking of a Personal God: An Essay in Philosophical Theology*. Cambridge: Cambridge University Press, 1992.

Bruner, Jerome. "The Ontogenesis of Speech Acts." *JCL* 2 (1975) 1–19.

Brunner, Emil. *The Divine-Human Encounter*. Translated by Amandus W. Loos. London: SCM, 1944.

Buber, Martin. *I and Thou*. Translated by Walter Kaufmann. New York: Scribner's, 1970.

Budé, Guillaume. *Omnia Opera*. 1557. Repr., Farnborough, UK: Gregg, 1966.

Bunge, Marcia J., ed. *The Child in Christian Thought*. Grand Rapids: Eerdmans, 2001

Burke, Edmund. *A Philosophical Enquiry into the Origin of Our Ideas of the Sublime and the Beautiful*. Edited by James T. Boulton. London: Routledge, 1958.

Bushman, Richard L. "Jonathan Edwards and Puritan Consciousness." *JSSR* 5 (1966) 383–96.

Bushnell, Horace. *Christian Nurture*. 4th ed. London: Dickinson, 1880.

Butin, Philip W. *Revelation, Redemption and Purpose: Calvin's Trinitarian Understanding of the Divine-Human Relationship*. Oxford: Oxford University Press, 1995.

Cairns, David. *The Image of God in Man*. London: SCM, 1953.

Carasik, Michael, ed. and trans. *The Commentators' Bible: The JPS Miqra'ot Gedolot: Exodus*. Philadelphia: JPS, 2005.

Cassuto, Umberto. *Commentary on the Book of Exodus*. Translated by Israel Abrahams. Jerusalem: Magnes, 1967.

Chadwick, Henry. *Early Christian Thought and Classical Tradition: Studies in Justin, Clement, and Origen*. Oxford: Clarendon, 1966.

Chenu, Marie-Dominique. *Toward Understanding Saint Thomas*. Translated by Albert M. Landry and Dominic Hughes. Chicago: Regnery, 1964.

Chillingworth, William. *The Religion of Protestants: A Safe Way to Salvation*. Oxford: Lichfield, 1638.

Cottret, Bernard. *Calvin: A Biography*. Translated by M. Wallace McDonald. London: T. & T. Clark, 2000.

Coveney, Peter. *The Image of Childhood. The Individual and Society: A Study of the Theme in English Literature.* Rev. ed. London: Penguin, 1967.

Crisp, Oliver D. "Jonathan Edwards on the Divine Nature." *JRT* 3 (2009) 175–91.

———. "Jonathan Edwards's God: Trinity, Individuation, and Divine Simplicity." In *Engaging the Doctrine of God,* edited by Bruce McCormack, 83–103. Grand Rapids: Baker, 2008.

———. "Jonathan Edwards's Ontology: A Critique of Sang Hyun Lee's Dispositional Account of Edwardsian Metaphysics." *RS* 46 (2010) 1–20.

D'Angelo, Mary R. *Moses in the Letter to the Hebrews.* Missoula, MT: Scholars, 1979.

Danaher, William J., Jr. "Beauty, Benevolence, and Virtue in Jonathan Edwards's *The Nature of True Virtue.*" *JR* 87 (2007) 386–410.

———. "'Fire Enfolding Itself': Jonathan Edwards, the *Merkabah,* and Reparative Reasoning." *JSR* (electronic) 8, no. 2 (2009). http://jsr.shanti.virginia.edu/back-issues/vol-8-no-2-august-2009-the-roots-of-scriptural-reasoning/fire-enfolding-itself-jonathan-edwards-the-merkabah-and-reparative-reasoning/.

———. *The Trinitarian Ethics of Jonathan Edwards.* Louisville: Westminster John Knox, 2004.

Daniel, Stephen H. "Edwards, Berkeley, and Ramist Logic." *IS* 31 (2001) 55–72.

Davies, Oliver. "Reading the Burning Bush: Voice, World and Holiness." *MT* 22 (2006) 439–48.

Davis, Ellen F., and Richard B. Hays, eds. *The Art of Reading Scripture.* Grand Rapids: Eerdmans, 2003.

de Kroon, Marijn. *The Honour of God and Human Salvation: Calvin's Theology according to His Institutes.* Translated by John Vriend and Lyle D. Bierma. Edinburgh: T. & T. Clark, 2001.

Le Déaut, Roger. *Targum du Pentateuque.* Vol. 2, *Exode et Lévitique.* Paris: Cerf, 1979.

Delattre, Roland A. "Aesthetics and Ethics: Jonathan Edwards and the Recovery of Aesthetics for Religious Ethics." *JRE* 31 (2003) 277–97.

———. *Beauty and Sensibility in the Thought of Jonathan Edwards: An Essay in Aesthetics and Theological Ethics.* New Haven: Yale University Press, 1968.

———. "Beauty and Theology: A Reappraisal of Jonathan Edwards." *Soundings* 51 (1968) 60–79.

Doherty, Sam. *Children: A Biblical Perspective.* Lisburn: CEF, 2011.

———. *How to Evangelize Children.* Lisburn: CEF, 2003.

Donaldson, Margaret. *Children's Minds.* New York: Norton, 1978.

Dowey, Edward A., Jr. *The Knowledge of God in Calvin's Theology.* 3rd ed. Grand Rapids: Eerdmans, 1994.

Driver, Samuel R. *Notes on the Hebrew Text and the Topography of the Books of Samuel.* Oxford: Clarendon, 1913.

Drummond, Henry. "Mr. Gladstone and Genesis." *NC* 19 (1886) 206–14.

Duncan, John. *In the Pulpit and at the Communion Table.* Edited by David Brown. Edinburgh: Edmonston & Douglas, 1874.

Dunn, James D. G. *Baptism in the Holy Spirit.* London: SCM, 1970.

Dylan, Bob. *Lyrics: 1962–2001.* London: Simon & Schuster, 2004.

Elwood, Douglas J. *The Philosophical Theology of Jonathan Edwards.* New York: Columbia University Press, 1960.

Engel, Mary P. *John Calvin's Perspectival Anthropology.* Atlanta: Scholars, 1988.

Erdt, Terrance. *Jonathan Edwards: Art and the Sense of the Heart*. Amherst: University of Massachusetts Press, 1980.

Erikson, Eric H. *Childhood and Society*. 2nd ed. London: Vintage, 1995.

Ezell, Margaret J. M. "John Locke's Images of Childhood." *ECS* 17 (1983/84) 139–55.

Farley, Edward. *Faith and Beauty: A Theological Aesthetic*. Aldershot: Ashgate, 2001.

Farrer, Austin. *Faith and Speculation: An Essay in Philosophical Theology*. London: A. & C. Black, 1967.

Fee, Gordon D. *God's Empowering Presence: The Holy Spirit in the Letters of Paul*. Peabody, MA: Hendrickson, 1994.

Field, Frederick. *Origenis Hexaplorum quae supersunt*. 2 vols. Oxford: Clarendon, 1875.

Fiering, Norman S. *Jonathan Edwards's Moral Thought and Its British Context*. Chapel Hill: University of North Carolina Press, 1981.

———. "Review of Delattre's *Beauty and Sensibility*." *WMQ* 28 (1971) 655–61.

Fleming, Daniel E. "The Etymological Origins of the Hebrew *nābî*': The One Who Invokes God." *CBQ* 55 (1993) 217–24.

———. "*Nābû* and *Munabbiātu*: Two New Syrian Religious Personnel." *JAOS* 113 (1993) 175–83.

Ford, David F. *Christian Wisdom: Desiring God and Learning in Love*. Cambridge: Cambridge University Press, 2007.

———. *Self and Salvation: Being Transformed*. Cambridge: Cambridge University Press, 1999.

———, ed. *The Modern Theologians*. 3rd ed. Oxford: Blackwell, 2005.

———, and Graham Stanton, eds. *Reading Texts, Seeking Wisdom: Scripture and Theology*. Grand Rapids: Eerdmans, 2003.

Francis, James M. M. *Adults as Children: Images of Childhood in the Ancient World and the New Testament*. Oxford: Lang, 2006.

Fredriksen, Paula. "Paul and Augustine: Conversion Narratives, Orthodox Traditions, and the Retrospective Self." *JTS* 37 (1986) 3–34.

Fynn. *Mister God, This Is Anna*. London: Fount, 1979.

Gadamer, Hans-Georg. *Truth and Method*. 2nd rev. ed. Translated by Joel Weinsheimer and Donald G. Marshall. London: Continuum, 1989.

Ganoczy, Alexandre. *The Young Calvin*. Translated by David L. Foxgrover and Wade Provo. Edinburgh: T. & T. Clark, 1987.

Gelman, Susan A. *The Essential Child: Origins of Essentialism in Everyday Thought*. Oxford: Oxford University Press, 2003.

Gerrish, Brian A. *The Old Protestantism and the New: Essays on the Reformation Heritage*. Edinburgh: T. & T. Clark, 1982.

Gnuse, Robert K. "A Reconsideration of the Form-Critical Structure in I Samuel 3: An Ancient Near Eastern Dream Theophany." *ZAW* 94 (1982) 379–90.

Gordon, Robert P. *1 & 2 Samuel: A Commentary*. Exeter: Paternoster, 1986.

Graham, Billy. *Just As I Am*. New York: HarperCollins, 1997.

Greenspan, Stanley I. *The Growth of the Mind and the Endangered Origins of Intelligence*. Reading, MA: Perseus, 1997.

Greßmann, Hugo. *Die älteste Geschichtsschreibung und Prophetie Israels (von Samuel bis Amos und Hosea)*. SAT 2/1. Göttingen: Vandenhoeck & Ruprecht, 1910.

Grislis, Egil. "Calvin's Use of Cicero in the *Institutes* I:1–5—A Case Study in Theological Method." *ARG* 62 (1971) 5–37.

Guillaume, Alfred. *Prophecy and Divination among the Hebrews and Other Semites.* London: Hodder & Stoughton, 1938.

Hadfield, James A. *Childhood and Adolescence.* London: Penguin, 1962.

Harbison, E. Harris. *Christianity and History: Essays.* Princeton: Princeton University Press, 1964.

Hardy, Daniel W. *Finding the Church.* London: SCM, 2001.

———. *God's Ways with the World: Thinking and Practising Christian Faith.* Edinburgh: T. & T. Clark, 1996.

Harman, Gilbert H. "The Inference to the Best Explanation." *PR* 74 (1965) 88–95.

Haroutunian, Joseph G. *Piety versus Moralism: The Passing of the New England Theology.* New York: Holt, 1932.

Hay, David, and Rebecca Nye. *The Spirit of the Child.* Rev. ed. London: Fount, 2006.

Hebblethwaite, Brian, and Douglas Hedley, eds. *The Human Person in God's World: Studies to Commemorate the Austin Farrer Centenary.* London: SCM, 2006.

Hebblethwaite, Margaret. *Motherhood and God.* London: Chapman, 1993.

Helm, Paul. *Calvin: A Guide to the Perplexed.* London: T. & T. Clark, 2009.

———. *Calvin at the Centre.* Oxford: Oxford University Press, 2010.

———. *John Calvin's Ideas.* Oxford: Oxford University Press, 2004.

Helm, Paul, and Oliver D. Crisp, eds. *Jonathan Edwards: Philosophical Theologian.* Aldershot, UK: Ashgate, 2003.

Hiebert, Paul G. "The Category "Christian" in the Missionary Task." *IRM* 72 (1983) 421–27.

Hofstadter, Douglas R. *Gödel, Escher, Bach: An Eternal Golden Band.* London: Penguin, 2000.

Hogg, James. *The Private Memoirs and Confessions of a Justified Sinner.* Edited by Peter D. Garside. Edinburgh: Edinburgh University Press, 2002.

Hoitenga, Dewey J., Jr. *John Calvin and the Will: A Critique and Corrective.* Grand Rapids: Baker, 1997.

Holbrook, Clyde A. *The Ethics of Jonathan Edwards: Morality and Aesthetics.* Ann Arbor: University of Michigan Press, 1973.

Holladay, William L. "The Background of Jeremiah's Self-understanding: Moses, Samuel, Jeremiah, and Psalm 22." *JBL* 83 (1964) 153–64.

Holmes, Stephen R. "Something Much Too Plain to Say': Towards a Defence of the Doctrine of Divine Simplicity." *Neue Zeitschrift für systematische Theologie und Religionsphilosophie* 43 (2003) 137–54.

Hopkins, Samuel. *The Life and Character of the Late Reverend, Learned, and Pious Mr. Jonathan Edwards.* 2nd ed. Glasgow: Duncan, 1785.

Howe, Daniel W. "The Cambridge Platonists of Old England and the Cambridge Platonists of New England." *CH* 57 (1988) 470–85.

Hutcheson, Francis. *An Essay on the Nature and Conduct of the Passions and Affections, with Illustrations on the Moral Sense.* Edited by Aaron Garrett. Indianapolis: Liberty Fund, 2002.

———. *An Inquiry into the Original of Our Ideas of Beauty and Virtue in Two Treatises.* Edited by Wolfgang Leidhold. Rev. ed. Indianapolis: Liberty Fund, 2008.

Hylander, Ivar. *Der Literarische Samuel-Saul-Komplex (I Sam. 1–15) traditionsgeschichtlich.* Uppsala: Almquist & Wiksell, 1932.

Ibn Ezra. *Commentary on the Pentateuch: Exodus (Shemot).* Translated by H. Norman Strickman and Arthur M. Silver. New York: Menorah, 1996.

Janz, Paul D. "Divine Causality and the Nature of Theological Questioning." *MT* 23 (2007) 317–48.

———. *God, the Mind's Desire: Reference, Reason and Christian Thinking.* Cambridge: Cambridge University Press, 2004.

Jewett, Robert. *Paul's Anthropological Terms.* Leiden: Brill, 1971.

Johnston, Frances M. *The Wordless Book Song.* Warrenton, MO: CEF, 1976.

Jones, Serene. *Calvin and the Rhetoric of Piety.* Louisville: Westminster John Knox, 1995.

Kagan, Jerome. *The Nature of the Child.* New York: Basic, 1984.

Kaiser, Christopher B. "Calvin's Understanding of Aristotelian Natural Philosophy: Its Extent and Possible Origins." In *Calviniana: Ideas and Influence of Jean Calvin,* edited by Robert V. Schnucker, 77–92. Kirksville, MO: Sixteenth Century Journal, 1988.

Kant, Immanuel. *Critique of the Power of Judgment.* Edited by Paul Guyer. Translated by Paul Guyer and Eric Matthews. Cambridge: Cambridge University Press, 2000.

———. *Critique of Pure Reason.* Translated and edited by Paul Guyer and Allen W. Wood. Cambridge: Cambridge University Press, 1998.

Kaufman, Gordon. *God the Problem.* Cambridge, MA: Harvard University Press, 1972.

Kennedy, Harry A. A. *St. Paul's Conceptions of the Last Things.* London: Hodder & Stoughton, 1904.

Kimnach, Wilson H., and Kenneth P. Minkema. "The Material and Social Practices of Intellectual Work: Jonathan Edwards's Study." *WMQ* 69 (2012) 699–730.

Kingdon, Robert M. "Catechesis in Calvin's Geneva." In *Educating People of Faith: Exploring the History of Jewish and Christian Communities,* edited by John van Engen, 294–313. Grand Rapids: Eerdmans, 2004.

Kirkpatrick, Alexander F. *The First Book of Samuel. The Cambridge Bible for Schools and College.* Rev. ed. Cambridge: Cambridge University Press, 1930.

Klauber, Martin I. "Continuity and Discontinuity in Post-Reformation Reformed Theology: An Evaluation of the Muller Thesis." *JETS* 33 (1990) 467–75.

Knight, George W. III. *The Pastoral Epistles: A Commentary on the Greek Text.* Carlisle, UK: Paternoster, 1992.

Lane, Anthony N. S. *John Calvin: Student of the Church Fathers.* Edinburgh: T. & T. Clark, 1999.

Lane, Belden C. "Jonathan Edwards on Beauty, Desire, and the Sensory World." *TS* 65 (2004) 44–72.

Lang, August. "The Sources of Calvin's *Institutes* of 1536." *EQ* 8 (1936) 130–41.

Lee, Sang H. *The Philosophical Theology of Jonathan Edwards.* Expand. ed. Princeton: Princeton University Press, 2000.

Lee, Sang H., ed. *The Princeton Companion to Jonathan Edwards.* Princeton: Princeton University Press, 2005.

Lee, Sang H., and Allen C. Guelzo, eds. *Edwards in Our Time: Jonathan Edwards and the Shaping of American Religion.* Grand Rapids: Eerdmans, 1999.

Lindbeck, George A. *The Nature of Doctrine: Religion and Theology in a Postliberal Age.* Philadelphia: Westminster, 1984.

Lock, Walter. *A Critical and Exegetical Commentary on the Pastoral Epistles: I & II Timothy and Titus.* ICC. Edinburgh: T. & T. Clark, 1924.

Locke, John. *Some Thoughts concerning Education.* Edited by John W. and Jean S. Yolton. Oxford: Oxford University Press, 1989.

————. *An Essay concerning Human Understanding.* Edited by Peter H. Nidditch. Oxford: Oxford University Press, 1975.

Loder, James E. *The Logic of the Spirit: Human Development in Theological Perspective.* San Francisco: Jossey-Bass, 1998.

Loder, James E., and Jim W. Neidhardt. *The Knight's Move: The Relational Logic of the Spirit in Theology and Science.* Colorado Springs: Helmers & Howard, 1992.

MacDonald, George. *Alec Forbes of Howglen.* 3 vols. London: Hurst & Blackett, 1865.

————. *A Dish of Orts.* London: Sampson Low, Marston, 1893.

————. *At the Back of the North Wind.* London: Strahan, 1871.

————. *David Elginbrod.* 3 vols. London: Hurst & Blackett, 1863.

————. "Dr. George MacDonald in Aberdeen." *Wingfold* 56 (2006) 3.

————. *The Princess and Curdie.* London: Chatto & Windus, 1883.

————. *The Princess and the Goblin.* London: Strahan, 1872.

————. *The Seaboard Parish.* 3 vols. London: Tinsley Brothers, 1868.

————. *Unspoken Sermons First Series.* London: Strahan, 1867.

————. *Unspoken Sermons Second Series.* London: Longmans, Green, & Co., 1885.

————. *Unspoken Sermons Third Series.* London: Longmans, Green, & Co., 1889.

————. *Weighed and Wanting.* 3 vols. London: Sampson Low, Marston, 1882.

Maritain, Jacques. *Creative Intuition in Art and Poetry.* Bollingen Series 25/1. Princeton: Princeton University Press, 1953.

Marsden, George M. *Jonathan Edwards: A Life.* New Haven: Yale University Press, 2003.

Marshall, I. Howard. *A Critical and Exegetical Commentary on the Pastoral Epistles.* ICC. Edinburgh: T. & T. Clark, 1999.

Mascall, Eric L. *Christian Theology and Natural Science: Some Questions in their Relations.* 2nd ed. London: Longmans & Green, 1957.

McClymond, Michael J. "God the Measure: Towards an Understanding of Jonathan Edwards' Theocentric Metaphysics." *SJT* 47 (1994) 43–59.

McKane, William. *A Critical and Exegetical Commentary on Jeremiah.* ICC. Edinburgh: T. & T. Clark, 1986.

McKee, Elsie A. "Exegesis, Theology, and Development in Calvin's *Institutio*: A Methodological Suggestion." In *Probing the Reformation: Historical Studies in Honor of Edward E. Dowey, Jr.*, edited by Elsie A. McKee and Brian G. Armstrong, 154–72. Louisville: Westminster John Knox, 1989.

Meyendorff, John, and Robert Tobias, eds. *Salvation in Christ: A Lutheran-Orthodox Dialogue.* Minneapolis: Augsburg Fortress, 1992.

Miles, Margaret R. "Theology, Anthropology, and the Human Body in Calvin's *Institutes of the Christian Religion*." *HTR* 74 (1981) 303–23.

Miller, Perry. *Jonathan Edwards.* New York: Sloane, 1949.

Miller, Ronald. *Vygotsky in Perspective.* Cambridge: Cambridge University Press, 2011.

Minkema, Kenneth P. "'Informing of the Child's Understanding, Influencing His Heart, and Directing Its Practice': Jonathan Edwards on Education." *Acta Theologica* 31 (2011) 159–89.

Mitchell, Louis J. *Jonathan Edwards on the Experience of Beauty.* Studies in Reformed Theology and History, N.S. 9. Princeton: Princeton Theological Seminary, 2003.

Moberly, R. Walter L. *The Bible, Theology, and Faith.* Cambridge: Cambridge University Press, 2000.

————. "To Hear the Master's Voice: Revelation and Spiritual Discernment in the Call of Samuel." *SJT* 48 (1985) 443–68.

————. *Prophecy and Discernment*. Cambridge: Cambridge University Press, 2006.

Molnar, Paul D. "Natural Theology Revisited: A Comparison of T. F. Torrance and Karl Barth." *ZDT* 20 (2005) 53–83.

Moltmann, Jürgen. *Experiences in Theology*. Translated by Margaret Kohl. London: SCM, 2000.

————. *In the End–The Beginning: The Life of Hope*. Translated by Margaret Kohl. Minneapolis: Fortress, 2004.

————. *Science and Wisdom*. Translated by Margaret Kohl. Minneapolis: Fortress, 2003.

Moody, William R. *The Life of Dwight L. Moody*. London: Morgan & Scott, 1900.

More, Hannah. *Strictures on the Modern System of Female Education*. 2 vols. 3rd ed. London: Cadell & Davies, 1799.

Muilenburg, James. "The 'Office' of the Prophet in Ancient Israel." In *The Bible in Modern Scholarship*, edited by J. Philip Hyatt, 74–97. London: Kingsgate, 1966.

Muller, Richard A. *After Calvin: Studies in the Development of a Theological Tradition*. Oxford: Oxford University Press, 2003.

————. *Calvin and the Reformed Tradition: On the Work of Christ and the Order of Salvation*. Grand Rapids: Baker, 2012.

————. "'Duplex cognitio Dei' in the Theology of Early Reformed Orthodoxy." *SCJ* 10 (1979) 51–61.

————. "The Starting Point of Calvin's Theology: An Essay-Review." *CTJ* 36 (2001) 314–41.

————. *The Unaccommodated Calvin: Studies in the Foundation of a Theological Tradition*. Oxford: Oxford University Press, 2000.

Murray, Ian H. *The Forgotten Spurgeon*. London: Banner of Truth, 1966.

Naphy, William G. "The Reformation and the Evolution of Geneva's Schools." In *Reformations Old and New: Essays on the Socio-Economic Impact of Religious Change, c.1470–1630*, edited by Beat A. Kümin, 185–202. Aldershot, UK: Scolar, 1996.

Neurath, Marie, and Robert S. Cohen, eds. *Otto Neurath: Empiricism and Sociology*. Boston: Reidel, 1973.

Neuser, Wilhelm H. "The Development of the *Institutes* 1536 to 1559." In *John Calvin's Institutes His Opus Magnum*, Proceedings of the Second South African Congress for Calvin Research July 31–August 3, 1984, edited by Barend J. Van der Walt, 33–54. Potchefstroom, South Africa: Potchefstroom University for Higher Education, 1986.

Newey, Edmund. *Children of God: The Child as Source of Theological Anthropology*. Farnham, UK: Ashgate, 2012.

Newton, Isaac. *Opticks: Or, a Treatise of the Reflections, Refractions, Inflections & Colours of Light*. New York: Cosimo, 2007.

————. *The Principia: Mathematical Principles of Natural Philosophy*. Translated by I. Bernard Cohen and Anne Whitman. London: University of California Press, 1999.

Niebuhr, Reinhold. *The Nature and Destiny of Man: A Christian Interpretation*. 2 vols. London: Nisbet, 1941.

Niebuhr, Richard R. "The Anachronism of Jonathan Edwards." In *Theology, History and Culture: Major Unpublished Writings*, edited by W. S. Johnson, 123–33. New Haven: Yale University Press, 1996.

————. *Streams of Grace: Jonathan Edwards, Samuel Taylor Coleridge, and William James*. Kyoto: Doshisha University Press, 1980.

Niesel, Wilhelm. *The Theology of Calvin*, translated by Harold Knight. London: Lutterworth, 1956.

Noll, Mark. *The Scandal of the Evangelical Mind*. Leicester: Intervarsity, 1994.

O'Donovan, Joan E. "Man in the Image of God: The Disagreement between Barth and Brunner Reconsidered." *SJT* 39 (1986) 433–59.

Oberlinner, Lorenz. *Die Pastoralbriefe: Kommentar zum Ersten Timotheusbrief*. Basel: Herder Freiburg, 1994.

Oberman, Heiko A. "*Via Antiqua* and *Via Moderna*: Late Medieval Prolegomena to Early Reformation Thought." *JHI* 48 (1987) 23–40.

Oliphint, K. Scott. "Jonathan Edwards on Apologetics: Reason and the Noetic Effects of Sin." In *The Legacy of Jonathan Edwards: American Religion and the Evangelical Tradition*, edited by Darryl G. Hart et al., 131–46. Grand Rapids: Baker, 2003.

Ortony, Andrew, ed. *Metaphor and Thought*. Cambridge: Cambridge University Press, 1979.

Osborne, Grant R. *The Hermeneutical Spiral: A Comprehensive Introduction to Biblical Interpretation*. Leicester: Intervarsity, 1991.

Otto, Rudolf. *The Idea of the Holy: An Inquiry into the Non-Rational Factor in the Idea of the Divine and Its Relation to the Rational*. Translated by John W. Harvey. 2nd ed. Oxford: Oxford University Press, 1950.

Overholtzer, J. Irvin. *A Handbook on Child Evangelism*. Rev. ed. Grand Rapids: CEF, 1955.

Overholtzer, Ruth. *From Then Till Now: Reminiscing with Mrs. O*. Warrenton, MO: CEF, 1990.

————. *The Wordless Book Visualized*. Warrenton, MO: CEF, 1999.

Pannenberg, Wolfhart. *Anthropology in Theological Perspective*. Translated by Matthew J. O'Connell. Edinburgh: T. & T. Clark, 1999.

Parker, Thomas H. L. *Calvin's Doctrine of the Knowledge of God*. Rev. ed. Edinburgh: Oliver & Boyd, 1969.

————. *John Calvin: A Biography*. 2nd ed. Oxford: Lion, 2006.

Partee, Charles. *Calvin and Classical Philosophy*. Louisville: Westminster John Knox, 1977.

————. "Predestination in Aquinas and Calvin." *RR* 32 (1978–79) 14–22.

————. *The Theology of John Calvin*. Louisville: Westminster John Knox, 2008.

Pascal, Blaise. *Pensées*. Edited and translated by Roger Ariew. Indianapolis: Hackett, 2005.

Paul, Ian. *Knowledge of God: Calvin, Einstein and Polanyi*. Edinburgh: Scottish Academic, 1987.

Pauw, Amy P. *The Supreme Harmony of All: The Trinitarian Theology of Jonathan Edwards*. Grand Rapids: Eerdmans, 2002.

Petit, Françoise, ed. *Catenae Graecae in Genesim et in Exodvm*. Corpus Christianorum, series graeca 2. Turnhout: Leuven University Press, 1977.

Piaget, Jean. *The Origin of Intelligence in the Child*. Translated by Margaret Cook. London: Routledge, 1953.

————. *Six Psychological Studies*. Edited by David Elkind, translated by Anita Tenzer. London: University of London Press, 1968.

Pierce, David C. "Jonathan Edwards and the "New Sense" of Glory." *NEQ* 41 (1968) 82–95.

Piper, John. *The Pleasures of God.* Rev. ed. Fearn, UK: Christian Focus, 2001.

Pitkin, Barbara. "Children and the Church in Calvin's Geneva." In *Calvin and the Church*, Papers Presented at the 13th Colloquium of the Calvin Studies Society, May 24–26, 2001, edited by David L. Foxgrover, 144–64. Grand Rapids: Calvin Studies Society, 2002.

———. "'The Heritage of the Lord': Children in the Theology of John Calvin." In *The Child in Christian Thought*, edited by Marcia J. Bunge, 160–93. Grand Rapids: Eerdmans, 2001.

———. "Nothing But Concupiscence: Calvin's Understanding of Sin and the *Via Augustini.*" *CTJ* 34 (1999) 347–69.

Plantinga, Alvin. "The Reformed Objection to Natural Theology." *Christian Scholars Review* 11 (1982), 187–211.

Plato. *Complete Works.* Edited by John M. Cooper. Indianapolis: Hackett, 1997.

Polanyi, Michael. *Knowing and Being.* Edited by Marjorie Grene. London: Routledge, 1969

———. *Personal Knowledge: Towards a Post-Critical Philosophy.* London: Routledge, 1962.

———. *The Tacit Dimension.* New York: Doubleday, 1966.

Pollock, John C. *The Good Seed: the Story of the Children's Special Service Mission and the Scripture Union.* London: Hodder & Stoughton, 1959.

Pope, Alexander. *An Essay on Man.* Edited by Mark Pattison. Oxford: Clarendon, 1884.

Propp, William H. C. *Exodus 1–18.* London: Anchor Bible, 1999.

Pruyser, Paul W. "Calvin's View of Man: A Psychological Commentary." *Theology Today* 26 (1969) 51–68.

Pseudo-Dionysius. *Pseudo-Dionysius: The Complete Works.* Translated by Colm Luibheid. New York: Paulist, 1987.

Putnam, Hilary. *Meaning and the Moral Sciences.* London: Routledge, 1978.

Rahner, Karl. "Ideas for a Theology of Childhood." Translated by David Bourke, in *TI* 8:33–50.

Ramsey, Bennett. "The Ineluctable Impulse: 'Consent' in the Thought of Edwards, James, and Royce." *USQR* 37 (1983) 302–22.

Rashbam's Commentary on Exodus: An Annotated Translation. Translated and edited by Martin I. Lockshin. Atlanta: Scholars, 1997.

Rashi, Solomon ben Isaac. *Commentary on the Pentateuch*; text and translation: *Nederlandsche Vertaling van den Pentateuch benevens eene Nederlandsche verklarende vertaling van Rashie's Pentateuch-Commentaur door A.S. Onderwijzer.* Amsterdam: van Creveld, 1895–1901.

———. *The Torah: With Rashi's Commentary Translated, Annotated, and Elucidated*, 2:1–51. Translated and annotated by Yisrael Isser Zvi Herczeg. Brooklyn: Mesorah, 1994.

Redford, Donald B. "The Literary Motif of the Exposed Child (cf. Ex. ii 1–10)." *Numen* 14 (1967) 209–28.

Reid, Jasper. "Jonathan Edwards on Space and God." *JHP* 41 (2003) 385–403.

———. "The Trinitarian Metaphysics of Jonathan Edwards and Nicolas Malebranche." *HJ* 43 (2002) 152–69.

Reynolds, Philip L. "The Infants of Eden: Scholastic Theologians on Early Childhood and Cognitive Development." *MS* 68 (2006) 89–102.

Richard, Lucien J. *The Spirituality of John Calvin*. Atlanta: Knox, 1974.

Richter, Wolfgang. *Die sogenannten vorprophetischen Berufsberichte*, FRLANT 101. Göttingen: Vandenhoeck & Ruprecht, 1970.

Robinson, John T. *Thou Who Art: The Concept of the Personality of God*. London: Continuum, 2006.

Roloff, Jürgen. *Der erste Brief an Timotheus*. Zürich: Benziger, 1988.

Ross, James F. "The Prophet as Yahweh's Messenger." In *Israel's Prophetic Heritage: Essays in Honor of James Muilenburg*, edited by Bernard W. Anderson and Walter Harrelson, 98–107. San Francisco: Harper & Row, 1962.

Rousseau, Jean-Jacques. *Émile or On Education*. Translated by Barbara Foxley. London: Everyman, 1993.

Rupp, George. "The "Idealism" of Jonathan Edwards." *HTR* 62 (1969) 209–26.

Salvesen, Alison. *Symmachus in the Pentateuch*. Manchester: University of Manchester Press, 1991.

Sarna, Nahum M. *The JPS Torah Commentary of Exodus*. Jerusalem: JPS, 1991.

Schafer, Thomas A. "The Concept of Being in the Thought of Jonathan Edwards." *CH* 24 (1955) 179–80.

Schaffer, H. Rudolph. *The Child's Entry into a Social World*. London: Academic, 1984.

Scheick, William J. "Family, Conversion, and the Self in Jonathan Edwards' *A Faithful Narrative of the Surprising Work of God*." *TSL* 19 (1974) 79–89.

———. *The Will and the Word: The Poetry of Edward Taylor*. Athens: University of Georgia Press, 1974.

Schreiner, Susan E. "Exegesis and Double Justice in Calvin's Sermons on Job." *CH* 58 (1988) 322–38.

———. *The Theater of His Glory: Nature and the Natural Order in the Thought of John Calvin*. Durham, NC: Labyrinth, 1991.

———. *Where Shall Wisdom Be Found? Calvin's Exegesis of Job from Medieval and Modern Perspectives*. Chicago: University of Chicago Press, 1994.

Schweitzer, Don, ed. *Jonathan Edwards as Contemporary: Essays in Honor of Sang Hyun Lee*. New York: Lang, 2010.

Scougal, Henry. *The Life of God in the Soul of Man*. 2nd ed. London: Dring, 1691.

Sederholm, Carl. "The Trouble with Grace: Reading Jonathan Edwards's Faithful Narrative." *NEQ* 85 (2012) 326–34.

Shaftesbury, Anthony, Earl of. *Characteristicks of Men, Manners, Opinions, Times*. 3 vols. 2nd edn. London: Darby, 1714.

Shea, Daniel B., Jr. "Jonathan Edwards: Historian of Consciousness." In *Major Writers of Early American Literature*, edited by E. Emerson, 179–204. Madison: University of Wisconsin Press, 1972.

Shier-Jones, Angela, ed. *Children of God: Towards a Theology of Childhood*. Peterborough, UK: Epworth, 2007.

Smith, George Adam, *The Life of Henry Drummond*. London: Hodder & Stoughton, 1904.

Smith, Henry P. *A Critical and Exegetical Commentary on the Books of Samuel*. ICC. Edinburgh: T. & T. Clark, 1977.

Smits, Luchesius A. H. *Saint Augustin dans l'œuvre de Jean Calvin*. 2 vols. Assen: van Gorcum, 1956–1957.

Spierling, Karen E. *Infant Baptism in Reformation Geneva: The Shaping of a Community, 1536–1564.* Aldershot, UK: Ashgate, 2005.

Steele, Richard B. *"Gracious Affection" and "True Virtue" according to Jonathan Edwards and John Wesley.* London: Scarecrow, 1994.

Stein, Stephen J., ed. *The Cambridge Companion to Jonathan Edwards.* Cambridge: Cambridge University Press, 2007.

Steinmetz, David C. *Calvin in Context.* 2nd ed. Oxford: Oxford University Press, 2010.

Stern, Daniel N. *The Interpersonal World of the Infant: A View from Psychoanalysis and Developmental Psychology.* London: Karnac, 1998.

Stout, Harry S., et al., eds. *Jonathan Edwards at 300: Essays on the Tercentenary of His Birth.* Lanham, MD: University Press of America, 2005.

Targum Pseudo-Jonathan: Exodus. The Aramaic Bible. 2 vols. Translated by Michael Maher. Edinburgh: T. & T. Clark, 1994.

Tatarkiewicz, Wladyslaw. "The Great Theory of Beauty and Its Decline." *JAAC* 31 (1972) 165–80.

Taylor, John. *The Scripture-Doctrine of Original Sin Proposed to Free and Candid Examination.* London: Wilson, 1740.

Taylor, Mary E. *George MacDonald Exposes False Conflicts: Jesus/God, Justice/Mercy, Science/Religion.* Bloomington, IN: AuthorHouse, 2004.

Terrien, Samuel. *The Elusive Presence: Towards a New Biblical Theology.* San Francisco: Harper & Row, 1978.

Thiselton, Anthony C. "Barr on Barth and Natural Theology: A Plea for Hermeneutics in Historical Theology." *SJT* 47 (1994) 519–28.

———. *Thiselton on Hermeneutics: The Collected Works and New Essays of Anthony Thiselton.* Aldershot, UK: Ashgate, 2006.

———. *The Two Horizons: New Testament Hermeneutics and Philosophical Description with Special Reference to Heidegger, Bultmann, Gadamer, and Wittgenstein.* Exeter, UK: Paternoster, 1980.

Thomas, John N. "The Place of Natural Theology in the Thought of John Calvin." *JRT* 15 (1958) 107–36.

Thomson, Andrew. *Thomas Boston of Ettrick: His Life and Times.* Edinburgh: Nelson, 1895.

Ticciati, Susannah. "Scriptural Reasoning and the Formation of Identity." *MT* 22 (2006) 421–38.

Tillich, Paul. *A History of Christian Thought.* Edited by C. E. Braaten. London: SCM, 1968

———. *Systematic Theology.* 3 vols. London: Nisbet, 1953.

Torrance, Thomas F. *Calvin's Doctrine of Man.* London: Lutterworth, 1949.

———. *Divine and Contingent Order.* Oxford: Oxford University Press, 1981.

———. *The Ground and Grammar of Theology.* Belfast: Christian Journals, 1980.

———. *The Hermeneutics of John Calvin.* Edinburgh: Scottish Academic, 1988.

———. *Karl Barth, Biblical and Evangelical Theologian.* Edinburgh: T. & T. Clark, 1990.

———. *Space, Time and Resurrection.* Edinburgh: Handsel, 1976.

———. *Theological Science.* London: Oxford University Press, 1969.

———. *Theology in Reconstruction.* London: SCM, 1965.

———. "The Transitive Significance of Beauty in Science and Theology." In *L'art, la Science et la Métaphysique,* edited by Luz G. Alonso et al., 393–418. Bern: Lang, 1993.

Towner, Philip H. *The Letters to Timothy and Titus*. Grand Rapids: Eerdmans, 2006.

Towner, W. Sibley. "Children and the Image of God." In *The Child in the Bible*, edited by Marcia J. Bunge, 307–23. Grand Rapids. Eerdmans, 2008.

Trevarthen, Colwyn. "Communication and Cooperation in Early Infancy: A Description of Primary Intersubjectivity." In *Before Speech: The Beginnings of Human Communication*, edited by Margaret Bullowa, 321–47. Cambridge: Cambridge University Press, 1979.

———. "The Foundation of Intersubjectivity: Development of Interpersonal and Cooperative Understanding in Infants." In *The Social Foundations of Language and Thought*, edited by David R. Olson, 316–42. New York: Norton, 1980.

Turretin, Francis. *Institutes of Elenctic Theology*. 3 vols. Edited by James T. Dennison, Jr. Translated by George M. Giger. Phillipsburg, NJ: P&R, 1992–1997.

van den Eynde, Ceslas, ed. *Commentaire d'Išo'dad de Merv sur l'Ancien Testament*. Vol. 2, *Exode-Deutéronome*. CSCO 179, *Scriptores Syri*, Tome 81. Louvain: Secrétariat du CorpusSCO, 1958.

van der Kooi, Cornelis. *As in a Mirror. John Calvin and Karl Barth on Knowing God: A Diptych*. Translated by Donald Mader. Leiden: Brill, 2005.

Vanier, Jean. *Becoming Human*. London: DLT, 1999.

Venema, Cornelis P. "The 'Twofold Knowledge of God' and the Structure of Calvin's Theology." *MAJT* 4 (1988) 156–82.

Vermes, Geza. *Scripture and Tradition in Judaism: Haggadic Studies*. Rev. ed. Leiden: Brill, 1973.

Vetö, Miklos. "Spiritual Knowledge according to Jonathan Edwards." *CTJ* 31 (1996) 161–81.

von Balthasar, Hans Urs. "Jesus as Child and His Praise of the Child." Translated by Adrian Walker. *Communio* 22 (1995) 625–34.

von Rad, Gerhard. *Wisdom in Israel*. Translated by James D. Martin. London: SCM, 1972.

Vischer, Wilhelm. "The Vocation of the Prophet to the Nations: An Exegesis of Jeremiah 1:4–10." Translated by Suzanne de Dietrich. *Interpretation* 9 (1955) 310–17.

Vygotsky, Lev S. *Mind in Society: The Development of Higher Psychological Processes*. Edited by Michael Cole et al. London: Harvard University Press, 1978.

———. *Thought and Language*. Edited and translated by Alex Kozulin. Rev. ed. London: MIT Press, 1986.

Wainwright, William J. "Jonathan Edwards and the Sense of the Heart." *FP* 7 (1990) 43–62.

Wall, John. "Fallen Angels: A Contemporary Christian Ethical Ontology of Childhood." *IJPS* 8 (2003) 160–84.

———. *Ethics in Light of Childhood*. Washington, DC: Georgetown University Press, 2010.

Waters, Kenneth L, Sr. "Saved through Childbearing: Virtues as Children in 1 Timothy 2:11–15." *JBL* 123 (2004) 703–35.

Watson, Francis. *Text, Church and World: Biblical Interpretation in Theological Perspective*. Edinburgh: T. & T. Clark, 1994.

———. *Text and Truth: Redefining Biblical Theology*. Edinburgh: T. & T. Clark, 1997.

Watt, Jeffrey R. "Calvinism, Childhood, and Education: The Evidence from the Genevan Consistory." *SCJ* 33 (2002) 439–56.

————. "Childhood and Youth in the Geneva Consistory Minutes." In *Calvinus Præceptor Ecclesiæ*, Papers of the International Congress on Calvin Research, Princeton, August 20–24, 2002, edited by Herman J. Selderhuis, 43–64. Geneva: Droz, 2004.

Weil, Simone. *The Need for Roots: Prelude to a Declaration of Duties towards Mankind.* Translated by Arthur Wills. London: Routledge, 1952.

Wellman, Henry M. *The Child's Theory of Mind.* London: MIT Press, 1990.

Wertsch, James V. *Vygotsky and the Social Formation of Mind.* London: Harvard University Press, 1985.

Westermann, Claus. *Genesis 1–11: A Commentary.* Minneapolis: Augsburg, 1984.

Westminster Confession of Faith. Glasgow: Free Presbyterian, 1985.

Westphal, Merold. "Taking St. Paul Seriously: Sin as an Epistemological Category." In *Christian Philosophy*, edited by Thomas P. Flint, 200–226. Notre Dame: University of Notre Dame Press, 1990.

Wevers, John W. *LXX: Notes on the Greek Text of Exodus.* Atlanta: Scholars, 1990.

Wickes, Frances G. *The Inner World of Childhood.* London: Coventure, 1977.

Wilberforce, William. *A Practical View of Christianity.* Peabody, MA: Hendrickson, 1996.

Williams, Anna P. "The Logic of Genre: Theological Method in East and West." *TS* 60 (1999) 679–707.

Williams, Stephen N. *Revelation and Reconciliation: A Window on Modernity.* Cambridge: Cambridge University Press, 1995.

Williamson, Ronald. *Philo and the Epistle to the Hebrews.* Leiden: Brill, 1970.

Willis, E. David. *Calvin's Catholic Christology: the Function of the So-Called Extra Calvinisticum in Calvin's Theology.* Leiden: Brill, 1966.

————. "Rhetoric and Responsibility in Calvin's Theology." In *The Context of Contemporary Theology: Essays in Honour of Paul Lehmann*, edited by Alexander J. McKelway and E. David Willis, 43–63. Atlanta: Knox, 1974.

Willis, W. Waite. *Theism, Atheism and the Doctrine of the Trinity.* Decatur, GA: Scholars, 1987.

Wilson, Stephen A. *Virtue Reformed: Rereading Jonathan Edwards's Ethics.* Leiden: Brill, 2005.

Witherington, Ben III. *The Acts of the Apostles: A Socio-Rhetorical Commentary.* Grand Rapids: Eerdmans, 1998.

Wood, Diana, ed. *The Church and Childhood: Papers Read at the 1993 Summer Meeting and the 1994 Winter Meeting of the Ecclesiastical History Society.* Oxford: Blackwell, 1994.

Wordsworth, William. *The Poetical Works of William Wordsworth.* Edited by Thomas Hutchinson. 2nd ed. London: Oxford University Press, 1936.

Wright, Nicholas Thomas. *The New Testament and the People of God.* London: SPCK, 1992.

Zizioulas, John D. *Being as Communion: Studies in Personhood and Communion.* New York: St. Vladimir's Seminary Press, 1997.

Index